TEACH
Lesson Plan Manual

for

The Language of Medicine
Ninth Edition

Davi-Ellen Chabner, BA, MAT

SAUNDERS

ELSEVIER

3251 Riverport Lane
Maryland Heights, Missouri 63043

TEACH Lesson Plan Manual
for The Language of Medicine 9e

ISBN: 978-1-4377-0571-3

Notice

Neither the Publisher nor the Editors assume any responsibility for any loss or injury and/or damage to persons or property arising out of or related to any use of the material contained in this book. It is the responsibility of the treating practitioner, relying on independent expertise and knowledge of the patient, to determine the best treatment and method of application for the patient.

The Publisher

International Standard Book Number: 978-1-4377-0571-3

Elsevier's Total Education and Curriculum Help, TEACH, includes Instructor Resource Manuals, Curriculum Guides, and faculty development resources. If you would like more information on how TEACH can become your link to curriculum success, please contact your Elsevier sales representative, or call Faculty Support at 1-800-222-9570.

http://TEACH.elsevier.com

Acquisitions Editor: Jeanne Olson
Developmental Editor: Rebecca Swisher
Publishing Services Manager: Gayle May
Project Manager: Stephen Bancroft

Printed in the United States of America

Last digit is the print number: 9 8 7 6 5 4 3 2 1

How to Use This Lesson Plan Manual

Welcome to TEACH, your Total Curriculum Solution!

This Lesson Plan Manual is designed to help you prepare for classes using **The Language of Medicine** by Davi-Ellen Chabner. We hope it will reduce your lesson preparation time, give you new and creative ideas to promote student learning, and help you to make full use of the rich array of resources in the **Chabner** teaching package.

The lesson plans, based on sound educational principles and written by experts in the field, are designed to promote active student learning and get students involved in class discussions and activities. They include assessment tools to help you gauge your students' understanding of the course material and adapt lessons to their needs.

Each textbook chapter is divided into 50-minute lessons — building blocks that can be sequenced to fit your class schedule. The lesson plans are available in electronic format so that you can customize them to fit the requirements of your course.

Every lesson includes a wide variety of teaching resources. In many cases, our subject matter experts have provided more resources and activities than can be covered in a 50-minute lesson. We encourage you to choose activities that match the needs of your students and your curriculum and the materials and resources available at your school.

Lesson plans can be a valuable tool for documenting how your curriculum covers and applies learning objectives required by accrediting organizations. Some accrediting organizations require that learning resources be integrated into a program's curriculum to enhance students' learning experiences. The activities in this Lesson Plan Manual will encourage your students to use learning resources, such as the library or the Internet, to complement their textbooks.

Lesson Plan Manual Format

The Lesson Plan Manual is available in 3 formats:

1. In print, with pages 3-hole punched and perforated for your convenience
2. On a CD-ROM included with the printed Lesson Plan Manual; files are in Microsoft Word and PowerPoint.
3. Online at http://evolve.elsevier.com.

Lesson Plan Manual Organization

TEACH lesson plans complement Elsevier textbooks; there is a lesson plan chapter for each book chapter. Each lesson plan chapter includes 3 sections:

1. **Preparation:** checklists to help you prepare classes based on the chapter
2. **Lessons:** Each chapter is divided into 50-minute lessons, to provide you with the building blocks for your curriculum
3. **Lecture Outlines:** also divided into 50-minute lessons

Preparation

The Preparation section ensures that you're well prepared for class. It includes the following checklists:

- o *Teaching Focus*—identifies key student learning goals for the chapter
- o *Materials and Resources*—lists materials needed for each lesson within the chapter
- o *Lesson Checklist*—includes instructor preparation suggestions
- o *Key Terms*—provides page references for each key term in the chapter
- o *Reference List*—lists instructor resources available for this chapter

Lessons

Each lesson includes the following sections:

Pretest and *Background Assessment*. The first lesson in each chapter includes a Pretest and two Background Assessment questions, designed to help you gauge your students' readiness for the lesson. Depending on students' responses, you may wish to modify your lesson. Students who are comfortable with the topic may need more challenging activities. Students who have difficulty with the topic may need to start by addressing more fundamental concepts.

Critical Thinking Question. Every lesson includes a Critical Thinking Question to motivate students by demonstrating real-world applications of the lesson content.

Lesson Roadmap. The heart of the TEACH lesson plan is the 3-column road map that links Objectives and Content from **Chabner's *The Language of Medicine*** with its Teaching Resources. Teaching Resources reference all the elements of the ancillary package and include additional teaching tips such as Class Activities, discussion topics, and much more. This section correlates your textbook and its ancillary materials with the objectives upon which your course is based.

Homework/Assignments, Instructor's Notes/Student Feedback. These sections are provided for you to add your own notes for assignments, for recording student feedback, and for other notes relating to the lesson.

Lecture Outline

The Lecture Outlines include PowerPoint slides to provide a compelling visual presentation and summary of the main chapter points. Lecture notes for each slide highlight key topics and provide questions for discussion – to help create an interactive classroom environment.

NEW Clicker Questions have been added to the Lecture Outlines. Within each chapter, there are multiple choice questions that can be used with iClicker classroom response system technology. The iClicker system encourages active engagement in the classroom and provides you with real-time feedback while enriching your lecture.

We encourage you to select material from the Lesson Plan Manual that meets your students' needs, to integrate TEACH into your existing lesson plans, and to put your own teaching approach into the plans. We hope TEACH will be an invaluable tool in your classroom.

Table of Contents

The Language of Medicine, 9th ed.

LESSON PLANS AND LECTURE OUTLINES

TEACHING FOCUS

Students will have the opportunity to learn how to analyze words by dividing them into their component parts. Students will be exposed to terms such as *root, suffix*, and *prefix*, and they will be shown how to combine them into medical terms. Students will be given the opportunity to learn how to relate medical terms to the structure and function of the human body, and they will be introduced to spelling and pronunciation problems.

MATERIALS AND RESOURCES

- ☐ Index cards (Lesson 1.1)
- ☐ Overhead projector (all Lessons)

LESSON CHECKLIST

Preparations for this lesson include:

- Lecture
- Demonstration
- Student performance evaluation of all entry-level skills required for student comprehension and application of basic word structure including:
  - o applying medical terminology
  - o knowing basic structure of medical words
  - o understanding word building and definitions
  - o dividing medical words into their component parts
  - o finding the meaning of basic combining forms, prefixes, and suffixes of the medical language
  - o using correct pronunciation of terms

KEY TERMS

Vocabulary (p. 6)
combining form
combining vowel
prefix
root
suffix

Combining Forms (pp. 8-11)
aden/o
arthr/o
bi/o
carcin/o
cardi/o
cephal/o
cerebr/o
cis/o
crin/o
cyst/o
cyt/o
derm/o
dermat/o
electr/o
encephal/o

enter/o
erythr/o
gastr/o
glyc/o
gnos/o
gynec/o
hemat/o
hem/o
hepat/o
iatr/o
leuk/o
log/o
nephr/o
neur/o
onc/o
ophthalm/o
oste/o
path/o
ped/o
psych/o
radi/o
ren/o
rhin/o

sarc/o
sect/o
thromb/o
ur/o

Suffixes (pp. 11-12)
-ac
-al
-algia
-cyte
-ectomy
-emia
-genic
-globin
-gram
-ic, -ical
-ion
-ist
-itis
-logy
-oma
-opsy
-osis
-pathy

-scope
-scopy
-sis
-tomy
-y

Prefixes (pp. 13-14)
a-, an-
aut-, auto-
dia-
end-, endo-
epi-
ex-, exo-
hyper-
hypo-
in-
peri-
pro-
re-
retro-
sub-
trans-

ELSEVIER

Chabner

REFERENCE LIST

PowerPoint slides (CD, Evolve): 1-58

LESSON 1.1

PRETEST
IRM Exercise Quiz A

BACKGROUND ASSESSMENT
Question: How can you use word components to relate medical terms to the structure and function of the human body?

Answer: Once you know the meaning of the root components, it will be easier to remember medical terms explained in their proper context. For example, when you encounter the term *hepatitis*, you will know the term means inflammation of the liver if you know that *hepat* means liver and *-itis* means inflammation. You do not need previous knowledge of biology, anatomy, or physiology to be able to understand medical terms.

Question: Why is it important to be able to break down medical terms into component parts? Why not just memorize each term?

Answer: The goal of understanding the components of medical terms is to make understanding complex terminology easier. Because you are able to separate both complicated and simple terms into understandable word elements, you will be able to decipher virtually all medical terms. As you become familiar with the word parts and learn what each one means, you will be able to recognize those word parts in totally new combinations in other terms.

CRITICAL THINKING QUESTION
Carol wants to become a medical assistant. She is wondering why it is necessary to spend the time learning the roots, suffixes, and prefixes of medical terms when it is faster to simply memorize the actual medical terms. She has commented to you that she is studying to be a medical assistant, not an English teacher, and that learning all the word components seems like a waste of time. How would you respond?

Guidelines: To begin with, by learning the tools of medical word analysis, it is easier to understand complex medical terminology. Medical terms are like jigsaw puzzles. They are constructed of small pieces that make each word unique, but the pieces can also be used in different combinations in other words. This understanding can also help avoid medical mistakes. If Carol only memorizes whole terms, she might confuse *hyperglycemia* with *hypoglycemia*. But if she knows that *hypo* means less than normal and *hyper* means more than normal, she will immediately understand the patient's condition and be able to take the appropriate action.

OBJECTIVES	CONTENT	TEACHING RESOURCES
Learn basic objectives to guide your study of the medical language.	■ Objectives in studying the medical language (p. 2) ☐ Analyze words by dividing them into component parts (p. 2) ☐ Relate the medical terms to the structure and function of the human body (p. 2) ☐ Be aware of spelling and pronunciation problems (p. 2)	➤ MTO Module 1, Section I, Lesson 1 Exercise A (p. 15) ***Class Activity** Present students with the terms for specialties that they may be familiar with:* **biology, cardiology, dermatology, and psychology.** *Ask them what they see that the terms have in common (*-logy*). Explain that this is a suffix that means "the process of study." Ask if they have an idea of what is being studied in each of the terms. Explain that these are word parts that mean* **life, heart, skin,** *and* **mind.** *Demonstrate how, by using the word parts, a definition can be made. Note that some of these "-logies" relate to parts of the body (*cardiology, dermatology,*

ELSEVIER

OBJECTIVES	CONTENT	TEACHING RESOURCES
		and psychology). *Ask students if they can hear which syllable is stressed in each of the terms.*
		Read the sentence: "Dr. Knowledge is a psychologist in Philadelphia who has pneumonia." Ask students to identify the words that begin with silent letters.
		Class Activity Have small groups study the three objectives on pp. 1-2 and compile a list of words they know that function the same way as medical words (words that can be defined by looking at their prefixes, suffixes, and combining forms, and words that have the same pronunciations but different spellings).
		Examples: pretest/posttest, appear/reappear
		Have students present their lists to the class and discuss how they relate to understanding medical terminology.
Divide medical words into their component parts.	■ Word analysis (p. 3)	PPT 4-20
		IRM Exercise Quiz C
		MTO Module 1, Section I, Lesson 2 Exercise D (p. 16)
		Class Activity Divide the class into groups of two. Have each student copy five medical terms on an index card. After trading cards with the partner, each student divides each word into its components. Ask students to label the component parts (prefix/suffix/ word root/combining vowel) and define the term.
Find the meaning of basic combining forms, prefixes, and suffixes of the medical language.	■ Combining forms, suffixes, and prefixes (p. 6) □ Combining forms (p. 6) □ Suffixes (p. 11) □ Prefixes (p. 13)	PPT 21-22, 24-27, 29-56
		IRM Exercise Quizzes A, B, D-H
		IRM Review Sheet Quiz
		MTO Module 1, Section I, Lessons 3-5 Combining Forms Exercise (pp. 6-11)
		Exercises B, C, E, G, H, K, L (pp. 16-18, 20)
		Review Sheet (pp. 30-31)
		Companion CD Exercises 1-1, 1-2, 1-3, 1-4, 1-5

The Language of Medicine, 9th ed.

Chabner

OBJECTIVES	CONTENT	TEACHING RESOURCES
		Class Activity Copy each of the combining forms, suffixes, and prefixes on pp. 8-13 on an index card. Have each student take a turn randomly selecting a term. Each student will read the term and discuss a way to remember that term. Alternately, use an online bingo card generator to construct cards to review student knowledge of word components.
Use these combining forms, prefixes, and suffixes to build medical words.	■ Practical applications (p. 14)	▦ PPT 23, 28, 42 Exercises F, J, M-P (pp. 16, 18, 20-21) ▸ MTO Module 1, Section I, Lesson 6 ◉ Companion CD Exercises 1-6, 1-7 *Class Activity Write each of the combining forms, prefixes, and suffixes on small slips of paper and place them in a "hat." Go around the room and have each student take a slip and use it to make a medical word. Continue until all slips are used. Ask them to use their terms in sentences so that pronunciation and context can be checked.* *Class Activity Divide the class into small groups and assign each group a combining form. Have them create as many medical terms as possible by adding prefixes, suffixes, and combining vowels. Ask one of the students in each of the groups to use a medical dictionary to confirm the terms.*
Use these combining forms, prefixes, and suffixes to build medical words.	■ Pronunciation of terms (p. 25)	▦ PPT 57-58 ◈ IRM Spelling Quiz ◈ IRM Pronunciation Quiz Pronunciation Exercise (pp. 25-27) ◉ Companion CD Exercise 1-8 ▤ iTerms Chapter 01 *Class Activity Read Spotlight 1-1 to the class. Ask them to spell and analyze* **polyuria, glycosuria, neuropathy, nephropathy,** *and* **ophthalmic.** *Have them underline the stressed syllables.* *Read Spotlight 1-2 and ask the students to spell and analyze* **hyperthyroidism, tachycardia, exophthalmos, antithyroid, thyroidectomy,** *and* **cardiac.** *Have them underline the stressed syllables.*

Chabner

OBJECTIVES	CONTENT	TEACHING RESOURCES
		Alternatively, ask students to take turns reading the sentences in Exercise O at the end of the chapter, correcting their pronunciation as necessary.
Performance Evaluation		IRM Multiple Choice Quiz
		IRM Exercise Quiz
		IRM Dictation and Comprehension Quizzes
		IRM Spelling Quiz
		IRM Pronunciation Quiz
		IRM Review Sheet Quiz
		IRM Medical Scramble
		IRM Crossword Puzzle
		ESLR Student Quiz Chapter 01
		MTO Module 1, Section I quiz
		MTO Module 1, Exam
		Companion CD Exercises 1-9, 1-10

1.1 Homework/Assignments:

1.1 Teacher's Notes:

The Language of Medicine, 9th ed.

Chabner

Slide 1

Slide 2

Slide 3

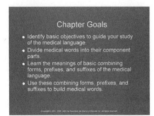

- Analyze words by dividing them into component parts.

- Relate the medical terms to the structure and function of the human body.

- Be aware of spelling and pronunciation problems.

Slide 4

Slide 5

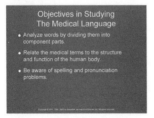

Chabner

Slide 6

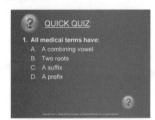

- Correct answer is C: all medical terms have a suffix.

Slide 7

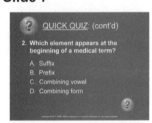

- Correct answer is B: the prefix is the element that appears at the beginning of a medical term.

Slide 8

Slide 9

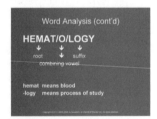

Slide 10

- A combining vowel has no meaning of its own.

Chabner

Slide 11

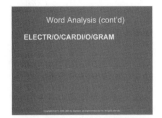

Slide 12

Slide 13

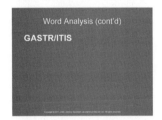

Slide 14

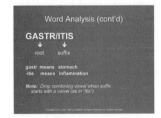

Slide 15

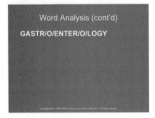

Slide 16

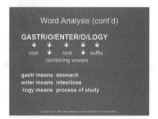

Slide 17

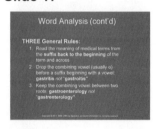

- When a term contains two or more roots related to parts of the body, what often determines which root is listed first? (*anatomical position*)

Slide 18

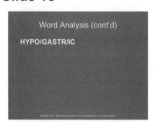

Slide 19

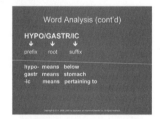

Slide 20

The Language of Medicine, 9th ed.

Chabner

Slide 21

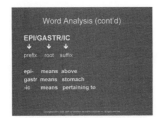

Slide 22

- Refer to pp. 6-7 for definitions and medical terms made with these combining forms.

Slide 23

- Refer to pp. 6-7 for definitions and medical terms made with these combining forms.

Slide 24

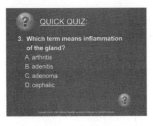

- The correct answer is B: adenitis

Slide 25

- Refer to pp. 7-8 for definitions and medical terms made with these combining forms.

ELSEVIER

The Language of Medicine, 9th ed.

Chabner

Slide 26

- Refer to pp. 7-8 for definitions and medical terms made with these combining forms.

Slide 27

- Refer to pp. 8-9 for definitions and medical terms made with these combining forms.

Slide 28

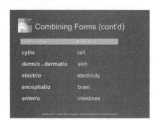

- Refer to pp. 8-9 for definitions and medical terms using these word parts

Slide 29

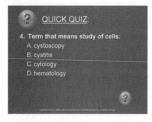

- Correct answer is C: cytology.

Slide 30

- Refer to p. 9 for definitions and medical terms made with these word parts.

ELSEVIER

The Language of Medicine, 9th ed.

Chabner

Slide 31

- Refer to p. 9 for definitions and medical terms made with these word parts.

Slide 32

- Refer to pp. 9-10 for definitions and medical terms made with these combining forms.

Slide 33

- Refer to pp. 9-10 for definitions and for medical terms from these combining forms.

Slide 34

- Refer to p. 10 for definitions and medical terms made with these combining forms.

Slide 35

- Refer to p. 10 for definitions and medical terms made with these combining forms.

ELSEVIER

The Language of Medicine, 9th ed.

Chabner

Slide 36

- Refer to pp. 10-11 for definitions and medical terms made with these combining forms.

Slide 37

- Refer to pp. 10-11 for definitions and medical terms made with these combining forms.

Slide 38

- Refer to p. 11 for definitions and medical terms made with these combining forms.
- Using the given combining forms, can you form and define other terms not listed in the slide?

Slide 39

- Refer to p. 11 for definitions and medical terms made with these combining forms.

Slide 40

- Refer to p. 11 for definitions and medical terms made with these suffixes.

The Language of Medicine, 9th ed.

Chabner

Slide 41

- Refer to p. 11 for definitions and for terms made with these suffixes.

Slide 42

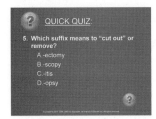

- Correct answer is A: -ectomy, meaning excision, or removal.

Slide 43

- Refer to pp. 11-12 for definitions and for terms made with these suffixes.
- Using the given combining forms, can you form and define other terms not listed in the slide?

Slide 44

- Refer to pp. 11-12 for definitions and for terms made with these suffixes.
- Using the given combining forms, can you form and define other terms not listed in the slide?

Slide 45

- Refer to p. 12 for definitions and for terms made with these suffixes.
- Using the given combining forms, can you form and define other terms not listed in the slide?

Slide 46

- Refer to p. 12 for definitions and for terms made with these suffixes.
- Using the given combining forms, can you form and define other terms not listed in the slide?

Slide 47

- Refer to p. 12 for definitions and for terms made with these suffixes.
- Using the given combining forms, can you form and define other terms not listed in the slide?

Slide 48

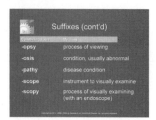

- Refer to p. 12 for definitions and for terms made with these suffixes.
- Using the given combining forms, can you form and define other terms not listed in the slide?

Slide 49

- Refer to p. 12 for definitions and for terms made with these suffixes.
- Using the given combining forms, can you form and define other terms not listed in the slide?

Slide 50

- Refer to p. 12 for definitions and for terms made with these suffixes.
- Using the given combining forms, can you form and define other terms not listed in the slide?

Slide 51

- Refer to p. 13 for definitions and for terms made with these prefixes.
- Using the given combining forms, can you form and define other terms not listed in the slide?

Slide 52

- Refer to p. 13 for definitions and for terms made with these prefixes.
- Using the given combining forms, can you form and define other terms not listed in the slide?

Slide 53

- Refer to pp. 13-14 for definitions and for terms made with these prefixes.
- Using the given combining forms, can you form and define other terms not listed in the slide?

Slide 54

- Refer to pp. 13-14 for definitions and for terms made with these prefixes.
- Using the given combining forms, can you form and define other terms not listed in the slide?

Slide 55

- Refer to p. 14 for definitions and for terms made with these prefixes.
- Using the given combining forms, can you form and define other terms not listed in the slide?

ELSEVIER

Slide 56

- Refer to p. 14 for definitions and for terms made with these prefixes.
- Using the given combining forms, can you form and define other terms not listed in the slide?

Slide 57

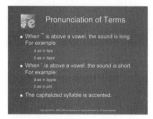

- Pronunciation of Terms section begins on p. 25 of the text.
- Review long and short vowel sounds with the students.
- The syllable that appears in all caps is the accented syllable.

Slide 58

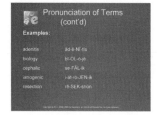

Chabner

2 Lesson Plan
Terms Pertaining to the Body as a Whole

TEACHING FOCUS

Students will have the opportunity to learn about the structural organization of the body, including cells, tissues, organs, and systems. Students will be presented with terminology relating to the body cavities and organs and will receive instruction on the terms associated with the anatomical divisions of the body and back, and the positions, directions, and planes of the body. Students will also have the opportunity to learn new medical word elements and use them to understand new medical terms.

MATERIALS AND RESOURCES

- ☐ Copies of diagrams of human bodies (Lesson 2.1)
- ☐ Copies of unlabeled spine diagram (Lesson 2.2)
- ☐ Flashcards or transparencies with a variety of combining forms, prefixes, and suffixes (Lesson 2.2)
- ☐ Overhead projector (all Lessons)
- ☐ Paper (all Lessons)
- ☐ Projector screen (all Lessons)
- ☐ Unlabeled diagrams of body cavities (Lesson 2.1)

LESSON CHECKLIST

Preparations for this lesson include:
- Lecture
- Guest speakers: medical assistant, physician, nurse
- Student performance evaluation of all entry-level skills required for student comprehension and application of medical terminology principles including:
  - ○ body cavities
  - ○ combining terms, definitions, and pronunciations
  - ○ directions and planes
  - ○ divisions of the body and back
  - ○ organs

KEY TERMS

Vocabulary (pp. 32-50)
abdominal
abdominal cavity
adipose tissue
anabolism
anterior (ventral)
cartilage
catabolism
cell membrane
cervical
chromosome
circulatory system
coccygeal
coccyx
connective tissue
cranial
cranial cavity
cytoplasm
deep
diaphragm
digestive system
disc/disk

distal
DNA
dorsal
endocrine system
endoplasmic reticulum
epigastric region
epithelial
epithelial cell
epithelial tissue
fat
fat cell
frontal (coronal)
genes
histologist
hypochondriac regions
hypogastric region
iliac
inferior (caudal)
inguinal
inguinal regions
karyotype
larynx

lateral
left lower quadrant
  (LLQ)
left upper quadrant
  (LUQ)
lumbar
lumbar regions
medial
mediastinum
metabolism
mitochondria
muscle cell
muscle tissue
musculoskeletal system
nerve cell
nerve tissue
nervous system
nucleus
pelvic
pelvic cavity
peritoneum
pharynx

pituitary gland
pleura
pleural cavity
posterior (dorsal)
prone
proximal
respiratory system
reproductive system
right lower quadrant
  (RLQ)
right upper quadrant
  (RUQ)
sacrum
sagittal (lateral)
skin system
slipped disk
spinal
spinal cavity
spinal column
spinal cord
superficial
superior
superior (cephalic)
supine
thoracic
thoracic cavity
thyroid gland
trachea
transverse (cross-sectional
  or axial)

umbilical region
ureter
urethra
urinary system
uterus
ventral
vertebra
viscera

**Combining Forms
(pp. 50-53)**
abdomin/o
adip/o
anter/o
bol/o
cervic/o
chondr/o
chrom/o
coccyg/o
crani/o
cyt/o
dist/o
dors/o
hist/o
ili/o
inguin/o
kary/o
later/o
lumb/o
medi/o

nucle/o
pelv/i
poster/o
proxim/o
sacr/o
sarc/o
spin/o
thel/o
thorac/o
trache/o
umbilic/o
ventr/o
vertebr/o
viscer/o
Prefixes (p. 53)
ana-
cata-
epi-
hypo-
inter-
meta-
Suffixes (p. 54)
-eal
-iac
-ior
-ism
-ose
-plasm
-somes
-type

REFERENCE LIST
PowerPoint slides (CD, Evolve): 1-54

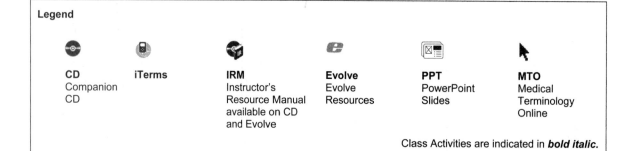

CD Companion CD	**iTerms**	**IRM** Instructor's Resource Manual available on CD and Evolve	**Evolve** Evolve Resources	**PPT** PowerPoint Slides	**MTO** Medical Terminology Online

Class Activities are indicated in **bold italic**.

Chabner

LESSON 2.1

PRETEST
IRM Quiz B

BACKGROUND ASSESSMENT
Question: The body is organized into a number of systems, for example, the cardiovascular system. Can you name any of its organs, tissues, or cells?
Answer: One of the organs of the cardiovascular system is the heart. The tissues in the heart are the endocardium, myocardium, and pericardium. The cells of the myocardium are heart muscle cells.

Question: How could you use a system of location similar to north/south and east/west to describe location on a patient's body? Why is this important?
Answer: Because a patient may change position, from standing to lying down, a system of describing location on the body is necessary for communication between members of the healthcare team. The concept of superior (above another structure) and inferior (below another structure), posterior (back of the body) and anterior (front of the body), and medial (pertaining to the middle) and lateral (pertaining to the side) are the human body's equivalents of directional terms.

CRITICAL THINKING QUESTION
Why is it important to have a universal scheme for describing regions of the abdomen?
Guidelines: Practitioners must have a common means of communicating that will describe locations in the abdomen.

OBJECTIVES	CONTENT	TEACHING RESOURCES
Define terms that apply to the structural organization of the body.	■ Structural organization of the body (p. 32) ☐ Cells (p. 32) ☐ Tissues (p. 36) ☐ Organs (p. 37) ☐ Systems (p. 37)	⊠ PPT 5-13 IRM Exercise Quizzes A, B ↖ MTO Module 2, Section I, Lessons 1-6 Figure 2-1 Major parts of a cell (p. 32) Figure 2-2 Egg and sperm cells (p. 33) Figure 2-3 Karyotype of a normal male (p. 33) Figure 2-4 (A) Karyotype of a Down syndrome female patient; (B) Photograph of a 3½-year-old girl (p. 34) Figure 2-5 Types of cells (p. 36) Study Section 1 (p. 35) Study Section 2 (p. 38) Exercises A-C (pp. 55-56) ⊙ Companion CD Exercise 2-1 *Class Activity **Divide the class into two teams. Give them a term relating to the structural organization of the body (e.g., heart, mitochondria, etc.) and ask them to name the larger structure or system it belongs to. The first team to answer correctly wins a point. The team with the most points wins.***

ELSEVIER

The Language of Medicine, 9th ed.

OBJECTIVES	CONTENT	TEACHING RESOURCES
		Class Activity Give the students a copy of Figure 2-1 and ask them to label the structures, including combining forms wherever appropriate.
Identify the body cavities and recognize the organs contained within those cavities.	■ Body cavities (p. 38)	PPT 14-18 IRM Exercise Quiz C IRM Diagram Quiz MTO Module 2, Section I, Lesson 7 Figure 2-6 Body cavities (p. 39) Figure 2-7 Divisions of the thoracic cavity (p. 39) Figure 2-8 Abdominal cavity (side view) (p. 40) Study Section 3 (p. 43) Figure 2-9 Organs of the abdominopelvic and thoracic cavities, anterior view (p. 41) Figure 2-10 Organs of the abdominopelvic and thoracic cavities, posterior view (p. 42) Exercise D (p. 56) Companion CD Exercises 2-2, 2-7 *Class Activity Divide students into teams. Give each team a copy of Figure 2-6 (p. 39) without the cavity labels. Have each team label the cavities and fill in the names of at least one organ in each cavity. The first team to complete a correct diagram wins. Have them present their diagram to the class.*
Locate and identify the anatomical and clinical divisions of the abdomen.	■ Abdominopelvic regions and quadrants (p. 44) ☐ Regions (p. 44) ☐ Quadrants (p. 44)	PPT 19-27, 32-33 IRM Exercise Quizzes E-F IRM Review Sheet Quiz MTO Module 2, Section I, Lesson 8 Figure 2-11 Abdominopelvic regions (p. 44) Figure 2-12 Abdominopelvic quadrants (p. 45) Exercise E (p. 57) Review Sheet, Label the regions and quadrants of the abdominopelvic cavity (p. 67) Companion CD Exercise 2-5

The Language of Medicine, 9th ed.

Chabner

OBJECTIVES	CONTENT	TEACHING RESOURCES
		Class Activity Make two copies of the figure of the human body in Figure 2-9 (p. 41) for each student. Have each student first draw and label the four quadrants of the body. On the next page, have each student draw and label the nine regions. Be sure to check the correct labeling for left and right sides.

2.1 Homework/Assignments:

2.1 Teacher's Notes:

LESSON 2.2

CRITICAL THINKING QUESTION

Judy is found lying on her back after a fall. The imaging studies show that she has injured her spine at T3. Where is this?

Guidelines: T3 is the third thoracic vertebra. The thoracic vertebrae are between the cervical and the lumbar vertebrae.

OBJECTIVES	CONTENT	TEACHING RESOURCES
Locate and name the anatomical divisions of the back.	■ Divisions of the back (spinal column) (p. 45)	PPT 29-31 IRM Exercise Quiz D MTO Module 2, Section I, Lesson 9 Figure 2-13 Anatomical divisions of the back (spinal column) (p. 46) Study Section 4 (p. 47) Exercise F (p. 57) Review Sheet, Name the divisions of the spinal column (p. 67) Companion CD Exercise 2-3 *Class Activity Divide the class into two teams. Show a transparency or PowerPoint slide of the anatomical divisions of the back (Figure 2-13, p. 46). Call out a number and ask them to name the division. The first team to answer correctly wins a point. Give an additional point to the team that can give the correct number of bones in this division. The team with the most points wins.* *Class Activity Make copies of the spine in Figure 2-13 (p. 46). Have students label the divisions of the spine with the numbers of bones in each division, including the correct term for the space between the vertebrae. Using the copies of the spine in Figure 2-14, choose a bone in each of the divisions and mark it on either a transparency or a PowerPoint slide. Ask students to identify the bone with its abbreviation where appropriate.*
Become acquainted with terms that describe positions, directions, and planes of the body.	■ Positional and directional terms (p. 48) ■ Planes of the body (p. 49)	PPT 34-40 IRM Exercise Quizzes G, H MTO Module 2, Section I, Lesson 10 Figure 2-14 Positional and directional terms (p. 48)

The Language of Medicine, 9th ed.

Chabner

OBJECTIVES	CONTENT	TEACHING RESOURCES
		Study Section 5 (pp. 50)
		Review Sheet, Name the planes of the head as pictured below (p. 68)
		Review Sheet, Name the positional and directional terms (pp. 68)
		⊙ Companion CD Exercise 2-4
		Class Activity Use sticky notes to mark a location on either a model of the body or a skeleton. Ask students to use the directional terms they have learned to describe the locations of the sticky notes.
		Class Activity Divide the class into two or more competing teams. Give them one of the terms that describe positions, directions, or planes of the body. Ask them to explain or demonstrate the meaning of the term and give an example of its use. The team with the most correct answers wins.
		Class Activity Find examples of illustrations of patients that can be described as an anterior or posterior view and supine or prone positions. Use these as PowerPoint or transparency slides Ask students to name the view. Ask the students to then give examples of how the terms proximal/distal and inferior/superior can be used with regard to these illustrations.
Performance Evaluation		🎲 IRM Multiple Choice Quiz
		🎲 IRM Exercise Quiz
		🎲 IRM Dictation and Comprehension Quiz
		🎲 IRM Spelling Quiz
		🎲 IRM Pronunciation Quiz
		🎲 IRM Diagram Quiz
		🎲 IRM Review Sheet Quiz
		🎲 IRM Medical Scramble
		🎲 IRM Crossword Puzzle
		🖉 ESLR Student Quiz Chapter 02
		➤ MTO Module 2, Section I Quiz

OBJECTIVES	CONTENT	TEACHING RESOURCES
		↖ MTO Module 2, Exam
		💿 Companion CD Exercises 2-11, 2-12

2.2 Homework/Assignments:

2.2 Teacher's Notes:

Slide 1

The Language Of Medicine
9th edition
Davi-Ellen Chabner

Slide 2

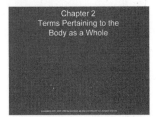

Chapter 2
Terms Pertaining to the
Body as a Whole

Slide 3

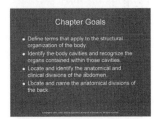

Chapter Goals

- Define terms that apply to the structural organization of the body.
- Identify the body cavities and recognize the organs contained within those cavities.
- Locate and identify the anatomical and clinical divisions of the abdomen.
- Locate and name the anatomical divisions of the back.

Slide 4

Chapter Goals (cont'd)

- Become acquainted with terms that describe positions, directions, and planes of the body.
- Identify the meanings for new word elements and use them to understand medical terms.

Slide 5

Chapter 2
Lesson 2.1

Chabner

Slide 6

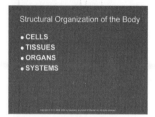

Slide 7

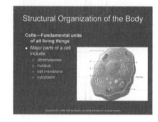

- What is karyotyping and when is it used? (*Chromosomes are analyzed to determine if they are normal in number and structure. Obstetricians often recommend an amniocentesis for a pregnant woman.*)

- Have students identify parts of the cell. *Answers appear on the following slide.*

- What is cytoplasm? (*It includes all material outside the nucleus.*)

- What are mitochondria? (*small, sausage-shaped bodies that produce energy by burning food*)

Slide 8

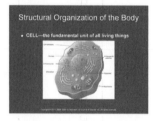

- What is karyotyping and when is it used? (*Chromosomes are analyzed to determine if they are normal in number and structure. Obstetricians often recommend an amniocentesis for a pregnant woman.*)

- What is cytoplasm? (*It includes all material outside the nucleus.*)

- What are mitochondria? (*small, sausage-shaped bodies that produce energy by burning food*)

Slide 9

Slide 10

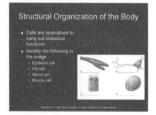

Chabner

Slide 11

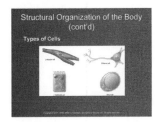

Slide 12

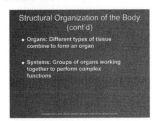

- What is the term for a scientist who specializes in the study of tissue? (*histologist*)

- Which tissue conducts impulses all over the body? (*nerve*)

- Examples of what type of tissue include fat and cartilage? (*connective*)

- What tissue forms the linings of internal organs and the outer surface of the skin? (*epithelial*)

Slide 13

- What defines a system? (*group of organs working together to perform complex functions*)

- Name the system in which these organs are found:

  - thyroid gland and pituitary gland (*endocrine*)

  - kidneys, ureters, urinary bladder urethra (*urinary or excretory*)

  - skin, hair, nails, sweat glands (*skin and sense organs*)

Slide 14

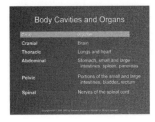

Slide 15

- Name the cavity in which these organs are found:

  - nerves of the spinal cord (*spinal*)

  - stomach, small and large intestines, spleen, pancreas, liver (*abdominal*)

  - brain (*cranial*)

  - lungs, heart, esophagus, trachea, bronchial tubes (*thoracic*)

  - portions of the small and large intestines, rectum, urinary bladder, urethra (*pelvic*)

Slide 16

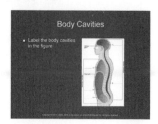

- Which cavities are dorsal and which are ventral? (*cranial and spinal are dorsal while thoracic, abdominal and pelvic are ventral*)

Slide 17

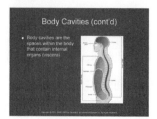

Slide 18

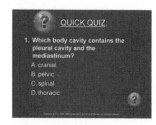

- Correct answer is D: thoracic cavity contains the pleural cavity and the mediastinum.

Slide 19

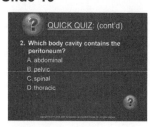

- Correct answer is A: the abdominal cavity contains the peritoneum.

Slide 20

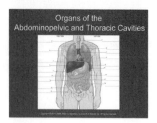

ELSEVIER

The Language of Medicine, 9th ed.

Chabner

Slide 21

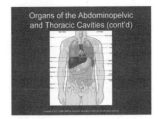

Slide 22

Slide 23

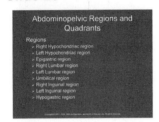

Slide 24

- Have students verbally label the regions of the abdominopelvic cavity.

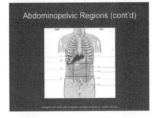

Slide 25

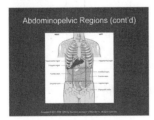

The Language of Medicine, 9th ed.
Chabner

Slide 26

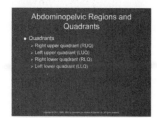

- Discuss the organs in each quadrant.

Slide 27

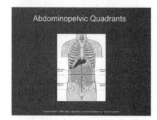

- Have students identify the quadrants of the adbominopelvic cavity.

Slide 28

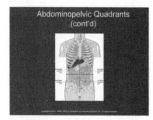

- Where is the appendix located?
- In which quadrant does the liver lie?

Slide 29

Slide 30

- What is cervical? (*the neck region*)
- What is thoracic? (*the chest region*)
- What is lumbar? (*waist or flank region*)
- What is sacral? (*Five bones are fused to form the sacrum.*)
- What is coccygeal? (*The tailbone is composed of four fused pieces.*)

ELSEVIER

The Language of Medicine, 9th ed.

Chabner

Slide 31

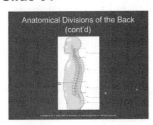

- Fill in the blanks. (*1. Cervical; 2. Thoracic; 3. Lumbar; 4. Sacral; 5. Coccygeal or tailbone*)
- What is a disk? (*a small pad of cartilage between the vertebrae*)

Slide 32

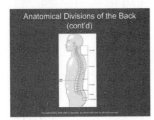

- What is a disk? (*a small pad of cartilage between the vertebrae*)

Slide 33

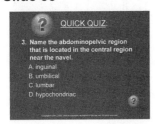

- Correct answer is B: umbilical

Slide 34

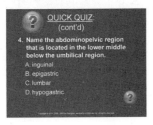

- Correct answer is D: hypogastric

The Language of Medicine, 9th ed.

Chabner

Slide 35

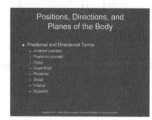

- Match the definition to one of these terms:
  - front side of the body (*anterior*)
  - the back side of the body (*posterior*)
  - away from the surface (*deep*)
  - on the surface (*superficial*)
  - near the point of attachment to the trunk or near the beginning of a structure (*proximal*)
  - far from the point of attachment to the trunk or far from the beginning of a structure (*distal*)
  - below another structure (*inferior*)
  - above another structure (*superior*)

Slide 36

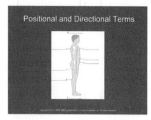

- How could the following conditions be identified?
  - a bruise on the forehead (*anterior; superficial*)
  - a cramp in the left ovary (*lateral; deep*)
  - a callus on the ball of the foot (*inferior*)

Slide 37

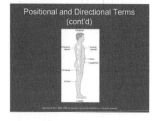

- How could the following conditions be identified?
  - a bruise on the forehead (*anterior; superficial*)
  - a cramp in the left ovary (*lateral; deep*)
  - a callus on the ball of the foot (*inferior*)

Slide 38

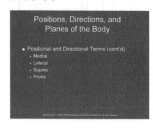

- Match the definition to one of these terms:
  - front side of the body (*anterior*)
  - the back side of the body (*posterior*)
  - away from the surface (*deep*)
  - on the surface (*superficial*)
  - near the point of attachment to the trunk or near the beginning of a structure (*proximal*)
  - far from the point of attachment to the trunk or far from the beginning of a structure (*distal*)
  - below another structure (*inferior*)
  - above another structure (*superior*)

The Language of Medicine, 9th ed.

Chabner

Slide 39

- a plane running across the body parallel to the ground (*transverse*)

- a vertical plane dividing the body into anterior and posterior portions (*frontal*)

- a lengthwise vertical plane dividing the body into right and left sides (*sagittal*)

Slide 40

- How could the following conditions be identified?

  - a bruise on the forehead (*anterior; superficial*)

  - a cramp in the left ovary (*lateral; deep*)

  - a callus on the ball of the foot (*inferior*)

Slide 41

- How could the following conditions be identified?

  - a bruise on the forehead (*anterior; superficial*)

  - a cramp in the left ovary (*lateral; deep*)

  - a callus on the ball of the foot (*inferior*)

Slide 42

- Refer to the Combining Forms Section beginning on p. 51 for terms using these combining forms.

Slide 43

- Refer to the Combining Forms Section beginning on p. 51 for terms using these combining forms.

Slide 44

- Refer to the Combining Forms Section beginning on p. 51 for terms using these combining forms.

Slide 45

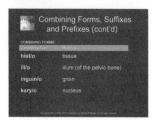

- Refer to the Combining Forms Section beginning on p. 51 for terms using these combining forms.

Slide 46

- Refer to the Combining Forms Section beginning on p. 51 for terms using these combining forms.

Slide 47

- Refer to the Combining Forms Section beginning on p. 51 for terms using these combining forms.

Slide 48

- Refer to p. 54 for terms using these combining forms.

Slide 49

- Refer to p. 55 for terms using these combining forms

Slide 50

- Refer to p. 55 for terms using these prefixes.

Slide 51

Slide 52

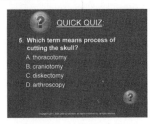

- Correct answer is B: craniotomy

Slide 53

- Long "a" vs. short "a": Cranial vs. Abdominal
- Ask students to provide additional examples from the terms and combining forms that have been discussed in this chapter.

Slide 54

• Write additional terms on the board and have students pronounce them.

Chabner

TEACHING FOCUS

Students will have the opportunity to learn many of the most common suffixes in the medical language. Students will also be shown new combining forms and instructions on how to use these to create words with suffixes. Finally, students will have the opportunity to expand their understanding of terminology beyond basic word analysis.

MATERIALS AND RESOURCES

☐ Projector (Lesson 3.1)
☐ Textbook (Lesson 3.1)

☐ Transparencies or flash cards with suffixes (Lesson 3.1)

LESSON CHECKLIST

Preparations for this lesson include:

- Lecture
- Method of student evaluation for entry-level knowledge to achieve competency, focusing on:
  - ○ new suffixes and review of those presented in previous chapters
  - ○ word analysis and combining word forms to build terms
  - ○ understanding new terminology and pronouncing it correctly
  - ○ names and functions of blood cells

KEY TERMS

Combining Forms (pp. 72-73)

abdomin/o	leuk/o
acr/o	lymph/o
acu/o	mamm/o
aden/o	mast/o
adip/o	morph/o
amni/o	muc/o
angi/o	my/o
arteri/o	myel/o
arthr/o	necr/o
axill/o	nephr/o
bi/o	neur/o
blephar/o	neutr/o
bronch/o	nucle/o
carcin/o	ophthalm/o
cardi/o	oste/o
chem/o	ot/o
chondr/o	path/o
chron/o	peritone/o
col/o	phag/o
cyst/o	phleb/o
encephal/o	plas/o
erythr/o	pleur/o
hem/o	pneumon/o
hepat/o	pulmon/o
hydr/o	radi/o
inguin/o	rect/o
isch/o	ren/o
lapar/o	rhin/o
laryng/o	sarc/o
	splen/o

staphyl/o
strept/o
thorac/o
thromb/o
tonsil/o
trache/o
ven/o

Suffixes and Terminology (pp. 74-78)
-algia
-cele
-centesis
-coccus, -cocci
-cyte
-dynia
-ectomy
-emia
-genesis
-gram
-graph
-graphy
-itis
-logy
-lysis
-malacia
-megaly
-oma
-opsy
-osis
-pathy
-penia
-phobia
-plasia
-plasty
-ptosis
-sclerosis
-scope
-scopy
-stasis
-stomy
-therapy
-tomy
-trophy

Shorter Noun Suffixes (p. 78)
-er
-ia
-ist
-ole
-ule
-um, -ium
-us
-y

Adjective Suffixes (p. 79)
-ac, -iac
-al
-ar
-ary
-eal
-genic
-ic, -ical
-oid
-ose
-ous
-tic

Appendix A: Hernia (p. 80)
cystocele
hernia
hiatal hernia
inguinal hernia
omphalocele
rectocele

Appendix B: Amniocentesis (p. 81)
amniocentesis

Appendix C: Streptococcus (pp. 82-83)
abscess
diplococci
gonococci
pneumococci
staphylococci
streptococcus

Appendix D: Blood Cells (p. 84)
basophils
eosinophils
erythrocytes
granulocytes
hemoglobin
leukocytes
lymphocytes
macrophages
monocytes
mononuclear leukocytes
neutrophils
phagocytes
platelets
polymorphonuclear
thrombocytes

Appendix E: Pronunciation Clue (p. 84)

Appendix F: Anemia (p. 84)
anemia
aplastic anemia

Appendix G: Ischemia (p. 84)
ischemia
ischemic

Appendix H: Tonsillitis (p. 84)
    tonsillectomy
    tonsillitis
Appendix I: Acromegaly (p. 84)
    acromegaly
    pituitary gland
Appendix J: Splenomegaly (p. 84)
    spleen
    splenectomy
Appendix K Achondroplasia (p. 85)
    achondroplasia
Appendix L: -ptosis (p. 86)
    blepharoptosis
    -ptosis

Appendix M: Laparoscopy (p. 86)
    laparoscopy
    MIS (minimally invasive surgery)
    peritoneoscopy
Appendix N: Tracheotomy (p. 86)
    incison
    -omy
    opening
    -stomy
Appendix O: Arteriole (p. 88)
    arterioles
    venules
Appendix P: Adenoids (p. 88)
    adenoids

REFERENCE LIST
PowerPoint slides (CD, Evolve): 1-37

Legend

CD	iTerms	IRM	Evolve	PPT	MTO
Companion CD		Instructor's Resource Manual available on CD and Evolve	Evolve Resources	PowerPoint Slides	Medical Terminology Online

Class Activities are indicated in **_bold italic_**.

LESSON 3.1

PRETEST
IRM Quiz A

BACKGROUND ASSESSMENT
Question: What suffixes are you familiar with at this time? What are the spelling rules that pertain to suffixes?
Answer: Students may answer any of the suffixes that have been used in the first two chapters. If a suffix begins with a vowel, drop the combining vowel; if the suffix begins with a consonant, keep the combining vowel.

Question: Which suffixes can be used to make a term into an adjective?
Answer: Suffixes such as *-al, -ose, -eal, -ior*, and *-iac* all mean *pertaining to*. Terms ending with these suffixes are adjectives.

CRITICAL THINKING QUESTION
Dr. Reilly has a patient, Jessica Adams, who needs to have a colonoscopy. The patient says that she knows of a friend of the family who had one, and she does not understand why she has to have surgery when she has not even had a diagnosis yet. What term is Jessica confusing with colonoscopy?
Guidelines: Jessica is confusing the term "colonostomy" with the term "colonoscopy". The first is a new opening of the colon, and the second is a visual examination of the colon. They are two very different procedures!

OBJECTIVES	CONTENT	TEACHING RESOURCES
Gain practice in word analysis by using these suffixes with combining forms to build and understand terms.	■ Introduction (p. 72) ■ Combining forms (p. 72)	PPT 4-15 IRM Exercise Quizzes B, E IRM Pronunciation Quiz C IRM Review Sheet Quiz MTO Module 3, Section I, Lessons 1-3 Exercise B (p. 90) Exercise E (p. 92) Exercises H, I (p. 94) Exercise K (p. 96) Review Sheet: Combining forms (pp. 106-107) Companion CD Exercises 3-3, 3-4 *Class Activity Divide the class into teams of three or four. During a timed session, call out the name of a suffix or combining form. Members of each team must create as many medical terms from the suffix or combining form as they can in a 60-second period. Check the terms for application of spelling rules. After 60 seconds, announce another suffix or combining form.*

OBJECTIVES	CONTENT	TEACHING RESOURCES
Define new suffixes and review those presented in previous chapters.	■ Suffixes and terminology (p. 74) ☐ Noun suffixes (p. 74) ☐ Adjective suffixes (p. 79)	PPT 4-15 IRM Multiple Choice Quiz IRM Exercise Quizzes A, D, F, G IRM Pronunciation Quiz B IRM Review Sheet Quiz A, B IRM Crossword Puzzle MTO Module 3, Section I, Lessons 2-3 Exercise A (p. 90) Exercise D (p. 91) Exercise G (p. 93) Review Sheet: Noun suffixes and adjective suffixes (pp. 105-106) Companion CD Exercises 3-1, 3-2 *Class Activity **Divide the class into three groups and have each choose a "contestant" for a quiz show. Using transparencies or flash cards, show the contestants a variety of suffixes one at a time. Ask them to state a word using the suffix. The first contestant to answer correctly wins a point. Give an additional point for correct spelling and a correct definition of the term.*** *Class Activity **Write the suffixes listed on pp. 74-79 on slips of paper. Put them in a "hat" and ask each student to draw out two or three slips. Go around the room and ask each student to state a medical term using each suffix he or she has drawn from the hat.***
Gain practice in word analysis by using these suffixes with combining forms to build and understand terms.	■ Appendices ☐ Hernia (p. 80) ☐ Amniocentesis (p. 81) ☐ Streptococcus (p. 82-83) ☐ Blood cells (p. 84) ☐ Pronunciation clue (p. 84) ☐ Anemia (p. 84) ☐ Ischemia (p. 84) ☐ Tonsillitis (p. 84)	PPT 4-15 IRM Multiple Choice Quiz IRM Dictation and Comprehension Quiz IRM Spelling Quiz IRM Pronunciation Quiz A MTO Module 3, Section II, Lessons 1-5 Figure 3-1 Cystocele and rectocele (p. 80)

ELSEVIER

OBJECTIVES	CONTENT	TEACHING RESOURCES
	☐ Acromegaly (p. 84)	Figure 3-2 Omphalocele (p. 80)
	☐ Splenomegaly (p. 84)	Figure 3-3 Amniocentesis (p. 81)
	☐ Achondroplasia (p. 85)	Figure 3-4 Types of coccal bacteria (p. 82)
	☐ -ptosis (p. 86)	Exercise F (p. 93)
	☐ Laparoscopy (p. 86)	Exercise K (p. 96)
	☐ Tracheotomy (p. 86)	Pronunciation Exercise (pp. 101-104)
	☐ Arteriole (p. 88)	◉ Companion CD Exercise 3-5
	☐ Adenoids (p. 88)	*Class Activity Divide the class into small groups. Ask a volunteer to read the report, using the correct pronunciation. Assign each group a medical term from the column to the left (such as "hernia" or "amniocentesis"). Each group will research that particular term and report it back to the rest of the class.*
		Class Activity Divide the class into two or more teams. Say a medical term that uses a suffix and ask them to write the term correctly on the board and underline the suffix. The first correct answer wins a point. Give an additional point for a definition of the suffix. The team with the most points wins the game.
		Class Activity Ask students to identify any of the suffixes that are easy to confuse. Divide them into groups for the numbers of pairs identified, and have them develop strategies to help remember the differences. Ask them to report their findings to the class.
		Class Activity Create a mock game show where you write a medical term on the board. You ask three "panelists" (i.e., students) to pronounce the term and privately tell each one how you want them to pronounce it. One student will pronounce the term correctly and the other two will pronounce it incorrectly. The other students will guess which panelist is pronouncing the term correctly.
Name and know the functions of the different types of blood cells in the body.	☐ Blood cells (p. 84)	▣ PPT 15-36
	☐ Pronunciation clue (p. 84)	IRM Multiple Choice Quiz
	☐ Anemia (p. 84)	IRM Exercise Quiz C
	☐ Ischemia (p. 84)	➤ MTO Module 3, Section III, Lessons 1-3
	☐ Tonsillitis (p. 84)	➤ MTO Module 3, Section V
	☐ Acromegaly (p. 84)	

ELSEVIER

The Language of Medicine, 9th ed.

Chabner

OBJECTIVES	CONTENT	TEACHING RESOURCES
	☐ Splenomegaly (p. 84)	Figure 3-5 Types of blood cells (p. 83)
	☐ Achondroplasia (p. 85)	Figure 3-6 Gigantism with acromegaly (p. 85)
	☐ -ptosis (p. 86)	Figure 3-7 A boy with achondroplasia (p. 85)
	☐ Laparoscopy (p. 86)	Figure 3-8 Ptosis of the upper eyelid (blepharoptosis) (p. 86)
	☐ Tracheotomy (p. 86)	Figure 3-9 Laparoscopy for tubal ligation (p. 87)
	☐ Arteriole (p. 88)	Figure 3-10 Tracheotomy and tracheostomy (p. 87)
	☐ Adenoids (p. 88)	Figure 3-11 Relationship of blood vessels (p. 88)
		Figure 3-12 Adenoids and tonsils (p. 88)
		Exercise C (p. 91)
		Exercise J (p. 95)
		◉ Companion CD Exercise 3-6
		*Class Activity **Divide the class into two or more teams. Play a Jeopardy-style game by giving them "answers" relating to blood cells, such as "Blood cell formed in the bone marrow that has three types." Award a point for the question, "What are granulocytes?" The team with the most points wins. Alternatively, use a Jeopardy-style game to ask questions about definitions, spelling, pronunciation, word analysis and word building for the chapter.***
		*Class Activity **Make copies of Figure 3-5 (p. 83), taking care to delete the labels. Ask each student to label the type of blood cell and describe its function Alternatively, read the appendices A-P. Ask the students to spell, analyze, and underline the stressed syllables in the boldfaced terms.***
Performance Evaluation		📦 IRM Multiple Choice Quiz
		📦 IRM Exercise Quiz
		📦 IRM Dictation and Comprehension Quiz
		📦 IRM Spelling Quiz
		📦 IRM Pronunciation Quiz
		📦 IRM Review Sheet Quiz
		📦 IRM Medical Scramble

OBJECTIVES	CONTENT	TEACHING RESOURCES
		IRM Crossword Puzzle
		ESLR Student Quiz Chapter 03
		MTO Module 3, Sections I-III quizzes
		MTO Module 3 Exam
		Practical Applications (p. 89)
		Companion CD Exercises 3-7, 3-8, 3-9
		iTerms Chapter 03

3.1 Homework/Assignments:

3.1 Teacher's Notes:

Slide 1

The Language Of Medicine
9th edition
Davi-Ellen Chabner

Slide 2

Chapter 3
Suffixes

Slide 3

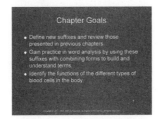

Chapter Goals

- Define new suffixes and review those presented in previous chapters.
- Gain practice in word analysis by using these suffixes with combining forms to build and understand terms.
- Identify the functions of the different types of blood cells in the body.

Slide 4

Chapter 3
Lesson 3.1

Slide 5

Suffixes and Terminology

NOUN SUFFIXES

-algia	pain
-cele	hernia
-centesis	surgical puncture to remove fluid
-coccus	berry-shaped bacterium
-cyte	cell

- Refer to section beginning on p. 74 for terms using these suffixes

Slide 6

- Refer to section beginning on p. 74 for terms using these suffixes

Slide 7

- Refer to section beginning on p. 74 for terms using these suffixes

Slide 8

- Refer to section beginning on p. 74 for terms using these suffixes

Slide 9

- Refer to section beginning on p. 74 for terms using these suffixes

Slide 10

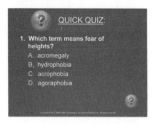

- Correct answer is C: acrophobia

Chabner

Slide 11

- Refer to section beginning on p. 74 for terms using these suffixes

Slide 12

- Refer to section beginning on p. 74 for terms using these suffixes

Slide 13

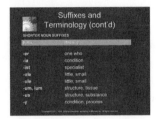

Slide 14

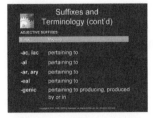

Slide 15

Slide 16

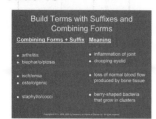

- What is Streptococcus?
- What are other berry-shaped bacteria?

Slide 17

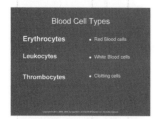

Slide 18

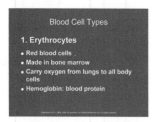

- What is hemoglobin? What purpose does it serve?

Slide 19

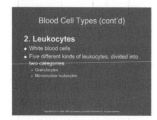

- What is the distinction between granulocytes and mononuclear leukocytes?
- An easy way to remember the names of the five leukocytes is: **N**ever (neutrophil) **L**et (lymphocyte) **M**onkeys (monocyte) **E**at (eosinophil) **B**ananas (basophil).

Slide 20

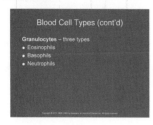

- Formed in the blood marrow
  - Eosinophils – active and elevated in allergic conditions such as asthma
  - Basophils – play a role in inflammation
  - Neutrophils – important disease-fighting cells
- What do the prefixes for each type reflect?
- What are some other names for neutrophils?

Slide 21

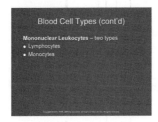

- Lymphocytes – fight disease by producing antibodies that destroy foreign bodies

- Monocytes – engulf and destroy cellular debris after neutrophils have attacked foreign cells

- What are two types of lymphocytes?

- What are macrophages?

Slide 22

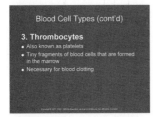

Slide 23

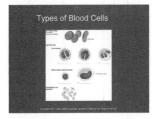

Slide 24

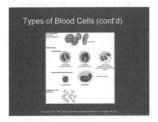

Slide 25

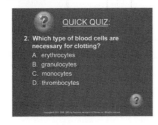

- Correct answer is D: thrombocytes, which are actually tiny fragments of cells formed in the bone marrow and necessary for blood clotting.

Chabner

Slide 26

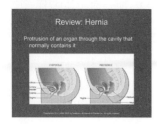

- See p. 82 for more information.
- A hernia is protrusion of an organ or the muscular wall of an organ through the cavity that normally contains it.

CYSTOCELE

- when part of the **urinary bladder herniates** through the vaginal wall.

RECTOCELE

- **protrusion of a portion of the rectum** toward the vagina

Slide 27

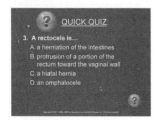

- Correct answer is B. See p. 82 for additional information on hernias.

Slide 28

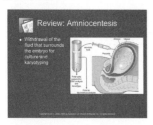

- When is an amniocentesis usually performed?

Slide 29

- What is the difference between streptococcus and staphylococcus?
- What is an abscess?
- What are the different types of hernias?
- When is an amniocentesis usually performed?

Slide 30

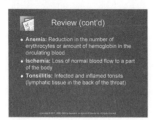

- What is the literal meaning of anemia?
- How are anemias classified?
- What is aplastic anemia?
- What happens to tissue that becomes ischemic?

Slide 31

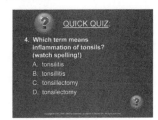

- Correct answer is B: tonsillitis. Although the term tonsil has only one "l", the combining form has a double letter "l". "ITIS" means inflammation. Choice A is incorrect because it has only one "l".

Slide 32

- What usually causes the excessive amount of growth hormone found in acromegaly?
- What is the spleen composed of, and what is its function?
- What is the difference between leukocytosis and leukemia? What do their suffixes mean?

Slide 33

- Laparoscope – a lighted telescopic instrument
- What causes achondroplasia?
- How is the suffix -ptosis pronounced?
- What are the specific uses of laparoscopy?

Slide 34

- What is the literal meaning of adenoids?
- What may happen if adenoids become enlarged?

Slide 35

- Correct answer is C: capillaries are the tiniest of blood vessels. See p. 88, appendix P for more information.

The Language of Medicine, 9th ed.

Chabner

Slide 36

Slide 37

- Are all students clear on the differences in short and long vowel sounds?

Chabner

4 Prefixes

TEACHING FOCUS

Students will have the opportunity to learn many of the most common prefixes in the medical language that provide a foundation for the study of body systems. Students will also be presented with additional combining forms that will aid in the analysis of terminology in this chapter. Students will have the opportunity to expand their understanding of terminology with reference to anatomy, physiology, and pathology.

MATERIALS AND RESOURCES

- ☐ Chalkboard or overhead projector (Lesson 4.1)
- ☐ Color photocopies (Lesson 4.1)
- ☐ Copies of unlabeled Figure 4-2 (Lesson 4.1)
- ☐ Textbook (Lesson 4.1)
- ☐ Transparencies or flash cards with words combining prefixes and other word elements (Lesson 4.1)

LESSON CHECKLIST

Preparations for this lesson include:

- Lecture
- Method of student evaluation for entry-level knowledge to achieve competency, focusing on:
  - o prefixes and suffixes, including those presented in previous chapters
  - o word analysis and combining word forms to build terms
  - o understanding new terminology and pronouncing it correctly
  - o terminology associated with Rh-factor conditions

KEY TERMS

Combining Forms (p. 110)
carp/o
cib/o
cis/o
cost/o
cutane/o
dactyl/o
duct/o
flex/o
furc/o
gloss/o
glyc/o
immun/o
morph/o
mort/o
nat/i
nect/o
norm/o
ox/o
pub/o
seps/o
somn/o
son/o
the/o
thel/o
thyr/o
top/o
tox/o

trache/o
urethr/o
Suffixes (p. 111)
-blast
-crine
-cyesis
-drome
-fusion
-gen
-lapse
-lysis
-meter
-mission
-or
-partum
-phoria
-physis
-plasia
-plasm
-pnea
-ptosis
-rrhea
-stasis
-trophy
Prefixes and Terminology (pp. 111-117)
a-, an-
ab-
ad-

ana-
ante-
anti-
auto-
bi-
brady-
cata-
con-
contra-
de-
dia-
dys-
ec-, ecto-
en-, endo-
epi-
eu-
ex-
hemi-
hyper-
hypo-
in- (not)
in- (into, within)
infra-
inter-
intra-
macro-
mal-
meta-
micro-
neo-
pan-
para-
per-
peri-
poly-
post-
pre-
pro-
pseudo-
re-
retro-
sub-
supra-
syn-, sym-
tachy-

trans-
ultra-
uni-

Appendix A: Adrenal Glands (p. 118)
  adrenal glands
Appendix B: Antigens and Antibodies; the Rh Condition (pp. 118-120)
  antibodies
  antigen
  bilirubin
  erythroblastosis fetalis
  hemolytic disease of the newborn (HDN)
  jaundice
  Rh condition
Appendix C: Autoimmune (p. 120)
  autoimmune
Appendix D: Congenital Anomaly (p. 120)
  congenital anomalies
Appendix E: Contralateral (p. 121)
  contralateral
  ipsilateral
Appendix F: Ectopic Pregnancy (p. 121)
  ectopic pregnancy
Appendix G: Prolapse (p. 122)
  -lapse
  prolapses
Appendix H: Recombinant DNA (p. 122)
  polymerase chain reaction (PCR)
  recombinant DNA
Appendix I: Syndactyly (p. 122)
  syndactyly
Appendix J: Syndrome (pp. 122-123)
  syndrome
Appendix K: Symbiosis (p. 123)
  parasitism
  symbiosis
Appendix L: Symphysis (p. 123)
  symphysis
Appendix M: Transurethral (p. 124)
  transurethral
Appendix N: Ultrasonography (p. 124)
  echocardiograms
  sonogram
  ultrasonography

Chabner

REFERENCE LIST
PowerPoint slides (CD, Evolve): 1-30

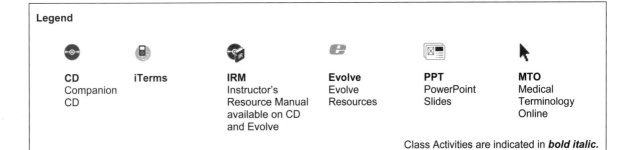

Legend

CD Companion CD	**iTerms**	**IRM** Instructor's Resource Manual available on CD and Evolve	**Evolve** Evolve Resources	**PPT** PowerPoint Slides	**MTO** Medical Terminology Online

Class Activities are indicated in ***bold italic.***

LESSON 4.1

PRETEST
IRM Quiz C

BACKGROUND ASSESSMENT
Question: What is a prefix? What is an example of a prefix? Give at least three examples of different medical terms that share that same prefix. Give an example of medical terms that share the same root but have different prefixes.

Answer: A prefix is a small word part that is attached to the beginning of a term. Not all medical terms contain prefixes, but the prefix can have an important influence on meaning. An example of a prefix is *hyper-*, which means "excessive" or "above." Three medical terms that use the prefix hyper- are hyperglycemia, which means excess of sugar in the blood; hyperplasia, which means increase in cell numbers; and hypertrophy, which means increase in size of individual cells. Subgastric and epigastric are examples of terms that share a root but have different prefixes and drastically different meanings. *Subgastric* means "pertaining to [something] under the stomach" and *epigastric* means "pertaining to [something] above the stomach."

Question: What is the medical term for a group of signs or symptoms that commonly occur together and indicate a particular disease or abnormal condition?

Answer: The term for a group of symptoms that occur together and indicate a particular disease is *syndrome*. The term syndrome is built from the suffix "syn" meaning "together, with" and from the Greek "dromos" meaning a cause for running.

CRITICAL THINKING QUESTION
Melinda is a student in a medical assisting program. She has difficulty reading an entry in a patient's chart that states that the patient has shown evidence of either hypertension or hypotension. She cannot read the physician's handwriting. Is there a difference between the two?

Guidelines: Yes! Hypertension would indicate high blood pressure, whereas hypotension would indicate abnormally low blood pressure. She needs to confirm which of the two is correct.

OBJECTIVES	CONTENT	TEACHING RESOURCES
Analyze medical terms that combine prefixes and other word elements.	■ Combining forms and suffixes (p. 110) ☐ Combining forms (p. 110) ☐ Suffixes (p. 111)	PPT 13-14 IRM Exercise Quiz G IRM Pronunciation Quiz C MTO Module 4, Section I, Lessons 1-2 Exercise J (pp. 130-131) Companion CD Exercises 4-3, 4-4 *Class Activity **Divide the class into teams of three or four. During a timed session, call out the name of a suffix or combining form.*** ***Each team must create as many medical terms from the suffix or combining form as it can in a 60-second period. After 60 seconds, announce another suffix or combining form.*** ***Alternatively, write each suffix or combining form on a card and its definition on another***

Chabner

OBJECTIVES	CONTENT	TEACHING RESOURCES
		card. Divide into as many piles as there are groups. Shuffle the cards and give to each group to match the suffix/combining form to its correct definition. Have students then shuffle the cards and pass to the next group until all suffixes and combining forms have been defined by all groups.
Define basic prefixes used in the medical language.	■ Prefixes and terminology (p. 111)	⊠■ PPT 1-12
		IRM Multiple Choice Quiz
		IRM Exercise Quizzes A, C, F
		IRM Pronunciation Quiz B
		IRM Crossword Puzzle
		➤ MTO Module 4, Section II, Lessons 1-4
		Prefixes and Terminology (pp. 111-117)
		Exercise A (p. 126)
		Exercise D (p. 127)
		Exercise G (p. 129)
		◉ Companion CD Exercises 4-1, 4-2
		Class Activity Go around the room and ask each student to name a prefix. Have the student give the prefix's meaning and name a medical term using that prefix. The next student must either name a new prefix or be able to name a term that has not been used yet.
		Class Activity Divide the class into two competing teams. Ask them to name a prefix, give the prefix's meaning, and name a medical term using that prefix. The first team to do so correctly wins a point. The team with the most points at the end of the game wins.
		Class Activity Divide the class into small groups. Write four prefixes on the chalkboard or overhead projector. Ask each group to come up with as many medical terms using those prefixes as possible. Ask one student in each group to be a fact checker to see if the terms are listed in a medical dictionary.

Chabner

OBJECTIVES	CONTENT	TEACHING RESOURCES
Analyze medical terms that combine prefixes and other word elements.	■ Appendixes (p. 118) □ Adrenal glands (p. 118)	PPT 15, 19, 20-22 IRM Multiple Choice Quiz IRM Exercise Quizzes A, C IRM Dictation and Comprehension Quiz IRM Spelling Quiz part A MTO Module 4, Section V Practical Applications (p. 125) Exercises B, C, I, J (pp. 126-127, 130-131) Companion CD Exercises 4-5, 4-6 ***Class Activity Divide the class into three groups and have each choose a contestant for a quiz show. Using transparencies or flash cards, show the contestants a variety of words one at a time. Ask them to pronounce each word correctly, spell the prefix and define it. The first contestant to answer correctly wins a point. When a contestant answers incorrectly, the team chooses a new contestant. The team with the most correct answers wins.***
Learn about the Rh condition as an example of an antigen-antibody reaction.	□ Antigens and antibodies; the Rh condition (p. 118)	PPT 16-18 Exercise A (p. 126) ***Class Activity Make copies of Figure 4-2 on p. 119, taking care to delete the labels. Divide the students into small groups. Ask each group to describe the scenario of the "second pregnancy" figure. Also ask them how this scenario can be prevented.***
Analyze medical terms that combine prefixes and other word elements.	■ Appendixes □ Autoimmune (p. 120) □ Congenital anomaly (p. 120) □ Contralateral (p. 121) □ Ectopic pregnancy (p. 121) □ Prolapse (p. 122) □ Recombinant DNA (p. 122) □ Syndactyly (p. 122) □ Syndrome (p. 122) □ Symbiosis (p. 123)	PPT 23-30 IRM Multiple Choice Quiz IRM Exercise Quizzes B, C, E, H IRM Spelling Quizzes A, B IRM Dictation and Comprehension Quiz IRM Pronunciation Quiz A Practical Applications (p. 125) Figure 4-1 Adrenal glands (p. 118)

Chabner

OBJECTIVES	CONTENT	TEACHING RESOURCES
	□ Symphysis (p. 123) □ Transurethral (p. 124) □ Ultrasonography (p. 124) ■ Pronunciation of terms (pp. 134-136)	Figure 4-3 Rh condition (p. 120) Figure 4-4 Sites of ectopic pregnancies (p. 121) Figure 4-5 First- and second-degree prolapse of the uterus (p. 122) Figure 4-6 Syndactyly (p. 123) Figure 4-7 Pubic symphysis (p. 123) Figure 4-8 Location of the prostate gland (p. 124) Figure 4-9 Ultrasonography (p. 124) Exercises B, C, E, F, H, I, K (pp. 126-131) Pronunciation Exercise (pp. 134-136) ⊙ Companion CD Exercise 4-7 ▯ iTerms Chapter 04 *Class Activity **Read any/all of the appendixes to the students. Ask them to spell, analyze, define, and underline the accented syllable in the boldfaced terms.*** *Class Activity **Spell a medical term to the class. Ask students to pronounce the word. Repeat this for 10 to 20 terms.***
Performance Evaluation		⬤ IRM Multiple Choice Quiz ⬤ IRM Exercise Quiz ⬤ IRM Dictation and Comprehension Quiz ⬤ IRM Spelling Quiz ⬤ IRM Pronunciation Quiz ⬤ IRM Review Sheet Quiz ⬤ IRM Medical Scramble ⬤ IRM Crossword Puzzle ⬤ ESLR Student Quiz Chapter 04 ⬈ MTO Module 4, Sections I-III quizzes ⬈ MTO Module 4 Exam Practical Applications (p. 125) ⊙ Companion CD Exercise 4-8

ELSEVIER

4.1 Homework/Assignments:

Divide the class into teams. Assign each of the terms in appendixes A through O. Have each team research the term and give a synopsis of their research to the class.

4.1 Teacher's Notes:

Slide 1

Slide 2

Slide 3

Slide 4

Slide 5

- Refer to section beginning on p. 111 for terms using these prefixes.

Slide 6

• Refer to section beginning on p. 111 for terms using these prefixes.

Slide 7

Slide 8

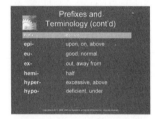

Slide 9

Slide 10

The Language of Medicine, 9th ed.

Chabner

Slide 11

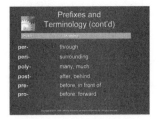

Slide 12

Slide 13

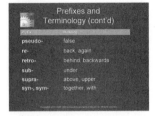

Slide 14

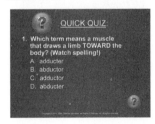

- Correct answer is C: adductor (answer A is misspelled. B means a muscle that draws a limb away from the body. D is misspelled.)

Slide 15

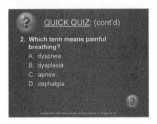

- Correct answer is A: dyspnea dys- means painful -pnea means breathing. Remember, medical terms do not need to have a root or combining form (as dyspnea, for example, has a prefix and a suffix with an imbedded root.)

Chabner

Slide 16

- What is the function of adrenal glands?

- What is adrenaline? What is another name for the term?

- What was the first antibiotic? (*penicillin*)

- What are some examples of autoimmune diseases? (*rheumatoid arthritis, lupus, Graves' disease*)

Slide 17

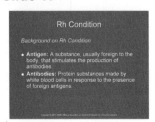

- Antigen examples: poison, flu virus, bacterium

- Immune reaction: reaction between an antigen and antibody

- What is a common name for an immune reaction against normally nonthreatening antigens?

Slide 18

- Discuss how Rh condition occurs.

  - First pregnancy with Rh+ baby: baby is not affected but Rh- mother is sensitized

  - Second pregnancy with Rh+ baby baby develops hemolytic disease of the newborn (HDN)

  - Symptom of HDN: Jaundice

- How can the condition be prevented? (*Prevent Rh condition with Rh immune globulin injection to Rh- woman within 72 hours of delivery, miscarriage, or abortion of an Rh+ fetus.*)

Slide 19

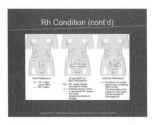

Slide 20

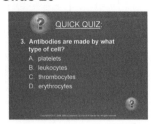

- Correct answer is B: leukocytes or white blood cells.

The Language of Medicine, 9th ed.

Chabner

Slide 21

- What are some examples of congenital anomalies?
- What are some causes of nonhereditary congenital anomalies?

Slide 22

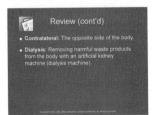

- Give some examples that demonstrate contralateral.
- What term means the same side? (*ipsilateral*)

Slide 23

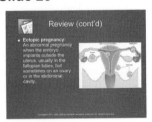

- See p. 118 for more details

Slide 24

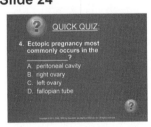

- Correct answer is D: fallopian tube. See p. 118 for more detail.

Slide 25

- What is the function of parathyroid hormone?

Slide 26

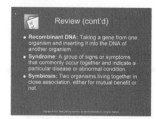

- Describe the recombinant DNA technique used to manufacture insulin outside the body.
- What is polymerase chain reaction (PCR)?
- List a syndrome example (other than Reye syndrome and fetal alcohol syndrome), and ask students to list the symptoms.
- What is parasitism?

Slide 27

- What are some examples of symphysis?

Slide 28

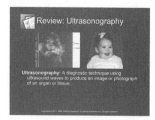

- Notice the facial features in the ultrasound image.
- What is an echocardiogram?

Slide 29

Slide 30

- Have students pronounce each term.
- Which syllable is accented (stressed) in each of these terms?

TEACHING FOCUS

Students will have the opportunity to learn the names of the organs of the digestive system, their locations and functions, and disease processes and symptoms that affect the digestive system organs. Furthermore, students will have the opportunity to learn how to define combining forms for organs, explain the meaning of related terminology using word parts, and learn how to properly pronounce new terms.

MATERIALS AND RESOURCES

- ☐ Copies of IRM Diagram Quiz (Lesson 5.1)
- ☐ Index cards (Lesson 5.1)
- ☐ Overhead projector (all Lessons)
- ☐ Paper (all Lessons)
- ☐ Projector screen (all Lessons)

- ☐ Transparencies or flash cards with a variety of words from the Combining Forms Section and Pathology Section (Lesson 5.2)
- ☐ Unlabeled diagrams of digestive organs (Lesson 5.2)

LESSON CHECKLIST

Preparations for this lesson include:

- Lecture
- Student performance evaluation of all entry-level skills required for student comprehension and application of anatomy and terminology related to the digestive system, including:
  - o the names, locations, and functions of the organs of the digestive system
  - o diseases and symptoms of the digestive system
  - o medical terminology, combining forms, and suffixes related to the digestive system
  - o the proper pronunciation of medical terms

KEY TERMS

Introduction (p. 142)
  absorption
  amino acids
  digested
  digestion
  elimination
  enzymes
  fatty acids
  gastrointestinal
  glucose
  triglycerides
Oral Cavity (pp. 142-145)
  buccal
  canine
  cheeks
  crown
  cementum
  deglutition
  dentin
  distal
  enamel
  enzymes
  facial
  gums
  hard palate
  incisal
  incisor

labial
lingual
lips
mastication
mesial
molar
occlusal
papillae
parotid gland
periodontal membrane
premolar
pulp
root
root canal
rugae
saliva
salivary glands
soft palate
sublingual gland
submandibular gland
teeth
tongue
tonsils
uvula
Pharynx (p. 145)
  deglutition
  esophagus

ELSEVIER

pharynx
throat

Esophagus (p. 146)

bolus
peristalsis
stomach

Stomach (p. 147)

antrum
body
fundus
hydrochloric acid
lower esophageal sphincter (cardiac sphincter)
pepsin
pyloric sphincter
rugae
sphincters

Small Intestine (Small Bowel) (p. 147)

bile
duodenum
gallbladder
ileum
jejunum
liver
pancreas
small intestine (small bowel)
villi

Large Intestine (Large Bowel) (p. 148)

anus
appendix
ascending colon
cecum
colon
defecation
descending colon
feces
rectum
sigmoid colon
transverse colon

Liver, Gallbladder, and Pancreas
(pp. 149-151)

amylase
bile
bilirubin
common bile duct
cystic duct
duodenum
emulsification
gallbladder
glycogen
glycogenolysis
gluconeogenesis
glucose
hepatic duct
insulin

jaundice (hyperbilirubinemia)
lipase
liver
pancreas
pancreatic duct
portal vein
protease

Terminology/Parts of the Body (pp. 155-159)

an/o
append/o
appendic/o
bucc/o
cec/o
celi/o
cheil/o
cholecyst/o
choledoch/o
col/o
colon/o
dent/i
duoden/o
enter/o
esophag/o
faci/o
gastr/o
gingiv/o
gloss/o
hepat/o
ile/o
jejun/o
labi/o
lapar/o
lingu/o
mandibul/o
odont/o
or/o
palat/o
pancreat/o
peritone/o
pharyng/o
proct/o
pylor/o
rect/o
sialaden/o
sigmoid/o
stomat/o
uvul/o

Terminology/Substances (pp. 159-160)

amyl/o
bil/i
bilirubin/o
chol/e
chlorhydr/o
gluc/o

glyc/o
glycogen/o
lip/o
lith/o
prote/o
sial/o
steat/o

Terminology/Suffixes (p. 160)
-ase
-chezia
-iasis
-prandial

Pathology (pp. 161-170)
anorexia
ascites
borborygmus
constipation
diarrhea
dysphagia
eructation
flatus
hematochezia
jaundice
melana
nausea
steatorrhea
achalasia

anal fistula
aphthous stomatitis
cholelithiasis
cirrhosis
colonic polyposis
colorectal cancer
Crohn's disease
dental caries
diverticulosis
dysentery
esophageal varices
gastric carcinoma
gastroesophageal reflux disease (GERD)
hemorrhoids
hernia
herpetic stomatitis
oral leukoplakia
ileus
intussusception
irritable bowel syndrome
pancreatitis
periodontal disease
peptic ulcer
ulcerative colitis
viral hepatitis
volvulus

REFERENCE LIST
PowerPoint slides (CD, Evolve): 1-53

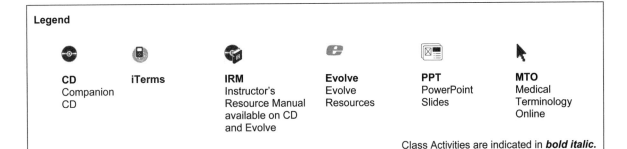

Legend

CD	iTerms	IRM	Evolve	PPT	MTO
Companion CD		Instructor's Resource Manual available on CD and Evolve	Evolve Resources	PowerPoint Slides	Medical Terminology Online

Class Activities are indicated in **bold italic**.

LESSON 5.1

PRETEST
IRM Quiz B

BACKGROUND ASSESSMENT
Question: What are the three functions of the digestive system? Describe each function.
Answer: The three functions of the system are digestion, absorption, and elimination. In the first step, digestion, food taken into the mouth is digested or broken down, mechanically and chemically, as it travels through the gastrointestinal tract. Digestive enzymes speed up chemical reactions and aid the breakdown of complex nutrients. In the second step, absorption, digested food passes into the bloodstream through the walls of the small intestine. Nutrients such as sugar, fatty acids, and amino acids travel to all cells of the body, which burn them for energy. The third function of the digestive system is elimination of solid waste materials that cannot be absorbed into the bloodstream. The large intestine concentrates these solid wastes, called feces, and passes them out of the body through the anus.

Question: What is the difference between the small intestine and the large intestine?
Answer: The small intestine connects the stomach to the large intestine. The small intestine is a 20-foot-long narrow tube that has millions of microscopic projections called villi that line its walls. The tiny capillaries (microscopic blood vessels) in the villi absorb the digested nutrients into the bloodstream and lymph vessels. The large intestine extends from the ileum, the third section of the small intestine, to the anus. The large intestine is 4 to 6 feet long and larger in diameter than the small intestine. It receives the fluid waste products of digestion (the material unable to pass into the bloodstream) and stores these wastes until they can be released from the body. Because the large intestine absorbs most of the water from the waste material, the body can expel solid feces.

CRITICAL THINKING QUESTION
Frank, a 72-year-old man with suspected colon cancer, underwent a colonoscopy. A large mass was found 12 centimeters proximal to the splenic flexure. In which part of the colon is this located? Trace the route of the colonoscope to the location of the mass.
Guidelines: The mass would be located in the transverse colon, between the ascending and descending colon. The colon is divided into several parts: the ascending colon, the transverse colon, the descending colon, and the sigmoid colon. The colonoscope would pass through the rectum, the sigmoid colon, the descending colon, and then finally past the splenic flexure to the transverse colon.

OBJECTIVES	CONTENT	TEACHING RESOURCES
Name the organs of the digestive system and describe their locations and functions.	■ Anatomy and physiology (p. 142) □ Oral cavity (p. 142) □ Pharynx (p. 145) □ Esophagus (p. 146) □ Stomach (p. 147) □ Small intestine (p. 147) □ Large intestine (p. 148) □ Liver, gallbladder, and pancreas (p. 149)	PPT 4-33 IRM Multiple Choice Quiz IRM Exercise Quiz A IRM Dictation and Comprehension Quiz: Vocabulary IRM Diagram Quiz MTO Module 5, Section I, Lessons 1-4 Figure 5-1 Oral cavity (p. 143) Figure 5-2 Upper permanent teeth (p. 143) Figure 5-3 Anatomy of a tooth (p. 144)

Chabner

OBJECTIVES	CONTENT	TEACHING RESOURCES
		Figure 5-4 Salivary glands (p. 145)
		Figure 5-5 Deglutition (p. 145)
		Figure 5-6 The gastrointestinal tract (p. 146)
		Figure 5-7 Parts of the stomach (p. 147)
		Figure 5-8 Villi in the lining of the small intestine (p. 148)
		Figure 5-9 Liver, gallbladder, and pancreas (p. 149)
		Figure 5-10 Bilirubin pathway (p. 150)
		Figure 5-11 The pancreas and its functions (p. 150)
		Figure 5-12 Pathway of food through the gastrointestinal tract (p. 151)
		Vocabulary Review (pp. 152-154)
		Exercises A, B (pp. 171)
		◉ Companion CD Exercises 5-1, 5-2, 5-3, 5-4, 5-5
		Class Activity Divide the class into teams. Give each team a blank copy of the IRM Diagram Quiz. The goal is to be the first team to complete the diagram correctly.
		Class Activity Divide the class into small teams and assign each team a category such as Oral Cavity, Pharynx, Esophagus, or Stomach. Ask each group to study the anatomy and function of the category, as well as investigate related combining forms and other word parts such as prefixes and suffixes. Have students summarize their findings for the class.
		Class Activity Write all the labels on Figure 5-12 (p. 151) on individual index cards. Randomly assign each student (or group of students) a card. Ask them to assemble themselves in specific order of the various systems in the digestion process.
Define combining forms for organs and the meaning of related terminology using these word parts.	■ Vocabulary (p. 152) ■ Terminology (p. 155) □ Parts of the body (p. 155) □ Substances (p. 159) □ Suffixes (p. 160)	⊠ PPT 34-37 🎲 IRM Multiple Choice Quiz 🎲 IRM Combining Forms, Suffixes, and Terminology Quiz 🎲 IRM Exercise Quizzes B-C

OBJECTIVES	CONTENT	TEACHING RESOURCES
		Exercise C (p. 172)
		Exercise D (pp. 172-173)
		Exercise F (p. 173)
		Exercise L (p. 177)
		◉ Companion CD Exercises 5-6, 5-7, 5-8
		***Class Activity** Divide the class into teams. During a timed session, call out the name of a combining form. Ask each team to create as many digestive system medical terms from the combining form as they can in a 60-second period. After 60 seconds, announce another combining form. If two teams have the same term, eliminate it and assign points for only the terms that appear once.*
		Using the diagram from the IRM Diagram Quiz in the first module, ask the students to label the diagrams using the combining forms.

5.1 Homework/Assignments:

Have students investigate the "camera pill" and report back to the class.

5.1 Teacher's Notes:

The Language of Medicine, 9ᵗʰ ed.

Chabner

LESSON 5.2

CRITICAL THINKING QUESTION

Anisha is studying her medical terms and is comparing examples. She finds the terms "gastroesophageal" and "esophagogastric." Should she assume that they are two ways of saying the same thing?

Guidelines: No! In systems that have directionality, "gastroesophageal" means *pertaining to the stomach and esophagus* and indicates that the direction is from the stomach toward the esophagus. "Esophagogastric" *means pertaining to the esophagus and stomach* and the direction is from the esophagus toward the stomach.

OBJECTIVES	CONTENT	TEACHING RESOURCES
Describe disease processes and symptoms that affect these organs.	■ Pathology of the digestive system (p. 160) □ Symptoms (p. 161) □ Pathological conditions (p. 162) — Oral cavity and teeth (p. 162) — Upper gastrointestinal tract (p. 164) — Lower gastrointestinal tract (p. 166) — Liver, gallbladder, and pancreas (p. 169)	PPT 39-53 IRM Multiple Choice Quiz IRM Pathology Quiz IRM Exercise Quizzes D-G IRM Dictation and Comprehension Quiz: Pathological Symptoms IRM Dictation and Comprehension Quiz: Pathological Conditions IRM Spelling Quiz IRM Crossword Puzzle MTO Module 5, Section II, Lessons 1-7 and Section III, Lesson 1 Figure 5-13 Stages of appendicitis (p. 155) Figure 5-14 Sigmoid colostomy (p. 156) Figure 5-15 Three types of anastomoses (p. 156) Figure 5-16 Mesentery (p. 157) Figure 5-17 Ascites (p. 161) Figure 5-18 Normal teeth and gums and diseased teeth and gums (p. 163) Figure 5-19 (A) Esophageal varices; (B) Advanced gastric carcinoma (p. 164) Figure 5-20 Hernias (p. 165) Figure 5-21 (A) Anal fistula and two types of polyps; (B) Multiple polyps of the colon (p. 166) Figure 5-22 Adenocarcinoma of the colon (p. 167) Figure 5-23 (A) Diverticula; (B) Diverticulosis (p. 167)

ELSEVIER

OBJECTIVES	CONTENT	TEACHING RESOURCES
		Figure 5-24 Intussusception and volvulus (p. 168)
		Figure 5-25 (A) Gallstones; (B) Liver with alcoholic cirrhosis (p. 168)
		Figure 5-26 Gallstone positions (p. 169)
		Figure 5-27 Trocars in place for laparoscopic cholecystectomy (p. 170)
		Exercises F-K (pp. 173-176)
		Companion CD Exercise 5-9
		Class Activity Pronounce the terms that describe the digestive system. Ask students to spell them and to underline the stressed syllable.
		Class Activity Show the class the drawings or photographs in the figures listed above, taking care to delete the labels. Ask the students to describe the condition being shown.
		Class Activity Divide the class into three groups and have each choose a contestant for a quiz show. Using transparencies or flash cards, show the contestants a variety of words one at a time. Ask them to pronounce each word correctly and define it. The first contestant to answer correctly wins a point. When a contestant answers incorrectly, the team chooses a new contestant. The team with the most correct answers wins.
Define combining forms for organs and the meaning of related terminology using these words.	■ Pronunciation of terms (p. 180) □ Vocabulary and terminology sections (p. 180 □ Pathological terminology (p. 184)	IRM Pronunciation Quiz Pronunciation Exercise (pp. 180-185) Companion CD Exercises 5-10, 5-11 iTerms Chapter 05 *Class Activity Spell a medical term to the class. Ask students to pronounce the word, along with analyzing the term and underlining the stressed syllable. Repeat this to cover 10 to 20 terms.* *Class Activity Divide the class into teams of two. Have each student practice pronouncing the terms on pp. 180-185 to each other.* *Alternatively, have students take turns reading the sentences in Exercise J of the text*

OBJECTIVES	CONTENT	TEACHING RESOURCES
		to the class, correcting their pronunciation as necessary. Ask them to analyze all terms that are appropriate.
Performance Evaluation		IRM Multiple Choice Quiz
		IRM Combining Forms, Suffixes, and Terminology Quiz
		IRM Pathology Quiz
		IRM Exercise Quiz
		IRM Dictation and Comprehension Quiz
		IRM Spelling Quiz
		IRM Pronunciation Quiz
		IRM Diagram Quiz
		IRM Vocabulary Quiz
		IRM Medical Scramble
		IRM Crossword Puzzle
		ESLR Body Spectrum Electronic Anatomy Coloring Book: Digestive
		ESLR Student Quiz Chapter 05
		MTO Module 5, Sections I-III quizzes
		MTO Module 5 Exam
		Companion CD Exercise 5-12

5.2 Homework/Assignments:

Have students write a two-page paper about the hepatitis B vaccine that children and healthcare workers receive. Why use that particular vaccine for those groups?

5.2 Teacher's Notes:

ELSEVIER

Slide 1

Slide 2

Slide 3

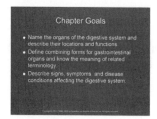

Slide 4

Slide 5

- Define, discuss, and describe the three main functions of the digestive system.

- What are enzymes, and what function do they serve in the digestive process?

Slide 6

Slide 7

Slide 8

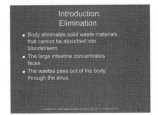

Slide 9

- In which major systems of the digestive tract do digestion, absorption, and elimination occur?

Slide 10

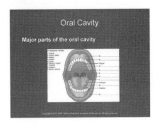

- Quiz students to complete labels.

- What is mastication?

- What is deglutition?

Chabner

Slide 11

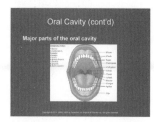

- Have students check answers using completed labels.
- What is mastication?
- What is deglutition?

Slide 12

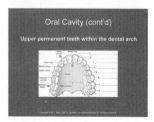

- Quiz students to complete labels.
- Discuss the following terms: labial surface, buccal surface, facial surface, lingual surface, mesial surface, distal surface, occlusal surface, and incisal edge.

Slide 13

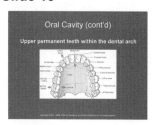

- Have students check answers using completed labels.
- Discuss the following terms: labial surface, buccal surface, facial surface, lingual surface, mesial surface, distal surface, occlusal surface, and incisal edge.

Slide 14

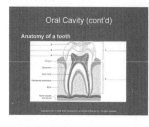

- Quiz students to complete labels.
- What is a root canal and why is it performed?

Slide 15

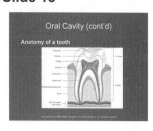

- Have students check answers using completed labels.
- What is a root canal and why is it performed?

The Language of Medicine, 9th ed.

Chabner

Slide 16

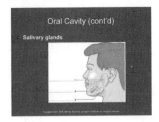

- Quiz students to complete labels.
- How many salivary glands surround the oral cavity?
- How do salivary enzymes aid digestion?

Slide 17

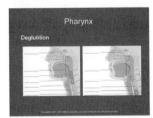

- The pharynx is the common passageway for both air and food.
- What potential problems do you see with this arrangement?
- How does the body address this problem?

Slide 18

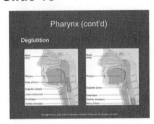

- The pharynx is the common passageway for both air and food.
- What potential problems do you see with this arrangement?
- How does the body address this problem?

Slide 19

- The esophagus is a 9 or 10 inch muscular tube extending from the pharynx to the stomach.
- What is a bolus?
- How does the esophagus move the bolus toward the stomach?
- What are the three parts of the stomach and what are their functions?

Slide 20

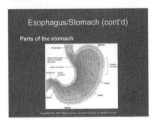

- The esophagus is a 9 or 10 inch muscular tube extending from the pharynx to the stomach.
- What is a bolus?
- How does the esophagus move the bolus toward the stomach?
- What are the three parts of the stomach and what are their functions?

Slide 21

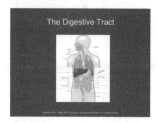

- Quiz students to complete labels.
- What is the name of the pigment produced from the breakdown of hemoglobin during red blood cell destruction?

Slide 22

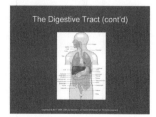

- Quiz students to check answers using completed labels.
- What is the name of the pigment produced from the breakdown of hemoglobin during red blood cell destruction?

Slide 23

- What is the function of the villi?

Slide 24

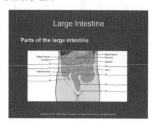

- Also known as the colon.
- The large intestine extends from the end of the ileum to the anus.
- The large intestine receives the fluid waste from digestion and stores it until it can be released from the body.
- What are the three sections of the colon and what are their functions?

Slide 25

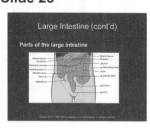

- Also known as the colon.
- The large intestine extends from the end of the ileum to the anus.
- The large intestine receives the fluid waste from digestion and stores it until it can be released from the body.
- What are the three sections of the colon and what are their functions?

ELSEVIER

The Language of Medicine, 9th ed.
Chabner

Slide 26

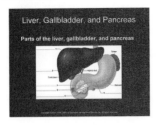

- Quiz students to complete labels in Fig. 5-9.
- What is emulsification?

Slide 27

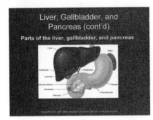

- Have students check answers using completed labels in Fig. 5-9.
- What is emulsification?

Slide 28

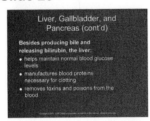

- How does the liver maintain blood glucose levels?

Slide 29

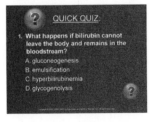

- Correct answer is C: hyperbilirubinemia (jaundice) which can show yellow discoloration of the skin, whites of the eyes, and mucous membranes.

Slide 30

- The pancreas is both an exocrine and endocrine organ.
- As an exocrine organ, it produces enzymes to digest starch (amylase), fat (lipase), and proteins (protease)
- As an endocrine organ it secretes insulin.
- What is the function of insulin?

Slide 31

- Quiz students by having them complete the flow chart of how food progresses through the GI tract.

Slide 32

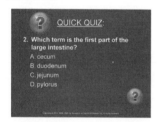

Slide 33

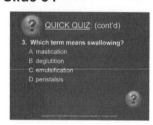

- Correct answer is A: the cecum is the first part of the large intestine.

Slide 34

- Correct answer is B: deglutition means swallowing.

Slide 35

- Define combining forms for organs and the meanings of related terminology using these word parts.

- Name two medical terms (not mentioned above) from the word forms listed.

Slide 36

- When -stomy is used with two or more combining forms for organs, it means the surgical creation of an opening between those organs inside the body.
- Anastomosis is the surgical connection between two body parts such as vessels, ducts, or bowel segments.
- In what other places might anastomoses be made?

Slide 37

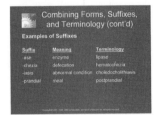

- Define suffixes for organs and the meanings of related terminology using these word parts.

Slide 38

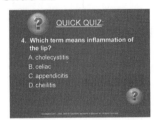

- Correct answer is D: cheilitis.

Slide 39

Slide 40

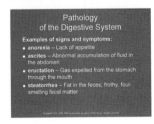

- Discuss symptoms such as ascites, borborygmus, constipation, diarrhea, dysphagia, flatus, hematochezia, jaundice, melena, and nausea.
- Based on your knowledge of the functions of the liver, how might cirrhosis cause ascites?
- For more signs and symptoms, see Chapter 5, Pathology Section.

Chabner

Slide 41

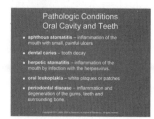

- Discuss herpetic stomatitis, oral leukoplakia, and periodontal disease.
- How does tooth decay progress? How is it treated?

Slide 42

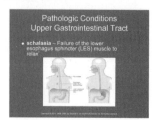

- What kind of diet do physicians recommend to relieve symptoms of achalasia?

Slide 43

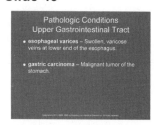

- Discuss the following terms: gastroesophageal reflux disease, hernia, and peptic ulcer.
- What is a major risk factor for gastric carcinoma? How is it treated?
- LES is lower esophagus sphincter.

Slide 44

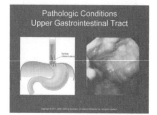

Slide 45

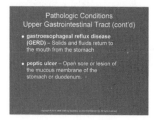

- Discuss the following terms: gastroesophageal reflux disease, hernia, and peptic ulcer.

Slide 46

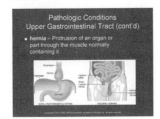

Pathologic Conditions
Upper Gastrointestinal Tract (cont'd)

- **hernia** – Protrusion of an organ or part through the muscle normally containing it.

Slide 47

Pathologic Conditions
Lower Gastrointestinal Tract:
Small and Large Intestines

- **anal fistula** – Abnormal tube-like passageway near the anus.

- **colonic polyposis** – Polyps protrude from the mucous membrane of the colon.

Slide 48

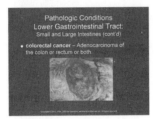

Pathologic Conditions
Lower Gastrointestinal Tract:
Small and Large Intestines (cont'd)

- **colorectal cancer** – Adenocarcinoma of the colon or rectum or both.

Slide 49

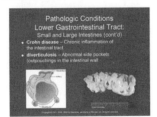

Pathologic Conditions
Lower Gastrointestinal Tract:
Small and Large Intestines (cont'd)

- **Crohn disease** – Chronic inflammation of the intestinal tract
- **diverticulosis** – Abnormal side pockets (outpouchings in the intestinal wall

Slide 50

Pathologic Conditions
Lower Gastrointestinal Tract:
Small and Large Intestines (cont'd)

- **dysentery** – Painful, inflamed intestines
- **hemorrhoids** – Swollen, twisted, varicose veins in the rectal region
- **ileus** – Failure of peristalsis with resulting obstruction of the intestines

Chabner

Slide 51

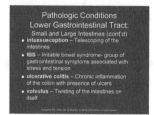

Slide 52

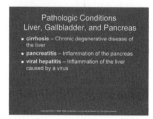

- What causes cirrhosis of the liver?

Slide 53

- What is biliary colic?
- What type of surgery is performed to remove the gallbladder and stones?

Chabner

6 Additional Suffixes and Digestive System Terminology

TEACHING FOCUS

Students will be introduced to a list of suffixes that commonly relate to the gastrointestinal system. With an understanding of these terms, students will have the opportunity to learn how terms are combined to define clinical terminology and procedures. Students will also have the opportunity to learn the laboratory tests and procedures, along with their abbreviated terms, that are related to gastrointestinal treatments. With a practical application, students will have the opportunity to gain an understanding of how terms are used within the context of one patient's case of a gastrointestinal disorder.

MATERIALS AND RESOURCES

- ☐ Bowl or hat (Lesson 6.1)
- ☐ Flash cards with names of laboratory tests, clinical procedures, or abbreviations related to the digestive system (Lesson 6.1)
- ☐ Transparencies or flash cards with a variety of suffixes and combining forms relating to the digestive system (Lesson 6.1)

LESSON CHECKLIST

Preparations for this lesson include:

- Lecture
- Demonstration
- Student performance evaluation of all entry-level skills required for student comprehension and application of digestive system terminology, including:
  - o new suffixes and how they relate to the digestive system
  - o laboratory tests, clinical procedures, and abbreviations that relate to the digestive system
  - o medical terms in reports and records

KEY TERMS

Suffixes (pp. 188-190)
- -ectasis, -ectasia
- -emesis
- -lysis
- -pepsia
- -phagia
- -plasty
- -ptosis
- -ptysis
- -rrhage, -rrhagia
- -rrhaphy
- -rrhea
- -spasm
- -stasis
- -stenosis
- -tresia

Terminology (pp. 191-192)
- bucc/o
- cec/o
- celi/o
- cheil/o
- chol/e
- cholangi/o
- cholecyst/o
- choledoch/o
- col/o
- colon/o
- dent/i
- duoden/o
- enter/o
- esophag/o
- gastr/o
- gingiv/o
- gloss/o
- gluc/o
- glyc/o
- hepat/o
- herni/o
- ile/o
- jejun/o
- labi/o
- lingu/o
- lip/o
- lith/o
- odont/o
- or/o
- palat/o
- pancreat/o
- proct/o
- pylor/o
- rect/o
- sialaden/o

splen/o
steat/o
stomat/o

Laboratory Tests (p. 193)
liver function tests (LFTs)
stool culture
stool guaiac or Hemoccult test

Clinical Procedures (pp. 193-199)
abdominal ultrasonography (ultrasound or
    sonography)
cholangiography

computed tomography (CT)
gastric bypass
gastrointestinal endoscopy
liver biopsy
liver scan
lower gastrointestinal series (barium enema)
magnetic resonance imaging (MRI)
nasogastric intubation
paracentesis (abdominocentesis)
upper gastrointestinal series

REFERENCE LIST
PowerPoint slides (CD, Evolve): 1-34

Chabner

LESSON 6.1

PRETEST
IRM Exercise Quiz A

BACKGROUND ASSESSMENT
Question: Using the suffixes that you have learned in previous chapters, build terms using the combining forms that were learned in Chapter 5.
Answer: Answers will vary, but may include gastroenteritis, gastralgia, cheiloplasty, esophagoscopy, and hepatectomy.

Question: Sometimes a suffix functions independently as a medical term. Give two examples of suffixes that are also terms, and explain how they are used.
Answer: The suffix "-lysis" means to break down. When used as a separate word, "lysis" is often used to describe a breakdown of cells. Similarly, the suffix "-spasm" refers to a sudden contraction of muscles, as in bronchospasm. However, the term "spasm" can be used alone to describe a sudden muscle contraction.

CRITICAL THINKING QUESTION
Sandra was admitted through the emergency department for a suspected bleeding ulcer. Her symptoms included gastralgia, dyspepsia, and hematemesis. What is the suffix that would tell you that she had been vomiting?
Guidelines: Hemat/o means blood and -emesis means vomiting. Hematemesis means that the patient has vomited blood. Gastralgia is stomach pain (gastr/o stomach; -algia pain) and dyspepsia is difficult or painful digestion (dys- bad, difficult, painful; -pepsia digestion).

OBJECTIVES	CONTENT	TEACHING RESOURCES
Define new suffixes and use them with digestive system combining forms.	■ Introduction (p. 188) ■ Suffixes (p. 188) ■ Terminology (p. 191)	PPT 4-13, 26-33 IRM Suffixes and Terminology Quiz IRM Exercise Quizzes A-E IRM Dictation and Comprehension Quiz IRM Spelling Quiz IRM Review Sheet Quiz IRM Crossword Puzzle MTO Module 6, Section I, Lessons 1-3 Figure 6-1 Esophageal atresia with tracheoesophageal fistula (p. 190) Exercises A-F, I (pp. 203-206) Review Sheet (pp. 214-215) Companion CD Exercises 6-1, 6-2, 6-3 *Class Activity Divide the class into three groups and have each choose a contestant for a game show. Using flash cards or transparencies, show the contestants a variety of suffixes and combining forms (relating to*

Chabner

OBJECTIVES	CONTENT	TEACHING RESOURCES
		the digestive system) one at a time. Ask them to define each word element correctly and give an example of its use in a term. Award a point to the first contestant to answer correctly. When a contestant answers incorrectly, the team chooses a new contestant. **Class Activity** *Distribute index cards with one suffix or combining form written on each. Have students pair up to create a combined-form term. Have the class decide what the new term means, and if it is an accepted term.* *Alternatively, write medical terms on index cards and tape one to each student's back. Have the students divide into pairs and have the pairs ask each other "yes/no" questions to determine the meaning of the term.* *Examples: Is it an A&P term? Is it a pathology term? Does it refer to the upper GI system? Does it have a prefix? Students may ask only one question at a time: then they must answer a question.*
List and explain laboratory tests, clinical procedures, and abbreviations common to the digestive system.	■ Laboratory tests, clinical procedures, and abbreviations (p. 193) ☐ Laboratory tests (p. 193) ☐ Clinical procedures (p. 193) ■ Abbreviations (p. 200)	PPT 14-25 IRM Exercise Quiz F MTO Module 6, Section II, Lessons 1-3 MTO Module 6, Section III, Lesson 1 Figure 6-2 (A) Barium enema; (B) small-bowel follow-through (p. 194) Figure 6-3 (A) Endoscopic retrograde cholangiopancreatography; (B) ERCP showing choledocholithiasis (p. 195) Figure 6-4 Computed tomographic images (p. 196) Figure 6-5 Gastric bypass (p. 197) Figure 6-6 Esophagogastroduodenoscopy (p. 198) Figure 6-7 Colonoscopy and polypectomy (p. 198) Exercises D, G, H (pp. 204, 206-207) Companion CD Exercise 6-6

The Language of Medicine, 9th ed.

Chabner

OBJECTIVES	CONTENT	TEACHING RESOURCES
		Class Activity Write the names of the various lab tests, clinical procedures, and abbreviations discussed in this section on slips of paper and place them in a bowl or hat. Have each student pull one out and describe the purpose or function of the term written on the slip. If a student does not know the answer, have the next student provide it.
		Class Activity Divide the class into two teams. Give each team a different set of flash cards with the names of laboratory tests, clinical procedures, or abbreviations related to the digestive system on them. The teams take turns showing a card to their opponents, who have to define the test or procedure, or give the abbreviated term. Award a point for each correct answer. However, the presenting team loses a point for accepting an incorrect answer or rejecting a correct answer.
Apply your new knowledge to understanding medical terms in their proper context, such as in medical reports and records.	■ Practical applications (p. 201)	🎲 IRM Pronunciation Quiz 🎲 IRM Practical Applications ⬆ MTO Module 6, Section V Exercise J (p. 208) 💿 Companion CD Exercises 6-4, 6-5 *Class Activity Read aloud the Colonoscopy Report (p. 201). When you read a word or phrase that is followed by a definition in brackets, ask students to write down a definition for the term or phrase you have just read. Have the students underline the accented syllable. Ask students to spell, analyze, define, and underline the accented syllables in the following terms included in the report: colonoscopy, polypectomy, coloproctoscopy, sigmoidoscopy, colonoscope, and pathology. As a concluding activity, have students form small groups to answer questions 1-4 in the report.*
Performance Evaluation		🎲 IRM Multiple Choice Quiz 🎲 IRM Suffixes and Terminology Quiz 🎲 IRM Exercise Quizzes A-F 🎲 IRM Dictation and Comprehension Quiz

OBJECTIVES	CONTENT	TEACHING RESOURCES
		IRM Spelling Quiz
		IRM Pronunciation Quiz
		IRM Review Sheet Quiz
		IRM Medical Scramble
		IRM Crossword Puzzle
		IRM Practical Applications
		ESLR Student Quiz Chapter 06
		MTO Module 6, Section I-III quizzes
		MTO Module 6 Exam
		Companion CD Exercises 6-7, 6-8
		iTerms Chapter 06

6.1 Homework/Assignments:

6.1 Teacher's Notes:

The Language of Medicine, 9th ed.

Chabner

Slide 1

Slide 2

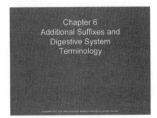

Slide 3

Slide 4

Slide 5

- Which suffix(es) describe(s) a position?

- Which suffix(es) describe(s) a motion?

- Which suffix is used in a term that describes uncontrolled eating?

- Which suffixes are surgical?

- What is the difference between hematemesis and hemoptysis?

Slide 6

- Which suffixes also stand alone as a word?
- Which suffix describes a motion?
- Which suffix is used in a term that describes flow or discharge?

Slide 7

- Use two of these terms in a sentence.

Slide 8

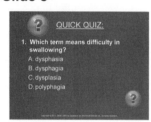

- Correct answer is B: dysphagia. (A, dysphasia means difficulty speaking; C, dysplasia means abnormal formation or development; D, polyphagia means excessive appetite.)

Slide 9

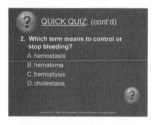

- Correct answer is A: hemostasis.

Slide 10

- "Col/o" is commonly combined with another form. What is it? (*colorectal*)
- What is a cholecystectomy?

The Language of Medicine, 9th ed.

Chabner

Slide 11

- Using the previous suffixes, combine forms to build terms.

- Which of these terms pertains to the liver?

- Which pertains to the tongue?

- Which terms refer to parts of the small intestine?

Slide 12

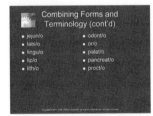

- Using the previous suffixes, combine forms to build terms.

- Which combining forms are not anatomical for a specific body part? (*lip/o, lith/o*)

Slide 13

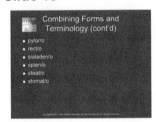

- What is sialadenitis?

- What is steatorrhea?

- What is stomatitis? (*Many students believe this is for stomach.*)

Slide 14

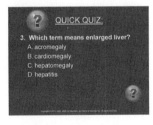

- Correct answer is C: hepatomegaly.

Slide 15

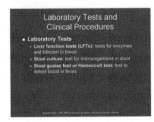

- What is a screening test for colon cancer? How does it work?

- Describe the enzymes LFTs measure.

Slide 16

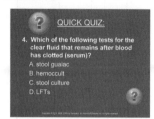

- Correct answer is D: LFTs—liver function tests which test for the presence of enzymes and bilirubin in serum.

Slide 17

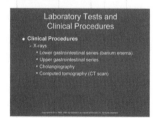

- Which test uses a contrast medium?

- In a cholangiography, how does the contrast material enter the body?

Slide 18

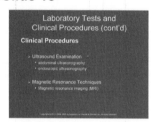

- Which test is used to examine the gallbladder?

- Which test creates a scan of the liver?

Slide 19

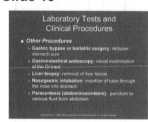

- Which procedure is a visual examination of the gastrointestinal tract?

- Which procedure removes fluid after surgery?

- Which procedure is also called gastrojejunostomy? What is this an example of? (*anastomosis*)

- Which procedure is used to pump out stomach contents?

Slide 20

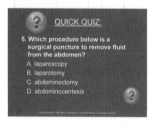

- Correct answer is D abdominocentesis—the suffix -centesis means to surgically puncture to remove fluid.

Chabner

Slide 21

- Use three of these abbreviations in sentences.
- Identify suffixes learned in this chapter.
- What is the medical term for BRBPR? (*hematochezia*)
- Which is an imaging test?
- Which are laboratory tests?

Slide 22

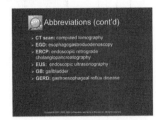

- What does tomography mean?

Slide 23

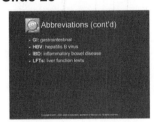

- Which of these abbreviations are pathologies?
- What is the purpose of liver function tests?

Slide 24

- What is the Latin term for "nothing by mouth"?

Slide 25

- What is the difference between the PEG tube and the PEJ tube?
- What are the probable locations of PUD? (*stomach, duodenum*)

Chabner

Slide 26

- Which enzymes are tested to detect liver disease?
- Which term describes intravenous nutrition? What is included in the formula?

Slide 27

Slide 28

Slide 29

Slide 30

Slide 31

Slide 32

Slide 33

Slide 34

Chabner

TEACHING FOCUS

Students will have the opportunity to learn the major organs of the urinary system, the waste conversion process, and the importance of urinalysis as a diagnostic tool. They will be given an opportunity to learn how the urinary system differs in men and women. Students will learn how the major organs of the urinary system function. They will also be introduced to the disorders of the urinary system and provided with information on related tests, procedures, and terminology.

MATERIALS AND RESOURCES

- ☐ Copies or transparency of one or more sample case reports (Lesson 7.2)
- ☐ Cystoscope (Lesson 7.2)
- ☐ Flash cards (Lesson 7.2)
- ☐ Poster of urinary system in females (Lesson 7.1)
- ☐ Poster of urinary system in males (Lesson 7.1)

- ☐ Poster with diagram of urinary system organs (Lesson 7.1)
- ☐ Ultrasound images of urinary system (Lesson 7.2)
- ☐ Urinalysis test results (Lesson 7.1)
- ☐ X-ray images of urinary system (Lesson 7.2)

LESSON CHECKLIST

Preparations for this lesson include:

- Lecture
- Demonstration
- Student performance evaluation of all entry-level skills required for student comprehension and application of medical terminology of the urinary system, including:
  - o knowledge of the locations, functions, and pathologies of the organs of the urinary system
  - o knowledge of the system's terminology
  - o urinalysis as a diagnostic test

KEY TERMS

Vocabulary (pp. 222-224)

arterioles
Bowman capsule
calyces/calices
calyx/calix
catheter
cortex
creatinine
electrolytes
erythropoietin (EPO)
filtration
glomerulus
hilum
kidney
meatus
medulla
micturition
nephron
nitrogenous waste
potassium (K+)
reabsorption
renal artery
renal pelvis

renal tubule
renal vein
renin
secretion
sodium (Na+)
trigone
urea
ureter
urethra
uric acid
urinary bladder
urine
urination
voiding

Terminology/Structures (pp. 225-228)

cali/o
calic/o
cyst/o
glomerul/o
meat/o
nephr/o
pyel/o
ren/o

trigon/o
ureter/o
urethr/o
vesic/o

**Terminology/Substances and Symptoms
(pp. 228-229)**
albumin/o
azot/o
bacteri/o
dips/o
kal/o
ket/o
keton/o
lith/o
natr/o
noct/i
olig/o
-poietin
py/o
-tripsy
ur/o
urin/o
-uria

Pathology (pp. 231-233)
bladder cancer
diabetes insipidus
diabetes mellitus
glomerulonephritis
interstitial nephritis

nephrolithiasis
nephrotic syndrome
polycystic kidneys
pyelonephritis
renal cell carcinoma (hypernephroma)
renal failure
renal hypertension
Wilms tumor

**Laboratory Tests and Clinical Procedures
(pp. 233-238)**
blood urea nitrogen (BUN)
creatinine clearance test
CT scan
cytoscopy
dialysis
extracorporeal shock wave lithotripsy
    (ESWL)
intravenous pyelogram (IVP)
kidneys, ureters, and bladder (KUB)
magnetic resonance imaging
radioisotope scan
renal angiography
renal angioplasty
renal biopsy
renal transplantation
retrograde pyelogram (RP)
ultrasonography
urinary catheterization
voiding cystourethrogram (VCUG)

REFERENCE LIST
PowerPoint slides (CD, Evolve): 1-115

Legend

  CD
Companion
CD

  iTerms

  IRM
Instructor's
Resource Manual
available on CD
and Evolve

  Evolve
Evolve
Resources

  PPT
PowerPoint
Slides

  MTO
Medical
Terminology
Online

Class Activities are indicated in ***bold italic.***

                                                                            Chabner

LESSON 7.1

PRETEST
IRM Exercise Quiz questions 1-10

BACKGROUND ASSESSMENT
Question: What are the functions of the kidneys?
Answer: A byproduct of protein metabolism in the body is ammonia, a nitrogenous waste product, which is secreted as urea. Urea is formed in the liver from the ammonia and travels via the bloodstream to the kidneys. There, it passes out of the bloodstream as a component of urine and travels through the bladder and out of the body. Besides removing urea from the blood, another important function of the kidneys is to maintain the proper balance of water, salts, and acids in the body fluids. Known as electrolytes, these substances are necessary for proper muscle and nerve cell function. The kidneys also secrete renin, an enzyme that controls blood pressure, and erythropoietin, a hormone that stimulates the production of red blood cells in bone marrow.

Question: What are the anatomical terms of the organs associated with the urinary system?
Answer: The organs in the urinary system are the kidneys, ureters, urinary bladder, and urethra.

CRITICAL THINKING QUESTION
Why would do women have a greater incidence of urinary tract infections (bladder infections) than men?
Guidelines: The male urethra is significantly longer (8 inches) than the female urethra (1.5 inches). Consequently, pathogens have a much shorter distance to travel to reach the urinary bladder in a female than in a male.

OBJECTIVES	CONTENT	TEACHING RESOURCES
Name the organs of the urinary system and describe their locations and functions.	■ Introduction (p. 218) ■ Anatomy of the major organs (p. 219) ■ How the kidneys produce urine (p. 220)	PPT 5-46 IRM Multiple Choice Quiz IRM Exercise Quiz A IRM Diagram Quiz IRM Crossword Puzzle MTO Module 7, Section I, Lessons 1-3 Figure 7-1 Organs of the urinary system in a male (p. 218) Figure 7-2 Female urinary system (p. 219) Figure 7-3 (A) Renal artery; (B) Glomerulus and Bowman capsule (p. 220) Figure 7-4 Three steps in the formation of urine (p. 221) Figure 7-5 Section of the kidney showing renal pelvis, calyces, and ureter (p. 222) Figure 7-6 Flow diagram illustrating the process of forming and expelling urine (p. 223) Exercises A-B (p. 242)

ELSEVIER

Chabner

OBJECTIVES	CONTENT	TEACHING RESOURCES
		⊙ Companion CD Exercise 7-1
		Class Activity Have four groups of students select a different organ of the urinary tract and describe its role. Have students discuss this in an order that demonstrates the urinary process.
		Alternatively, have the students label diagrams of the urinary system with the correct terms.
Define combining forms, prefixes, and suffixes of the system's terminology.	■ Vocabulary (p. 222) ■ Terminology (p. 225) □ Structures (p. 225) □ Substances and symptoms (p. 228)	PPT 47-62 IRM Multiple Choice Quiz IRM Terminology Quiz IRM Dictation and Comprehension Quiz A IRM Vocabulary Quiz Figure 7-7 Acute cystitis (p. 225) Figure 7-8 Hydronephrosis and hydroureter (p. 226) Figure 7-9 Ileostomy (p. 227) Exercises C, D (pp. 243) ⊙ Companion CD Exercise 7-2 ▶ Discuss the relevance of learning combining forms and their roots. *Class Activity Divide the class into teams. During a timed session, have one team call out the name of a combining form. Each team needs to create as many urinary system medical terms from the combining form as they can in a 60-second period. After 60 seconds, announce another combining form.* *Ask students to use the same diagram as in the first module, but to include the combining forms for the structures illustrated.*
Recognize the use and interpretation of urinalysis as a diagnostic test.	■ Urinalysis (p. 230)	PPT 63-65 IRM Multiple Choice Quiz IRM Exercise Quiz C ➤ MTO Module 7, Section II, Lesson 1

Chabner

OBJECTIVES	CONTENT	TEACHING RESOURCES
		Exercise F (p. 243)
		Figure 7-10 pH scale (p. 230)
		Class Activity **Divide the class into two or more teams. Give them both the name of a urinalysis test (e.g. color, pH, etc.) and ask them to describe the use and interpretation of this test. Award a point to the first team to answer correctly.**

7.1 Homework/Assignments:

7.1 Teacher's Notes:

LESSON 7.2

CRITICAL THINKING QUESTION

Cathy, a 60-year-old woman, has been diagnosed with a stone in her left ureter. Why is this a potentially serious condition?

Guidelines: Stones in the ureter can block the outflow of urine from the kidney. If urine cannot be excreted, the waste will build up and can lead to kidney failure.

OBJECTIVES	CONTENT	TEACHING RESOURCES

Give the meaning of various pathologic conditions affecting the system.	■ Pathologic terminology for kidney, bladder, and associated conditions (p. 231)
	
	☐ Kidney (p. 231)
	  – Glomerulonephritis (p. 231)
	  – Interstitial nephritis (p. 231)
	  – Nephrolithiasis (p. 231)
	  – Nephrotic syndrome (p. 231)
	  – Polycystic kidneys (p. 232)
	  – Pyelonephritis (p. 232)
	  – Renal cell carcinoma (hypernephroma) (p. 232)
	  – Renal failure (p. 232)
	  – Renal hypertension (p. 233)
	  – Wilms tumor (p. 233)
	
	☐ Urinary bladder (p. 233)
	  – Bladder cancer (p. 233)
	
	☐ Associated conditions (p. 233)
	  – Diabetes insipidus (p. 233)
	  – Diabetes mellitus (p. 233)
		PPT 67-72
		
		IRM Multiple Choice Quiz
		
		IRM Pathology Quiz
		
		IRM Dictation and Comprehension Quiz B
		
		IRM Spelling Quiz A
		
		IRM Pronunciation Quiz A-C
		
		MTO Module 7, Section II, Lessons 2-4
		
		Figure 7-11 (A) Polycystic kidney disease; (B) Chronic pyelonephritis (p. 232)
		
		Exercises G, H (p. 244)
		
		Companion CD Exercises 7-3, 7-4
		
		Class Activity Use the terms listed to practice analyzing, defining, and pronouncing them.
		
		Class Activity Divide the class into several groups. Describe the symptoms associated with a pathologic condition of the urinary system. Give each group 20 seconds to come up with the name of the disease and write it down on a piece of paper. Repeat for five rounds and provide the correct answers. Have each group share the total number of correct answers with the rest of the class, using correct pronunciation to call out the answers.

List and explain some clinical procedures, laboratory tests, and abbreviations that pertain to the urinary system.	■ Laboratory tests, clinical procedures, and abbreviations (p. 233)
	
	☐ Laboratory tests (p. 233)
	  – Blood urea nitrogen (BUN) (p. 233)
	  – Creatinine clearance test (p. 234)
		PPT 73-82
		
		IRM Multiple Choice Quiz
		
		IRM Laboratory Tests Quiz
		
		IRM Exercise Quiz F
		
		IRM Abbreviations Quiz

OBJECTIVES	CONTENT	TEACHING RESOURCES

	☐ Clinical procedures: x-rays (p. 234)
	
	  – CT scan (p. 234)
	  – Kidneys, ureters, and bladder (KUB) (p. 234)
	  – Renal angiography (p. 234)
	  – Retrograde pyelogram (RP) (p. 234)
	  – Voiding cystourethrogram (VCUG) (p. 235)
	
	☐ Clinical procedures: ultrasound (p. 235)
	
	  – Ultrasonography (p. 235)
	
	☐ Clinical procedures: radioactive (p. 235)
	
	  – Radioisotope scan (p. 235)
	
	☐ Clinical procedures: magnetic imaging (p. 235)
	
	  – Magnetic resonance imaging (MRI) (p. 235)
	
	☐ Clinical procedures: other procedures (p. 235)
	
	  – Cystoscopy (p. 235)
	  – Dialysis (p. 236)
	  – Lithotripsy (ESWL) (p. 237)
	  – Renal angioplasty (p. 237)
	  – Renal biopsy (p. 237)
	  – Renal transplantation (p. 238)
	  – Urinary catheterization (p. 238)
	
	■ Abbreviations (p. 239)
		↖ MTO Module 7, Section III, Lessons 1-2
		
		Figure 7-12 CT scan and voiding cystourethrogram (p. 234)
		
		Figure 7-13 Cystoscopy (p. 235)
		
		Figure 7-14 Patient receiving hemodialysis (p. 236)
		
		Figure 7-15 Continuous ambulatory peritoneal dialysis (CAPD) (p. 237)
		
		Figure 7-16 Renal (kidney) transplantation (p. 238)
		
		Figure 7-17 A Foley catheter in place in the urinary bladder (p. 238)
		
		Exercises I-J (p. 245)
		
		⊙ Companion CD Exercises 7-5, 7-6
		
		▸ Discuss the types of tests used for urinary system diagnosis and which ones are categorized as lab tests, x-rays, ultrasound, radioactive, and others.
		
		***Class Activity** Have students split up into pairs and create flash cards with definitions for the terms in this section. Have the students analyze the terms, underlining the stressed syllable in each term. Have pairs quiz each other on the key terms.*
		
		***Class Activity** Divide the class into two teams. Give each team a set of different flash cards with the names of laboratory tests, clinical procedures, or abbreviations pertaining to the urinary system on them. The teams take turns showing a card to the opponent, who must define the test or procedure or give the abbreviated term. Award a point for each correct answer. However, the presenting team loses a point for accepting an incorrect answer or rejecting a correct answer.*

Apply your new knowledge to understanding medical terms in their proper contexts, such as medical reports and records.	■ Practical applications (p. 240)	⊞ PPT 83-115 ⊛ IRM Practical Applications A-B ↖ MTO Module 7, Section V Practical Applications (p. 240-241) Exercises E, K (pp. 237, 239)

OBJECTIVES	CONTENT	TEACHING RESOURCES
		Companion CD Exercise 7-7
		▸ Discuss how the medical assistant's role is critical to the physician in evaluating and diagnosing urinary system disorders.
		Class Activity Divide the class into two or more teams. Give them copies (or show a transparency) of one or more sample Case Reports similar to the one in the chapter. Ask the first team to read the first sentence and to define the first highlighted term (if there is more than one in the sentence). Award a point for a correct answer. Ask the next team to define the next highlighted term.
		Class Activity Divide the students into small groups and have each group create a fictional medical report using terms learned from the chapter. See Case Report for an example of a medical report. Have a representative from each group read the report to the rest of the class. Be sure to correct pronunciation when appropriate.
		Alternatively, have students take turns reading sentences from Exercise M in the text. Ask them to correctly pronounce, analyze (where appropriate), and define the term that completes the sentence.
Performance Evaluation		IRM Multiple Choice Quiz
		IRM Terminology Quiz
		IRM Pathology Quiz
		IRM Laboratory Tests Quiz
		IRM Exercise Quiz
		IRM Dictation and Comprehension Quiz B
		IRM Spelling Quiz B
		IRM Pronunciation Quiz
		IRM Diagram Quiz
		IRM Vocabulary Quiz
		IRM Review Sheet Quiz
		IRM Medical Scramble

OBJECTIVES	CONTENT	TEACHING RESOURCES
		IRM Crossword Puzzle
		IRM Practical Applications
		ESLR Body Spectrum Electronic Anatomy Coloring Book, Urinary
		ESLR Student Quiz Chapter 7
		MTO Module 7, Section I-III quizzes
		MTO Module 7, Exam
		Companion CD Exercises 7-8, 7-9, 7-10
		iTerms Chapter 07

7.2 Homework/Assignments:

7.2 Teacher's Notes:

Slide 1

The Language Of
Medicine
9th edition
Davi-Ellen Chabner

Slide 2

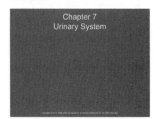

Chapter 7
Urinary System

Slide 3

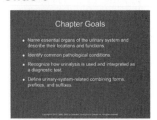

Chapter Goals

- Name essential organs of the urinary system and describe their locations and functions.
- Identify common pathological conditions.
- Recognize how urinalysis is used and interpreted as a diagnostic test.
- Define urinary-system-related combining forms, prefixes, and suffixes.

Slide 4

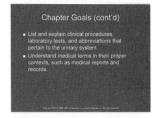

Chapter Goals (cont'd)

- List and explain clinical procedures, laboratory tests, and abbreviations that pertain to the urinary system.
- Understand medical terms in their proper contexts, such as medical reports and records.

Slide 5

Chapter 7
Lesson 7.1

Chabner

Slide 6

- Why is nitrogenous waste excreted from the body in a soluble rather than gaseous form?

- By what medium does urea travel to the kidneys?

Slide 7

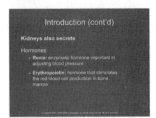

- Kidneys also adjust amount of water and electrolytes for proper muscle and nerve function.

- Are there other important functions performed by the kidneys?

Slide 8

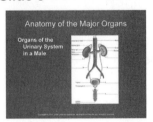

- Have students name the organs of the urinary system labeled 1-4 in the figure.

- What is the size and weight of a normal kidney?

- What function is performed by the ureters?

- What function is performed by the urinary bladder?

- What function is performed by the urethra?

Slide 9

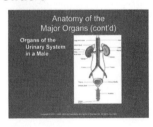

- Have students name the organs of the urinary system labeled 1-4 in the figure.

- What is the size and weight of a normal kidney?

- What function is performed by the ureters?

- What function is performed by the urinary bladder?

- What function is performed by the urethra?

Slide 10

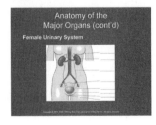

- How does the female urinary system differ from the male urinary system?

- What is the trigone and what function does it perform?

- What is micturition?

Slide 11

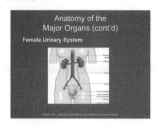

- How does the female urinary system differ from the male urinary system?
- What is the trigone and what function does it perform?
- What is micturition?

Slide 12

- Correct answer is B: urination

Slide 13

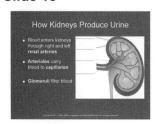

- The renal artery branches into smaller arteries, arterioles, and glomeruli located throughout the cortex of the kidneys.
- What is a glomerulus?
- There are approximately one million glomeruli in the cortex of each kidney.
- How does the kidney regulate blood pressure?
- Why is maintenance of proper blood pressure important to the kidneys' function?

Slide 14

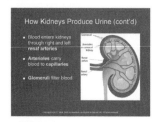

- The renal artery branches into smaller arteries, arterioles, and glomeruli located throughout the cortex of the kidneys.
- What is a glomerulus?
- There are approximately one million glomeruli in the cortex of each kidney.
- How does the kidney regulate blood pressure?
- Why is maintenance of proper blood pressure important to the kidneys' function?

Slide 15

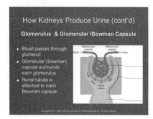

- What functions do the glomerulus, Bowman capsule, and renal tubule perform in the production of urine?
- Why don't proteins and blood cells usually appear in the urine?
- What is the process of reabsorption?
- What is secretion?
- What substances make up urine? (Note: These substances become toxic if allowed to accumulate.)

ELSEVIER

The Language of Medicine, 9th ed.

Chabner

Slide 16

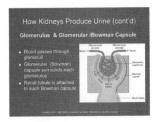

- What functions do the glomerulus, Bowman capsule, and renal tubule perform in the production of urine?

- Why don't proteins and blood cells usually appear in the urine?

- What is the process of reabsorption?

- What is secretion?

- What substances make up urine? (Note: These substances become toxic if allowed to accumulate.)

Slide 17

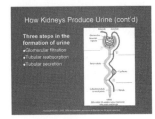

- What functions are performed in each of the three steps in the formation of urine?

- The combination of a glomerulus and a renal tubule is called a nephron. (There are more than one million nephrons in a kidney.)

Slide 18

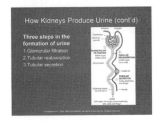

- What functions are performed in each of the three steps in the formation of urine?

- The combination of a glomerulus and a renal tubule is called a nephron. (There are more than one million nephrons in a kidney.)

Slide 19

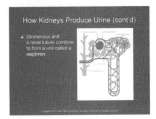

Slide 20

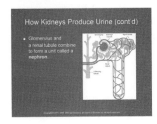

ELSEVIER

The Language of Medicine, 9th ed.
Chabner

Slide 21

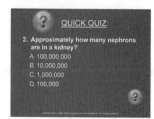

- Correct answer is C: one million

Slide 22

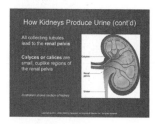

- Notice how secretion and reabsorption are functions of the same organs.
- Cup-like regions in the renal pelvis are called calyces or calices.
- Where do all connecting tubules lead?
- The renal pelvis narrows to form the ureter.
- To which organ does the ureter lead?

Slide 23

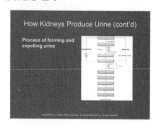

- Notice how secretion and reabsorption are functions of the same organs.
- Cup-like regions in the renal pelvis are called calyces or calices.
- Where do all connecting tubules lead?
- The renal pelvis narrows to form the ureter.
- To which organ does the ureter lead?

Slide 24

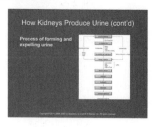

- How is urine flow from the bladder to the urethra controlled?
- What triggers the need to urinate?
- Urine finally exits the body through the urinary meatus.

Slide 25

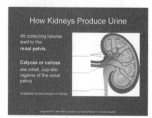

- How is urine flow from the bladder to the urethra controlled?
- What triggers the need to urinate?
- Urine finally exits the body through the urinary meatus.

The Language of Medicine, 9th ed.

Chabner

Slide 26

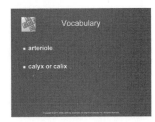

- How do each of these terms play a role in the urinary system?
- Which organs are involved in filtering urine?

Slide 27

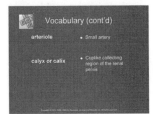

- Refer to p. 216 for more detailed definitions.
- How do each of these terms play a role in the urinary system?
- Which organs are involved in filtering urine?

Slide 28

- How do each of these terms play a role in the urinary system?
- Which organs are involved in filtering urine?

Slide 29

- How do each of these terms play a role in the urinary system?
- Which organs are involved in filtering urine?

Slide 30

- How do each of these terms play a role in the urinary system?
- Which organs are involved in filtering urine?

Slide 31

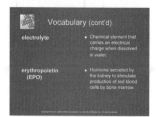

- How do each of these terms play a role in the urinary system?
- Which organs are involved in filtering urine?

Slide 32

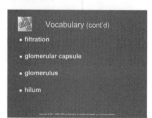

- How do each of these terms play a role in the urinary system?
- Which organs are involved in filtering urine?

Slide 33

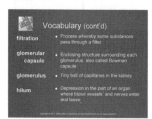

- How do each of these terms play a role in the urinary system?
- Which organs are involved in filtering urine?

Slide 34

- What path does waste take through the urinary system?

Slide 35

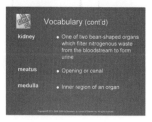

- What path does waste take through the urinary system?

The Language of Medicine, 9th ed.

Chabner

Slide 36

• What path does waste take through the urinary system?

Slide 37

• What path does waste take through the urinary system?

Slide 38

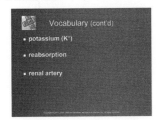

• What path does waste take through the urinary system?

Slide 39

• What path does waste take through the urinary system?

Slide 40

• What path does waste take through the urinary system?

Chabner

Slide 41

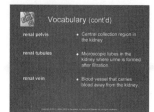

- What path does waste take through the urinary system?

Slide 42

- What is another term for urination?
- What is renin and where is it formed?
- Where is the trigone located?

Slide 43

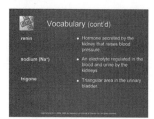

- What is another term for urination?
- What is renin and where is it formed?
- Where is the trigone located?

Slide 44

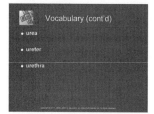

Slide 45

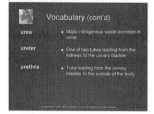

Slide 46

- What is another term for urination?

Slide 47

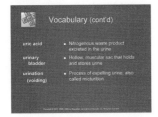

Slide 48

- Using the given combining forms, can you form and define other terms not listed in the slide?

Slide 49

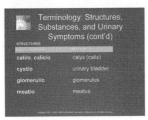

- Using the given combining forms, can you form and define other terms not listed in the slide?

Slide 50

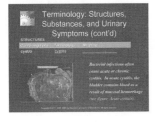

- Define the term cystitis.
- Using the given combining forms, can you form and define other terms not listed in the slide?

Slide 51

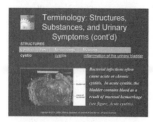

- Using the given combining forms, can you form and define other terms not listed in the slide?

Slide 52

- Using the given combining forms, can you form and define other terms not listed in the slide?

Slide 53

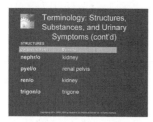

- Using the given combining forms, can you form and define other terms not listed in the slide?

Slide 54

- Define the term hydronephrosis
- Using the given combining forms, can you form and define other terms not listed in the slide?

Slide 55

Chabner

Slide 56

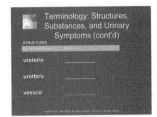

- Using the given combining forms, can you form and define other terms not listed in the slide?

Slide 57

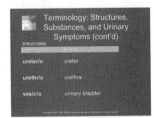

- Using the given combining forms, can you form and define other terms not listed in the slide?

Slide 58

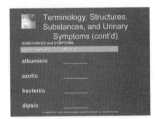

- Using the given combining forms, can you form and define other terms not listed in the slide?

Slide 59

- Using the given combining forms, can you form and define other terms not listed in the slide?

Slide 60

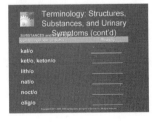

- Using the given combining forms, can you form and define other terms not listed in the slide?

The Language of Medicine, 9th ed.

Chabner

Slide 61

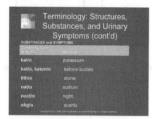

- Using the given combining forms, can you form and define other terms not listed in the slide?

Slide 62

- Using the given combining forms, can you form and define other terms not listed in the slide?

Slide 63

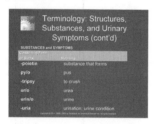

- Using the given combining forms, can you form and define other terms not listed in the slide?

Slide 64

- Colorless urine = large amount of water in urine. Smoky-red or brown indicates presence of blood in urine.
- Normal pH is 6.5 (slightly acidic).
- Protein test looks for albumin, which indicates a leak in the glomerular membrane.
- Glucose presence signals possibility of diabetes.

Slide 65

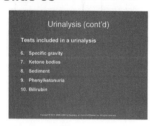

- Specific gravity reflects amounts of wastes and minerals.
- Ketone bodies appear when the body breaks down fat.
- Sediment are abnormal particles.
- Phenylketonuria indicates a lack of enzyme, especially in infants. PKU test measures this.
- Bilirubin results from a hemoglobin breakdown.

The Language of Medicine, 9th ed.

Chabner

Slide 66

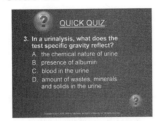

- Correct answer is D: specific gravity compares the density of urine with that of water.

Slide 67

Slide 68

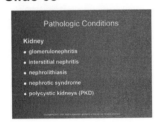

- Glomerulonephritis is the inflammation of the glomeruli within the kidney due to infection; it can lead to hypertension and renal failure if untreated.

- What is interstitial nephritis?

- What procedure might a physician recommend for a patient with nephrolithiasis?

- Nephrotic syndrome is a collection of symptoms caused by excessive protein loss in urine.

- Polycystic kidneys are a hereditary condition of progressive growth of cysts. There are two types of hereditary PKD. One type is usually asymptomatic until middle age and then is marked by maturia, urinary tract infections and nephrolithiasis. The other type of PKD occurs in infants or children and results in renal failure.

Slide 69

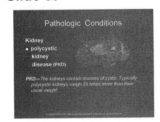

- Polycystic kidneys are a hereditary condition of progressive growth of cysts.

Chabner

Slide 70

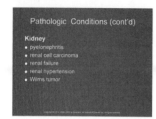

- See p. 229.

- Pyelonephritis is the inflammation of the lining of the renal pelvis and renal parenchyma.

- Renal cell carcinoma is adult cancer of the kidney—2% of all adult cancers.

- What occurs during renal failure?

- How does renal hypertension differ from essential hypertension?

- Wilms tumor is a malignant tumor of the kidney occurring in childhood and is an example of an eponym.

Slide 71

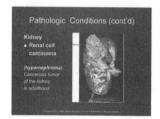

Slide 72

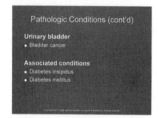

- What risk factors are associated with bladder cancer?

- Diabetes insipidus: Antidiuretic hormone is not secreted adequately or the kidney is resistant to its effect.

- Diabetes mellitus: Insulin is not secreted adequately or not used properly in the body.

- How does each of these conditions affect the kidneys?

Slide 73

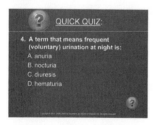

- Correct answer is B: nocturia.

Slide 74

- Which procedure tests for uremia?

- Which test measures the rate at which creatinine is cleared from the blood?

- What is azotemia?

- What role do the kidneys play in BUN levels?

Slide 75

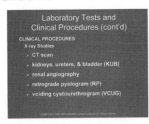

- How do these x-rays differ?
- Which tests require contrast material?
- Why is it important to measure the size of the kidneys (KUB)?
- Which tests require urinary catheterization?
- Why would someone have RP instead of IVP?

Slide 76

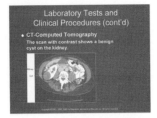

Slide 77

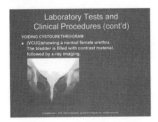

Slide 78

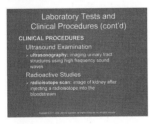

- What is hydronephrosis?
- What might cause the kidney to be enlarged?
- What can be diagnosed in the urinary system using sound waves?

Slide 79

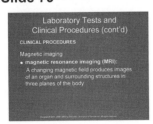

- How is an MRI of the kidney performed?

The Language of Medicine, 9th ed.

Chabner

Slide 80

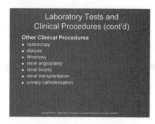

- Cystoscopy allows for visual examination through a hollow metal tube.
- What is the difference between hemodialysis and peritoneal dialysis?
- What procedure might be required to remove kidney stones?
- Describe the process of catheterization.

Slide 81

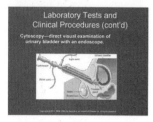

- How is a cytoscopy performed?

Slide 82

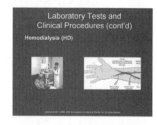

- How is a cytoscopy performed?

Slide 83

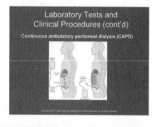

- CAPD can be performed continuously by the patient without artificial support.
- What other peritoneal dialysis procedures may be performed?

Slide 84

- Which abbreviations stand for disorders, which are measurements, and which are procedures?

Chabner

Slide 85

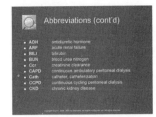

- Which abbreviations stand for disorders, which are measurements, and which are procedures?

Slide 86

- Which items are pathologies, and which are treatments?

Slide 87

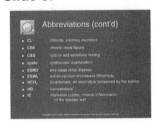

- Which items are pathologies, and which are treatments?

Slide 88

- Ask students to identify the category of metabolite, treatment, condition, or test.

Slide 89

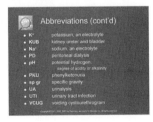

- Ask students to identify the category of metabolite, treatment, condition, or test.

Slide 90

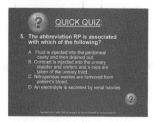

- Correct answer is B: abbreviation is for retrograde pyelogram
- Incorrect answer A is CAPD, continuous ambulatory periotoneal dialysis
- Incorrect answer C is HD, hemodialysis
- Incorrect answer D is K+ potassium

Slide 91

Slide 92

Slide 93

Slide 94

The Language of Medicine, 9th ed.

Chabner

Slide 95

Slide 96

Slide 97

Slide 98

Slide 99

Slide 100

Slide 101

Slide 102

Slide 103

Slide 104

Slide 105

Review Sheet (cont'd)
Suffixes

-plasty
-poietin
-ptosis
-rrhea
-sclerosis
-stomy

Slide 106

Review Sheet (cont'd)
Suffixes

-plasty	surgical repair
-poietin	substance that forms
-ptosis	droop; sag
-rrhea	flow; discharge
-sclerosis	hardening
-stomy	new opening (to form a mouth)

Slide 107

Review Sheet (cont'd)
Suffixes

-tomy
-tripsy
-uria

Slide 108

Review Sheet (cont'd)
Suffixes

-tomy	process of cutting
-tripsy	to crush
-uria	urination

Slide 109

Review Sheet
Prefixes

a-, an-
anti-
dia-
dys-

ELSEVIER

The Language of Medicine, 9th ed.
Chabner

Slide 110

Slide 111

Slide 112

Slide 113

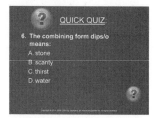

- C, Thirst is the correct answer

Slide 114

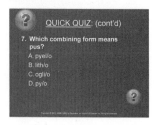

- D, py/o is the correct answer

Chabner

Slide 115

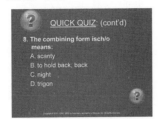

- B, to hold back; back is the correct answer

Chabner

Lesson Plan

8 Female Reproductive System

TEACHING FOCUS

Students will have the opportunity to learn about locations and functions of the female reproductive organs. They will also explore how the organs interact with hormones and function in the processes of menstruation and pregnancy. Students will have the opportunity to identify abnormal conditions of the system and conditions affecting newborns. In this context, they will be introduced to the laboratory tests, clinical procedures, and abbreviations related to gynecology and obstetrics. Students can apply this knowledge to understanding terms in the context of patient care, such as completing and processing medical reports and records.

MATERIALS AND RESOURCES

- ☐ Film showing birth (Lesson 8.1)
- ☐ Fetal monitor (Lesson 8.2)
- ☐ Flash cards (Lesson 8.2)
- ☐ ICR (all Lessons)
- ☐ Intrauterine device (IUD) (Lesson 8.1)
- ☐ Mammogram film (Lesson 8.3)
- ☐ Norplant device (Lesson 8.2)
- ☐ Oral contraceptives (Lesson 8.2)
- ☐ Poster of female reproductive anatomy (Lesson 8.1)
- ☐ Projector (all Lessons)
- ☐ Speculum (Lesson 8.3)
- ☐ Ultrasound of pelvic area (Lesson 8.3)
- ☐ Uterine dilator (Lessons 8.1 and 8.3)
- ☐ X-rays (Lesson 8.3)

LESSON CHECKLIST

Preparations for this lesson include:

- Lecture
- Demonstration
- Student performance evaluation of entry-level skills required for comprehension and application of female reproductive system terminology, including:
  - o knowledge of anatomy and physiology
  - o terminology associated with abnormal conditions of the female reproductive system
  - o understanding how clinical tests and procedures are used
  - o basic structure of medical words, including word building and definitions
  - o use of appropriate medical terminology in preparing patient for, and assisting with, procedures and treatments,

KEY TERMS

Vocabulary (pp. 266-268)

adnexa uteri
amnion
areola
Bartholin glands
cervix
chorion
clitoris
coitus
corpus luteum
cul-de-sac
embryo
endometrium
estrogen
fallopian tube
fertilization
fetus
fimbriae
follicle-stimulating hormone (FSH)

gamete
genitalia
gestation
gonad
gynecology
human chorionic gonadotropin (HCG)
hymen
labia
lactiferous ducts
luteinizing hormone (LH)
mammary papilla
menarche
menopause
menstruation
myometrium
neonatology
obstetrics
orifice
ovary

Chabner

ovulation
ovum
parturition
perineum
pituitary gland
placenta
pregnancy
progesterone
puberty
uterine serosa
uterus
vagina
vulva
zygote

Terminology (pp. 268-273)

amni/o
cervic/o
chori/o, chorion/o
colp/o
culd/o
episi/o
galact/o
gynec/o
hyster/o
lact/o
mamm/o
mast/o
men/o
metr/o, metri/o
my/o
myom/o
nat/i
obstetr/o
o/o
oophor/o
ov/o
ovari/o
ovul/o
perine/o
phor/o
salping/o
uter/o
vagin/o
vulv/o
-arche
-cyesis
-gravida
-parous
-rrhea
-salpinx
-tocia
-version
dys-
endo-

in-
intra-
multi-
nulli-
pre-
primi-
retro-

Pathology (pp. 274-282)

abruptio placentae
carcinoma of the breast
carcinoma of the cervix
carcinoma of the endometrium
cervicitis
choriocarcinoma
Down syndrome
ectopic pregnancy
endometriosis
erythroblastosis fetalis
fibrocystic disease
fibroids
hyaline membrane disease
hydrocephalus
meconium aspiration syndrome
multiple gestation
ovarian carcinoma
ovarian cysts
pelvic inflammatory disease
placenta previa
preeclampsia
pyloric stenosis

Tests/Procedures (pp. 282-287)

abortion
amniocentesis
aspiration
breast ultrasound imaging
cauterization
cesarean section
chorionic villus sampling
colposcopy
conization
cryosurgery
culdocentesis
dilation and curettage
exenteration
fetal monitoring
hysterosalpingography
in vitro fertilization
laparoscopy
mammography
Pap smear
pelvic utrasonography
pelvimetry
pregnancy test
tubal ligation

REFERENCE LIST
PowerPoint slides (CD, Evolve): 1-91

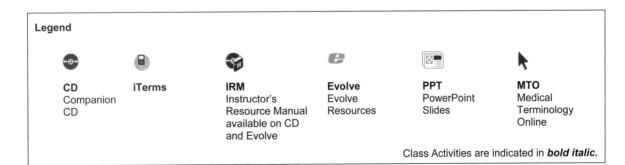

Legend

CD Companion CD	**iTerms**	**IRM** Instructor's Resource Manual available on CD and Evolve	**Evolve** Evolve Resources	**PPT** PowerPoint Slides	**MTO** Medical Terminology Online

Class Activities are indicated in ***bold italic.***

ELSEVIER

The Language of Medicine, 9th ed.

Chabner

LESSON 8.1

PRETEST
IRM Exercise A questions 1-10

BACKGROUND ASSESSMENT
Question: What are the terms for the organs in the female reproductive system?
Answer: Answers will vary, but should include at least the following: breast, uterus, vagina, cervix, fallopian tubes, and ovaries.

Question: What are the combining forms that are used with the female reproductive system?
Answer: Answers will vary, but students may recognize hyster/o for uterus, colp/o for vagina, mast/o and mamm/o for breast.

CRITICAL THINKING QUESTION
Why would uterine artery embolization be used to treat fibroids?
Guidelines: Uterine artery embolization is a method whereby the blood supply to a fibroid is blocked, which causes the fibroids to shrink in size.

OBJECTIVES	CONTENT	TEACHING RESOURCES

Name the organs of the female reproductive system, their locations, and their combining forms.	■ Introduction (p. 258)
	
	■ Organs of the female reproductive system (p. 258)
	
	   □ Uterus, ovaries, and associated organs (p. 258)
	
	   □ The breast (accessory organ of reproduction) (p. 261)
		PPT 5-14
		
		IRM Exercise Quiz A
		
		IRM Diagram Quiz
		
		MTO Module 8, Section I, Lessons 1-3
		
		Figure 8-1 Organs of the female reproductive system, lateral view (p. 259)
		
		Figure 8-2 Female external genitalia (p. 259)
		
		Figure 8-3 Organs of the female reproductive system, anterior view (p. 260)
		
		Figure 8-4 Views of the breast (p. 261)
		
		Exercise A (p. 291)
		
		Exercise B (p. 292)
		
		Companion CD Exercises 8-1, 8-2
		
		▸ Discuss the differences between the disciplines of obstetrics, gynecology, and neonatology. For what conditions would a patient seek a practitioner of each discipline?
		
		Class Activity Give each student copies of Figures 8-1 and 8-3. Divide students into small groups and have them fill in the missing organs without using their books. After a reasonable amount of time, determine which group has correctly named the most organs, and discuss any errors that were made. Ask students to include combining forms along with the names of the organs.

OBJECTIVES	CONTENT	TEACHING RESOURCES
Explain how these organs and their hormones function in the processes of menstruation and pregnancy.	■ Menstruation and pregnancy (p. 262) ☐ Menstrual cycle (p. 262) ☐ Pregnancy (p. 263) ■ Hormonal interactions (p. 265)	⊠ PPT 15-26 IRM Spelling Quiz MTO Module 8, Section I, Lessons 4-5 Figure 8-5 The menstrual cycle (p. 262) Figure 8-6 Implantation of the embryo (p. 263) Figure 8-7 Sagittal sections of pregnancy (p. 264) Figure 8-8 Cephalic presentation (p. 264) Figure 8-9 Newborn (p. 265) Exercise C (p. 292) ▸ Discuss how contraceptives work, using textual information on reproductive physiology and hormonal interactions. *Class Activity **Having the students use their knowledge of the menstrual cycle and pregnancy, ask them to describe how the different methods of contraception work.***

8.1 Homework/Assignments:

8.1 Teacher's Notes:

Chabner

LESSON 8.2

CRITICAL THINKING QUESTION

Jean's gynecologist has suggested that she undergo salpingolysis in order to increase her odds of becoming pregnant. What disorder may be in Jean's medical history? How could salpingolysis help her become pregnant?

Guidelines: A common cause of blocked fallopian tubes is pelvic inflammatory disease. Salpingolysis is a procedure to remove adhesions and restore patency in the tubes. Once the tubes are open, the ova can travel freely to the uterus.

OBJECTIVES	CONTENT	TEACHING RESOURCES
Apply your new knowledge to understanding medical terms in their proper contexts, such as medical reports and records.	■ Vocabulary (p. 266) ■ Terminology (p. 268) □ Combining forms (p. 268) □ Suffixes (p. 272) □ Prefixes (p. 273)	PPT 28-49 IRM Terminology Quiz IRM Exercise Quizzes B, D, G IRM Dictation and Comprehension Quiz: Vocabulary and Terminology IRM Pronunciation Quiz C Figure 8-10 Hysterectomies (p. 269) Figure 8-11 Total hysterectomy (p. 271) Exercises D, E, H, L (pp. 293, 295, 298) Review Sheet (p. 308-309) Companion CD Exercises 8-3, 8-4, 8-5 *Class Activity Divide the class into teams. During a timed session, call out the name of a combining form. Each team must create as many reproductive system medical terms from the combining form as it can in a 60-second period. After 60 seconds, announce another combining form.* *Class Activity Create bingo boards for the students, using an online generator. Divide the terms into prefixes, combining forms, suffixes, abbreviations, and medical terms. Call out the meanings and have them cover the appropriate answer.*
Identify abnormal conditions of the female reproductive system and of the newborn child.	■ Pathology: gynecological/breast, pregnancy, neonatal (p. 274) □ Gynecologic and breast (p. 274) – Uterus (p. 274) – Ovaries (p. 276)	PPT 50-54 IRM Pathology Quiz IRM Exercise Quizzes C, E MTO Module 8, Section II, Lessons 1-2, 5

OBJECTIVES	CONTENT	TEACHING RESOURCES
	– Fallopian tubes (p. 277) – Breast (p. 278)	Figure 8-12 (A) Intrauterine device; (B) Cervix, nulliparous and parous (p. 273) Figure 8-13 Cervical intraepithelial neoplasia (p. 274) Figure 8-14 Location of uterine fibroids (p. 276) Figure 8-15 Dermoid cyst of the ovary (p. 277) Figure 8-16 (A) Mammogram; (B) cut section (p. 278) Figure 8-17 Mastectomy scar (p. 279) Exercises F, G (pp. 294-295) ⊙ Companion CD Exercise 8-6 ▸ Discuss tampons and their link to endometriosis. ***Class Activity** **Make or have students make flash cards with names of gynecologic and breast pathologies on one side and the description of the condition on the other. Distribute the cards to pairs or small groups of students and have them quiz one other.***

8.2 Homework/Assignments:

8.2 Teacher's Notes:

Chabner

LESSON 8.3

CRITICAL THINKING QUESTION

At 24 weeks into her pregnancy, Terry visits her OB/GYN complaining of headaches, accelerated weight gain, and swelling in her ankles. The physician tells her that he suspects preeclampsia and directs her to the emergency room. How can the medical assistant help prepare Terry for her visit to the ER?

Guidelines: Remaining calm and positive, the medical assistant should reassure Terry that the ER has facilities that can help confirm or rule out the preeclampsia diagnosis. If confirmed, the ER can start treatment immediately. The medical assistant can reinforce the fact that prompt treatment is important to help keep Terry and her baby healthy during the pregnancy.

OBJECTIVES	CONTENT	TEACHING RESOURCES
Identify abnormal conditions of the female reproductive system and of the newborn child.	☐ Pregnancy (p. 279) ☐ Neonatal (p. 281)	PPT 56-58 IRM Dictation and Comprehension Quiz: Pathological Conditions, Clinical Tests, and Procedures IRM Spelling Quiz IRM Crossword Puzzle MTO Module 8, Section II, Lessons 3-4 Figure 8-18 Placenta previa (p. 280) Figure 8-19 Apgar scoring chart (p. 281) Exercise I (p. 296) Exercise K (p. 297) *Class Activity Make, or have students make, flash cards with names of pathologies found during pregnancy and in neonates on one side and the description of the condition on the other. Distribute the cards to pairs or small groups of students and have them quiz each other.*

Explain important laboratory tests, clinical procedures, and abbreviations related to gynecology and obstetrics.	■ Clinical tests, procedures, and abbreviations (p. 282)
	
	☐ Clinical tests (p. 282)
	
	☐ Procedures (p. 282)
	
	  – X-rays (p. 282)
	
	  – Ultrasound (p. 283)
	
	  – Gynecological procedures (p. 283)
	
	  – Procedures related to pregnancy (p. 286)
		PPT 59-62
		
		IRM Exercise Quiz F
		
		IRM Pronunciation Quiz
		
		IRM Abbreviations Quiz
		
		MTO Module 8, Section III, Lessons 1-4
		
		Figure 8-20 Pap smear (p. 282)
		
		Figure 8-21 Mammography (p. 283)
		
		Figure 8-22 Colposcopy (p. 284)

Chabner

OBJECTIVES	CONTENT	TEACHING RESOURCES
	☐ Abbreviations (p. 288)	Figure 8-23 Conization of the cervix (p. 284)
		Figure 8-24 Dilation and curettage (p. 285)
		Figure 8-25 Laparoscopic oophorectomy (p. 286)
		Figure 8-26 Amniocentesis (p. 287)
		Exercises J, M (pp. 296, 298)
		💿 Companion CD Exercise 8-7
		▶ Discuss various clinical tests and procedures. Compare and contrast the tests, and identify symptoms and other factors that help a practitioner decide which test or procedure is most appropriate.
		*Class Activity **Divide the class into teams. Write the abbreviations for various terms on the board and have a scribe for each team write the abbreviations on a piece of paper. Then give the groups a short time to tell the scribe to write the full term next to the abbreviation. The team with the most correct explanations wins.***
Apply your new knowledge to understanding medical terms in their proper contexts, such as medical reports or records.	■ Practical applications (p. 289)	PPT 63-90
		IRM Multiple Choice Quiz
		IRM Practical Applications
		MTO Module 8, Section V
		Exercise N (pp. 299)
		*Class Activity **Read the report in Practical Applications. Have students practice spelling, analyzing, and defining the terms in this report. Terms should include at least the following: endocervical, endometrial, leiomyomata, hysterectomy, and myomectomy sections.***
		Write medical terms from this chapter on small slips of paper and place them in a hat. Have each student draw a term. Go around the room and have students first provide a context for their terms and then use the terms in sentences. If students become stuck, have the rest of the class offer suggestions.

OBJECTIVES	CONTENT	TEACHING RESOURCES
Performance Evaluation		IRM Multiple Choice Quiz
		IRM Terminology Quiz
		IRM Pathology Quiz
		IRM Exercise Quiz
		IRM Dictation and Comprehension Quizzes
		IRM Spelling Quiz
		IRM Pronunciation Quiz
		IRM Abbreviations Quiz
		IRM Diagram Quiz
		IRM Vocabulary Quiz
		IRM Review Sheet Quiz
		IRM Medical Scramble
		IRM Crossword Puzzle
		IRM Practical Applications
		ESLR Body Spectrum Electronic Anatomy Coloring Book, Reproductive
		ESLR Student Quiz Chapter 8
		MTO Module 8, Sections I-III quizzes
		MTO Module 8 Exam
		Companion CD Exercises 8-8, 8-9, 8-10, 8-11
		iTerms Chapter 08

8.3 Homework/Assignments:

8.3 Teacher's Notes:

Slide 1

The Language Of Medicine
9th edition
Davi-Ellen Chabner

Slide 2

Chapter 8
Female Reproductive System

Slide 3

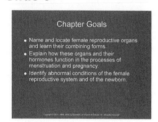

Chapter Goals

- Name and locate female reproductive organs and learn their combining forms.
- Explain how these organs and their hormones function in the processes of menstruation and pregnancy.
- Identify abnormal conditions of the female reproductive system and of the newborn.

Slide 4

Chapter Goals (cont'd)

- Describe important laboratory tests and clinical procedures used in gynecology and obstetrics, and recognize related abbreviations.
- Understand medical terms in their proper contexts, such as medical reports and records.

Slide 5

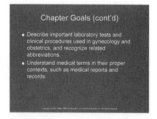

Chapter 8
Lesson 8.1

The Language of Medicine, 9th ed.

Chabner

Slide 6

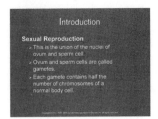

Slide 7

Slide 8

Slide 9

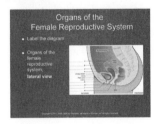

- Students should label the figure: 1. ovaries, 2. fallopian tube 3. uterus, 4. cul-de-sac, 5. vagina, 6. Bartholin glands, 7. clitoris, 8. perineum

Slide 10

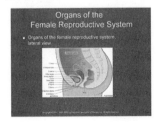

The Language of Medicine, 9th ed.

Chabner

Slide 11

- Correct answer is D: zygote

Slide 12

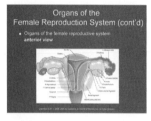

- See next slide for answers.

Slide 13

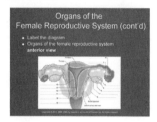

- Refer to p. 254 in text

Slide 14

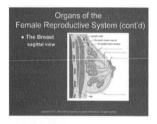

- What is the role of sinuses in the breast?
- Name the parts of the breast nipple.
- Which hormones stimulate lactation?

Slide 15

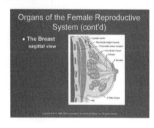

- What is the role of sinuses in the breast?
- Name the parts of the breast nipple.
- Which hormones stimulate lactation?

Chabner

Slide 16

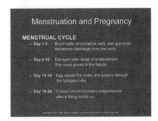

- Describe the menstrual cycle.
- What is the first menstrual cycle called? (*menarche*)

Slide 17

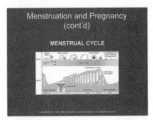

- Does lack of fertilization cause low or high levels of progesterone and estrogen?
- At what stage is the egg most likely to be fertilized?

Slide 18

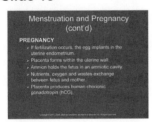

- What is the placenta derived from?
- What are the chorion and the amnion?
- What is amniotic fluid?

Slide 19

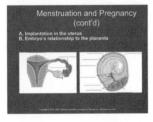

- See next slide for labels

Slide 20

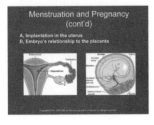

Chabner

Slide 21

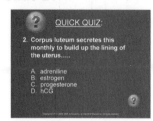

- Correct answer is C: progesterone

Slide 22

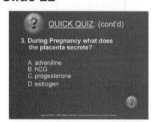

- Correct answer is B: hGC, human chorionic gonadotropin

Slide 23

- Which hormone does the placenta produce?
- What does a pregnancy test look for? (*urine vs. blood*)
- How long does it take the fetus to reach the epigastric region?

Slide 24

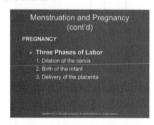

- Which hormone does the placenta produce?
- What does a pregnancy test look for? (*urine vs. blood*)
- How long does it take the fetus to reach the epigastric region?

Slide 25

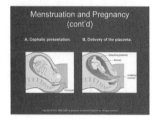

Chabner

Slide 26

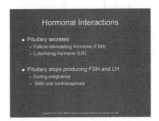

- What is negative feedback?
- How do oral contraceptives work?

Slide 27

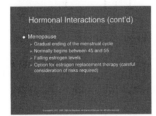

- How does the IUD function to prevent pregnancy?
- How does the diaphragm work to prevent pregnancy?
- What are the risks of either method?

Slide 28

Slide 29

- See Vocabulary section beginning of p. 266 for answers

Slide 30

- See Vocabulary section beginning of p. 266 for answers

ELSEVIER

Chabner

Slide 31

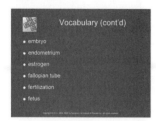

• See Vocabulary section beginning of p. 266 for answers

Slide 32

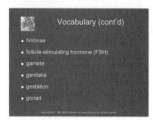

• See Vocabulary section beginning of p. 266 for answers

Slide 33

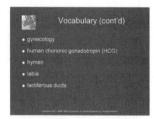

• See Vocabulary section beginning of p. 266 for answers

Slide 34

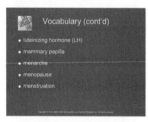

• See Vocabulary section beginning of p. 266 for answers

Slide 35

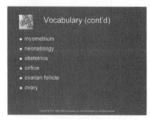

• See Vocabulary section beginning of p. 266 for answers

Chabner

Slide 36

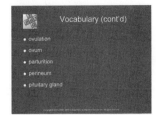

- See Vocabulary section beginning of p. 266 for answers

Slide 37

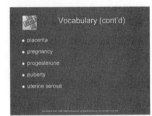

- See Vocabulary section beginning of p. 266 for answers

Slide 38

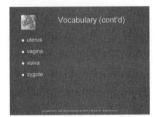

- See Vocabulary section beginning of p. 266 for answers

Slide 39

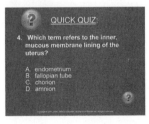

- Correct answer is A: endometrium

Slide 40

Slide 41

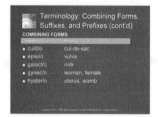

Terminology: Combining Forms, Suffixes, and Prefixes (cont'd)

COMBINING FORMS

Combining Form	Meaning
culd/o	cul-de-sac
epis/o	vulva
galact/o	milk
gynec/o	woman, female
hyster/o	uterus, womb

Slide 42

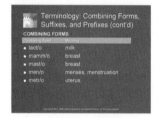

Terminology: Combining Forms, Suffixes, and Prefixes (cont'd)

COMBINING FORMS

Combining Form	Meaning
lact/o	milk
mamm/o	breast
mast/o	breast
men/o	menses, menstruation
metr/o	uterus

Slide 43

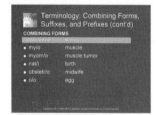

Terminology: Combining Forms, Suffixes, and Prefixes (cont'd)

COMBINING FORMS

Combining Form	Meaning
my/o	muscle
myom/o	muscle tumor
nat/i	birth
obstetr/o	midwife
o/o	egg

Slide 44

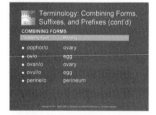

Terminology: Combining Forms, Suffixes, and Prefixes (cont'd)

COMBINING FORMS

Combining Form	Meaning
oophor/o	ovary
ov/o	egg
ovari/o	ovary
ovul/o	egg
perine/o	perineum

Slide 45

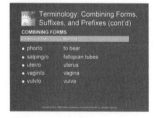

Terminology: Combining Forms, Suffixes, and Prefixes (cont'd)

COMBINING FORMS

Combining Form	Meaning
phor/o	to bear
salping/o	fallopian tubes
uter/o	uterus
vagin/o	vagina
vulv/o	vulva

ELSEVIER

The Language of Medicine, 9th ed.

Chabner

Slide 46

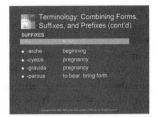

Slide 47

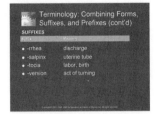

Slide 48

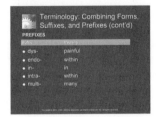

Slide 49

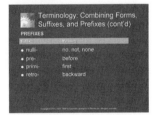

Slide 50

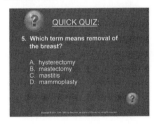

- Correct answer is B: mastectomy. Mammoplasty means surgical repair of the breast, while mastitis means inflammation of the breast and hysterectomy means removal of the uterus.

Slide 51

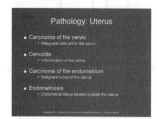

- Name the risk factors for carcinoma of the cervix.

Slide 52

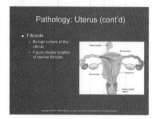

- Name the risk factors for carcinoma of the cervix.
- What is conization?
- How is conization used to diagnose and treat CIS?

Slide 53

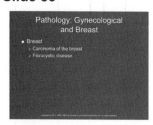

- What is the most common type of breast cancer?

Slide 54

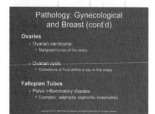

Slide 55

Slide 56

Slide 57

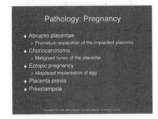

- What is an ectopic pregnancy?
- Which term describes the emergence of the placenta before the baby?

Slide 58

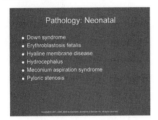

Slide 59

Slide 60

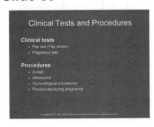

- For what tests is a speculum used?
- What types of x-rays are used to examine the reproductive organs?
- What is the purpose of hysterosalpingography (HSG)?

Slide 61

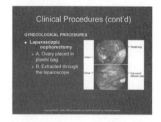

Slide 62

Slide 63

Slide 64

- Answers on next slide.

Slide 65

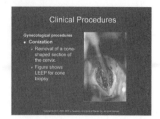

ELSEVIER

The Language of Medicine, 9th ed.

Chabner

Slide 66

- Answers on next slide.

Slide 67

Slide 68

- Answers on next slide.

Slide 69

Slide 70

- Answers on next slide.

The Language of Medicine, 9th ed.

Chabner

Slide 71

Slide 72

- Answers on next slide.

Slide 73

Slide 74

- Answers on next slide.

Slide 75

Slide 76

- Answers on next slide.

Slide 77

Slide 78

- Answers on next slide.

Slide 79

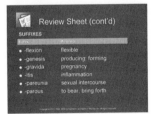

Slide 80

- Answers on next slide.

Slide 81

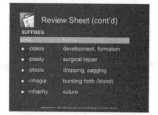

Review Sheet (cont'd)

SUFFIXES

Suffix	Meaning
-plasia	development, formation
-plasty	surgical repair
-ptosis	dropping, sagging
-rrhagia	bursting forth (blood)
-rrhaphy	suture

Slide 82

Review Sheet (cont'd)

SUFFIXES

Suffix	Meaning
-rrhea	
-salpinx	
-scopy	
-stenosis	
-stomy	

- Answers on next slide.

Slide 83

Review Sheet (cont'd)

SUFFIXES

Suffix	Meaning
-rrhea	discharge
-salpinx	uterine tube
-scopy	visual examination
-stenosis	tightening
-stomy	new opening

Slide 84

Review Sheet (cont'd)

SUFFIXES

Suffix	Meaning
-tocia	
-tomy	
-tresia	
-version	

- Answers on next slide.

Slide 85

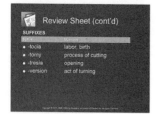

Review Sheet (cont'd)

SUFFIXES

Suffix	Meaning
-tocia	labor, birth
-tomy	process of cutting
-tresia	opening
-version	act of turning

Chabner

Slide 86

- Answers on next slide.

Slide 87

Slide 88

- Answers on next slide.

Slide 89

Slide 90

- Answers on next slide.

Chabner

Slide 91

ELSEVIER

The Language of Medicine, 9th ed.

Chabner

9 Male Reproductive System

TEACHING FOCUS

Students will have the opportunity to learn the major organs of the male reproductive system, define some abnormal and pathological conditions that affect the male system, and learn to differentiate between several types of sexually transmitted infections. Students will also be given the opportunity to define many combining forms used to describe the structures of the male system and to explain various laboratory tests, clinical procedures, and abbreviations that are pertinent to the system. Students will then be given the opportunity to apply their new knowledge to understanding medical terms in their proper contexts, such as medical reports and records.

MATERIALS AND RESOURCES

☐ Flash cards (Lesson 9.1)
☐ Copies of Figure 9-1 (Lesson 9.1)

LESSON CHECKLIST

Preparations for this lesson include:

- Lecture
- Method of student evaluation of comprehension and application of terminology relating to the male reproductive system including:
  - anatomical terminology for the male reproductive system
  - pathologies associated with the male reproductive system
  - common laboratory tests and clinical procedures
  - combining forms, prefixes, and suffixes

KEY TERMS

Vocabulary (pp. 315-316)

bulbourethral gland
ejaculation
ejaculatory duct
epididymis, epididymides
erectile dysfunction
flagellum
fraternal twins
glans penis
identical twins
impotence
parenchyma
penis
perineum
prepuce (foreskin)
prostate gland
scrotum
semen
seminal vesicle
seminiferous tubules
spermatozoon, spermatozoa
sterilization
stroma
testis, testes
testosterone
vas deferens

Terminology (pp. 317-319)

andr/o
balan/o
cry/o
crypt/o
epididym/o
gon/o
hydr/o
orch/o, orchi/o, orchid/o
pen/o
prostat/o
semin/i
sperm/o, spermat/o
terat/o
test/o
varic/o
vas/o
zo/o
-genesis
-one
-pexy
-stomy

Pathological Conditions; Sexually Transmitted Infections (pp. 319-324)

benign prostate hyperplasia
carcinoma of the prostate
carcinoma of the testes

chlamydial infection
cryptorchism; cryptorchidism
gonorrhea
herpes genitalis
human papillomavirus infection
hydrocele
hypospadias; hypospadia
prostatic hyperplasia
phimosis
syphilis
testicular torsion
varicocele

Laboratory Tests, Clinical Procedures, and Abbreviations (pp. 324-326)
castration
circumcision
digital rectal examination (DRE)
GreenLight PVP
PSA test
semen analysis
transurethral resection of the prostate (TURP)
vasectomy

REFERENCE LIST
PowerPoint slides (CD, Evolve): 1-41

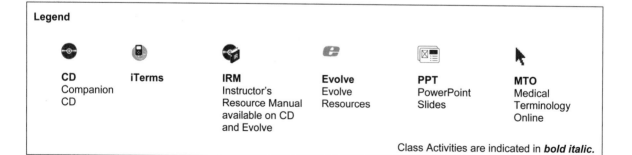

Legend

CD Companion CD

iTerms

IRM Instructor's Resource Manual available on CD and Evolve

Evolve Evolve Resources

PPT PowerPoint Slides

MTO Medical Terminology Online

Class Activities are indicated in ***bold italic.***

LESSON 9.1

PRETEST
IRM M/C Quiz questions 15-25

BACKGROUND ASSESSMENT
Question: What are the terms for the organs in the male reproductive system?
Answer: Answers will vary, but students may mention the penis, testicles, prostate.

Question: What are some of the disorders that can occur to the male reproductive system?
Answer: Answers may vary, but students may mention prostatic hyperplasia, erectile dysfunction, and cryptorchism. STDs are also a possibility, but be sure to mention that these also occur in females.

CRITICAL THINKING QUESTION
Victor, a 25-year-old man, has had surgery to remove one of his testicles due to seminoma. Can he still father a child?
Guidelines: Yes. As long as he has not had additional radiation, he will still be able to produce sperm with the remaining testicle.

OBJECTIVES	CONTENT	TEACHING RESOURCES
Name, locate, and describe the functions of the organs of the male reproductive system.	■ Introduction (p. 312) ■ Anatomy (p. 312) ■ Vocabulary (p. 315)	PPT 5-13 IRM Exercise Quizzes B-C IRM Spelling Quiz IRM Pronunciation Quiz IRM Diagram Quiz IRM Vocabulary Quiz IRM Crossword Puzzle MTO Module 9, Section I, Lessons 1-3 Figure 9-1 Male reproductive system (p. 313) Figure 9-2 Internal structure of a testis and the epididymis (p. 314) Figure 9-3 The passage of sperm (p. 314) Figure 9-4 Fraternal twins (p. 315) Exercises B, C, I, J (pp. 329-330, 332-333) Companion CD Exercise 9-1 *Class Activity **Using the terms for the male reproductive anatomy, have the students identify the singular/plural forms of each.*** *Class Activity **Make copies of Figure 9-1 and pass them out to students. In small groups, have students fill in the missing labels. After allowing a reasonable amount of time, have***

The Language of Medicine, 9th ed.
Chabner

OBJECTIVES	CONTENT	TEACHING RESOURCES
		groups share their figures with the class for discussion and corrections.
		Class Activity Have students make flash cards for vocabulary terms.
Define the many combining forms used to describe the structures of this system.	■ Terminology (p. 317)	▦ PPT 14-21
		▣ IRM Exercise Quiz
		▣ IRM Exercise Quiz G
		Exercise G (pp. 331)
		⦿ Companion CD Exercise 9-2
		Class Activity Use the diagram for the male reproductive system for labeling, using the appropriate combining forms.
		Class Activity Discuss the relevance of learning combining forms and their roots to help facilitate students' learning of the system's vocabulary terms.

9.1 Homework/Assignments:

9.1 Teacher's Notes:

LESSON 9.2

CRITICAL THINKING QUESTION

John is a 53-year-old man who is otherwise healthy, but recently he has had difficulty urinating. His physician performs a digital rectal exam and reports that it appears that John's prostate is enlarged. How would this cause problems with urination?

Guidelines: The prostate is an organ that surrounds the urethra. When it enlarges, it can squeeze the urethra, causing narrowing and difficulty with urination.

OBJECTIVES	CONTENT	TEACHING RESOURCES
Define some abnormal and pathological conditions that affect the male system.	■ Pathological conditions; sexually transmitted infections (p. 319) ☐ Abnormal and pathological conditions (p. 319) – Testes (p. 319) – Prostate gland (p. 320) – Penis (p. 322)	▣ PPT 23-25 ⊕ IRM Pathology Quiz ⊕ IRM Exercise Quiz A, B, D ⊕ IRM Dictation and Comprehension Quiz ↖ MTO Module 9, Section II, Lesson 1 Figure 9-5 A, Balanitis B, Cryptorchism (p. 317) Figure 9-6 Seminoma and carcinoma (p. 319) Figure 9-7 Hydrocele, testicular torsion, and varicocele (p. 320) Figure 9-8 The prostate gland with carcinoma and benign prostatic hyperplasia (BPH) (p. 321) Figure 9-10 Hypospadias, phimosis, and circumcision (p. 322) Exercises A, B, D, E (pp. 329-331) ***Class Activity** Assign small groups of students one or two of the following conditions: carcinoma of the testes, cryptorchism, hydrocele, testicular torsion, varicocele, carcinoma of the prostate, prostatic hyperplasia, hypospadias, or phimosis. Have students discuss each condition, explaining what they are, how and why they occur, and how they are treated. Students should also draw illustrations of what they think the condition looks like based on its description. Have groups present their lists of conditions to the class.*
Differentiate among several types of sexually transmitted infections.	☐ Sexually transmitted infections (p. 322)	▣ PPT 26 ⊕ IRM Exercise Quiz E ⊕ IRM Dictation and Comprehension Quiz

ELSEVIER

The Language of Medicine, 9th ed.

Chabner

OBJECTIVES	CONTENT	TEACHING RESOURCES
		➤ MTO Module 9, Section II, Lesson 2
		Figure 9-11 Gonorrhea and herpes (p. 323)
		Figure 9-12 Syphilis (p. 324)
		Class Activity In groups, have students discuss sexually transmitted infections. They should explain what the symptoms are of each, whether they are viral or bacterial, how they are treated, and whether or not they are curable. After allowing ample discussion time, call on groups at random to discuss one of the infections with the class. Do this for each infection.
		Class Activity Have students develop posters to describe one of the sexually transmitted diseases, the cause, prevention, signs, symptoms, and treatments.
Explain various laboratory tests, clinical procedures, and abbreviations that are pertinent to the system.	■ Laboratory tests, clinical procedures, and abbreviations (p. 324) □ Laboratory tests (p. 324) □ Clinical procedures (p. 325) □ Abbreviations (p. 326)	⊠ PPT 27-31 IRM Laboratory Tests and Clinical Procedures Quiz IRM Exercise Quiz F, H IRM Abbreviations Quiz ➤ MTO Module 9, Section III, Lessons 1-3 Figure 9-9 Digital rectal examination (p. 321) Figure 9-13 Transurethral resection of the prostate (TURP) (p. 325) Figure 9-14 Vasectomy (p. 326) Exercises F, H, J (pp. 331-333) ⬤ Companion CD Exercises 9-3, 9-4 *Class Activity In pairs or small groups, have students role-play a physician recommending a laboratory test or clinical procedure for a patient. Groups can include any combination of patients, medical assistants, nurses, or physicians. Have students perform their scenarios for the class.* *Class Activity Discuss the types of clinical procedures and which ones are invasive, noninvasive, radiation-based, or surgical.*

The Language of Medicine, 9th ed.

Chabner

OBJECTIVES	CONTENT	TEACHING RESOURCES
Apply your new knowledge to understanding medical terms in their proper contexts, such as medical reports and records.	■ Practical applications (p. 327)	PPT 32-40 IRM Practical Applications MTO, Module 9, Section V Review Sheet (p. 339) *Class Activity Have small groups of students choose two to three conditions or infections discussed in this chapter and present their symptoms to the class. Remaining groups will record the symptoms in a mock patient chart, using relevant vocabulary and abbreviations, and guess which condition is being described.* *Class Activity Read to the class the Case Report: A Man with Post-TURP Complaints. Ask them the following questions: What do the abbreviations PSA, DRE and TURP mean? Spell, analyze, and define the terms postvoid, sonogram, adenopathy, and adenocarcinoma.*
Performance Evaluation		IRM Multiple Choice Quiz IRM Terminology Quiz IRM Pathology Quiz IRM Laboratory Tests and Clinical Procedures Quiz IRM Exercise Quiz IRM Dictation and Comprehension Quiz IRM Spelling Quiz IRM Pronunciation Quiz IRM Diagram Quiz IRM Vocabulary Quiz IRM Review Sheet Quiz IRM Medical Scramble IRM Crossword Puzzle IRM Practical Applications

ELSEVIER

OBJECTIVES	CONTENT	TEACHING RESOURCES
		e ESLR Body Spectrum Electronic Anatomy Coloring Book: Reproductive
		e ESLR Student Quiz Chapter 09
		🔦 MTO Module 9, Sections I-III quizzes
		🔦 MTO Module 9 Exam
		💿 Companion CD Exercises 9-5, 9-6, 9-7
		📟 iTerms Chapter 07

9.2 Homework/Assignments:

9.2 Teacher's Notes:

Chabner

Slide 1

Slide 2

Slide 3

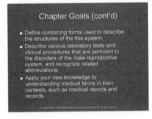

Slide 4

Slide 5

Slide 6

- What are the parts of a sperm cell and what is the sperm cell's purpose?
- How does sperm navigate?

Slide 7

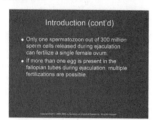

- Ask students to describe the process of fertilization.

Slide 8

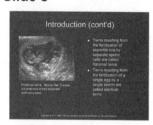

- What is the difference between fraternal and identical twins?
- Which twins are a perfect genetic match?

Slide 9

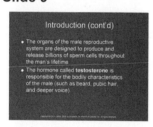

- Describe the role of testosterone.
- What is the difference between the number of eggs vs. sperm cells?

Slide 10

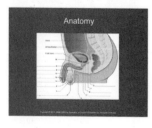

- What are the male gonads called and where are they located?
- How does temperature affect the scrotum?
- What is the function of the interstitial cells and where are they located?
- What are the supportive tissues of the testes?
- Answers are on next slide

Slide 11

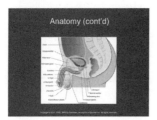

Slide 12

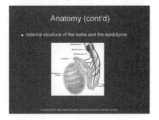

Slide 13

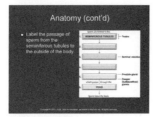

Slide 14

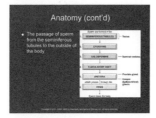

Slide 15

- The bulbourethral gland is also called Cowper gland.
- Which terms relate to the ejaculatory process?
- What type of twin can produce conjoined twins?
- What is impotence?

Chabner

Slide 16

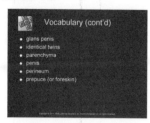

- What is the difference between a bulbourethral gland and the Cowper gland?
- Which terms relate to the ejaculatory process?
- What type of twin can produce conjoined twins?
- What is impotence?

Slide 17

- What is the difference between a bulbourethral gland and the Cowper gland?
- Which terms relate to the ejaculatory process?
- What type of twin can produce conjoined twins?
- What is impotence?

Slide 18

- Which terms relate to the ejaculatory process?
- What type of twin can produce conjoined twins?
- What is impotence?

Slide 19

- Correct answer is C: prepuce.

Slide 20

Chabner

Slide 21

Slide 22

Slide 23

Slide 24

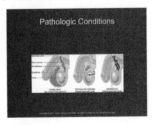

- How is hydrocele treated?
- What are the risks of an undescended testis?
- How common is carcinoma of the testes?
- What are varicoceles?
- What is the treatment for testicular torsion?

Slide 25

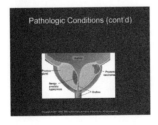

- How are carcinomas of the prostate and prostatic hyperplasia diagnosed?
- How are they treated?

Slide 26

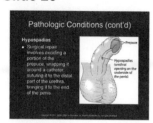

- What are the odds of a male having hypospadias?
- How is hypospadias treated?
- How is phimosis treated?

Slide 27

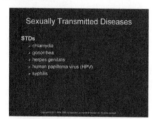

- What are the symptoms of a chlamydial infection? Gonorrhea? Herpes genitalis? Syphilis?
- What types of drugs are given to treat these infections?
- Which infections can occur without symptoms?

Slide 28

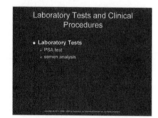

- What does the PSA test measure?
- What does a semen analysis look for? When might this test be performed?

Slide 29

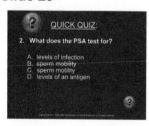

- Correct answer is D. PSA tests for prostate-specific antigen (PSA) in the blood. Elevated levels of PSA are associated with enlargement of the prostate gland and may be a sign of prostate cancer.

Slide 30

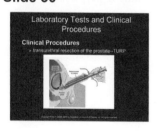

- What procedure treats prostatic hyperplasia (BPH)? How is it performed?
- What is the purpose of a digital rectal exam?

The Language of Medicine, 9th ed.

Chabner

Slide 31

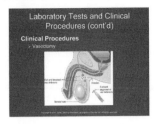

- How does the urologist perform a vasectomy?
- Are there any side affects to a vasectomy?
- What is reversal of a vasectomy? (*Vasovasostomy*)

Slide 32

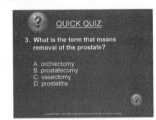

- Correct answer is B.

Slide 33

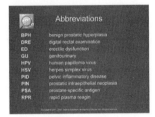

Slide 34

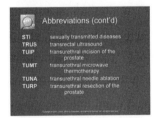

Slide 35

- Answers on next slide.

Slide 36

Slide 37

- Answers on next slide.

Slide 38

Slide 39

Slide 40

Chabner

Slide 41

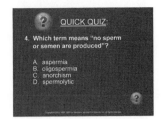

- Correct answer is A: aspermia

Chabner

TEACHING FOCUS

Students will have the opportunity to learn the nervous system's major organs, its functions, and its parts. Students will be introduced to several pathological conditions affecting the nervous system and the laboratory tests, clinical procedures, and terms and abbreviations associated with those conditions. Furthermore, students will have an opportunity to practice understanding medical terms in their proper contexts, such as in medical reports and records.

MATERIALS AND RESOURCES

- ☐ EEG (Lesson 10.3)
- ☐ Flash cards (Lessons 10.1-10.2)
- ☐ List of terms (Lessons 10.3)
- ☐ MRI image of the brain (Lesson 10.3)
- ☐ Unlabeled photocopies of Figures 10-5, 10-7, and 10-8 (Lesson 10.2)
- ☐ Myelography images (Lesson 10.3)
- ☐ Unlabeled posters of the nervous system (Lesson 10.1)
- ☐ X-ray images of the brain (Lesson 10.3)

LESSON CHECKLIST

Preparations for this lesson include:
- Lecture
- Student performance evaluation of all entry-level skills required for student comprehension of the nervous system and application of associated terms, including:
  - o naming nervous system anatomy and functions of major organs
  - o applying knowledge of combining forms to define organs and structures of the nervous system
  - o defining pathological conditions of the nervous system
  - o identifying and describing lab tests, clinical procedures, and abbreviations that pertain to the nervous system

KEY TERMS

Vocabulary (pp. 353-355)

acetylcholine
afferent nerve
arachnoid membrane
astrocyte
autonomic nervous system
axon
blood-brain barrier
brainstem
cauda equina
cell body
central nervous system (CNS)
cerebellum
cerebral cortex
cerebrospinal fluid (CSF)
cerebrum
cranial nerves
dendrite
dura mater
efferent nerve
ependymal cell
ganglion, ganglia
glial cells
gyrus, gyri

hypothalamus
medulla oblongata
meninges
microglial cell
motor nerves
myelin sheath
nerve
neuron
neurotransmitter
oligodendroglial cell
parasympathetic nerves
parenchyma
peripheral nervous system
pia mater
plexus, plexuses
pons
receptor
sciatic nerve
sensory nerve
stimulus, stimuli
stroma
sulcus, sulci
sympathetic nerve
synapse

ELSEVIER

Chabner

thalamus
vagus nerve
ventricles of the brain
Terminology (pp. 356-361)
cerebell/o
cerebr/o
dur/o
encephal/o
gli/o
lept/o
mening/o, meningi/o
my/o
myel/o
neur/o
pont/o
radicul/o
thalam/o
thec/o
vag/o
alges/o, -algesia
-algia
caus/o
comat/o
esthesi/o, -esthesia
kines/o, -kinesia
-kinesis, -kinetic
-lepsy
lex/o
-paresis
-phasia
-plegia
-praxia
-sthenia
syncop/o
tax/o

Pathologic Conditions (pp. 361-369)
Alzheimer disease (AD)
amyotrophic lateral sclerosis (ALS)
brain tumor
cerebral concussion
cerebral contusion
cerebrovascular accident (CVA)
epilepsy
herpes zoster (shingles)
human immunodeficiency virus (HIV) with
    encephalopathy
Huntington disease
hydrocephalus
meningitis
migraine
multiple sclerosis (MS)
myasthenia gravis
palsy
Parkinson disease
spina bifida
Tourette syndrome
**Laboratory Tests and Clinical Procedures
(pp. 371-373)**
cerebral angiography
cerebrospinal fluid analysis
computed tomography (CT) of the brain
Doppler/ultrasound studies
electroencephalography (EEG)
lumbar (spinal) puncture (LP)
magnetic resonance imaging of the brain
myelography
positron emission tomography
stereotactic radiosurgery

REFERENCE LIST
PowerPoint slides (CD, Evolve): 1-67

Legend

CD	**iTerms**	**IRM**	**Evolve**	**PPT**	**MTO**
Companion CD		Instructor's Resource Manual available on CD and Evolve	Evolve Resources	PowerPoint Slides	Medical Terminology Online

Class Activities are indicated in ***bold italic.***

LESSON 10.1

PRETEST
IRM Exercise Quiz A

BACKGROUND ASSESSMENT
Question: What is the function and basic structure of the nervous system?
Answer: One of the most complex systems in the body, the nervous system processes information from both external and internal stimuli and responds accordingly. The nervous system is divided structurally into two major divisions. The first division, the central nervous system, includes the brain and spinal cord. The second division, the peripheral nervous system, consists of 12 cranial nerves and 31 pairs of spinal nerves. Together, these systems operate all voluntary and involuntary functions of the body.

Question: What are some neurological disorders that you are familiar with?
Answer: Answers may vary, but students may answer Alzheimer's disease, Parkinson's disease, paraplegia, paralysis, multiple sclerosis, stroke, and epilepsy.

CRITICAL THINKING QUESTION
How is a severed electrical cord similar to a nerve that has been cut?
Guidelines: An electrical cord that has been cut can no longer transmit an electrical impulse.

OBJECTIVES	CONTENT	TEACHING RESOURCES
Name, locate, and describe the functions of the major organs and parts of the nervous system.	■ Introduction (p. 342) ■ General structure of the nervous system (p. 342) ■ Neurons, nerves, and glia (p. 346)	⊠▤ PPT 5-15 🎲 IRM Exercise Quiz A 🎲 IRM Diagram Quiz ↖ MTO Module 10, Section I, Lessons 1-6 Figure 10-1 The brain and the spinal cord, spinal nerves, and spinal plexuses (p. 343) Figure 10-2 Cranial nerves and their functions (p. 344) Figure 10-3 Actions of parasympathetic and sympathetic nerves (p. 345) Figure 10-4 Divisions of the central nervous system (CNS) and peripheral nervous system (PNS) (p. 346) Figure 10-5 Parts of a neuron (p. 347) Figure 10-6 Glial cells (p. 348) Exercise A (p. 377) 💿 Companion CD Exercise 10-1 ▸ Discuss how the nervous system functionally differs from other organs. *Class Activity **Divide the class into several teams. Assign each team to an unlabeled poster of the nervous system. Provide each team with several flash cards with the names***

OBJECTIVES	CONTENT	TEACHING RESOURCES
		of the different parts of the nervous system written on them. Within a 5-minute time limit, have each team arrange as many of the flash cards as possible in the correct position on their respective posters.
		Class Activity *Have students develop their own charts that illustrate the structure of the nervous system. Working in pairs, have them cover up one part and see if the other student can remember what is missing.*

10.1 Homework/Assignments:

10.1 Teacher's Notes:

LESSON 10.2

CRITICAL THINKING QUESTION

Dan, a 50-year-old man, is experiencing muscle stiffness and shaky hands. In the office, you also note his stooped posture. Tests reveal a deficiency of dopamine levels, which helps confirm a diagnosis of Parkinson's disease. Knowing that there is no cure, Dan is upset and ambivalent about taking medication. How can you help Dan understand his condition and how his medication, levodopa plus carbidopa (Sinemet), will help him?

Guidelines: When Dan has a better understanding of Parkinson's disease, he will be able to see the importance of this medication. You can tell him that the disease progresses very slowly and is caused by a deficiency of dopamine, which is produced by cells in the basal ganglia. The drug he has been prescribed increases dopamine levels in the brain, which can help slow the process. You can also reassure him that there are many people who have Parkinson's disease and that research in this area is very active.

OBJECTIVES	CONTENT	TEACHING RESOURCES
Name, locate, and describe the functions of the major organs and parts of the nervous system.	■ The brain (p. 348) ■ The spinal cord and meninges (p. 351) □ Spinal cord (p. 351) □ Meninges (p. 352)	PPT 17-26 IRM Crossword Puzzle MTO Module 10, Section I, Lessons 7-10 Figure 10-7 Left cerebral hemisphere (p. 349) Figure 10-8 Circulation of cerebrospinal fluid (p. 349) Figure 10-9 Parts of the brain (p. 350) Figure 10-10 The spinal cord (p. 351) Figure 10-11 The meninges (p. 352) ▶ Discuss the back and forth direction of messages traveling across the brain and how this is represented in learning disabilities, such as dyslexia. *Class Activity Provide students with unlabeled copies of Figures 10-6, 10-8, and 10-9. In groups, have students fill in the missing information without using their texts. After groups have completed the task, have them present their figures to the class, working together to correct any mistakes.* *Class Activity Have small groups of students work together to create two sets of cards for brain parts. They should list the functions of the parts on one set and the names of the parts on the other. Then ask them to shuffle the cards and practice matching the name with the function.*

ELSEVIER

OBJECTIVES	CONTENT	TEACHING RESOURCES
Recognize nervous system combining forms and make terms using them with new and familiar suffixes.	■ Vocabulary (p. 353) ■ Terminology (p. 356) □ Organs and structures (p. 356) □ Symptoms (p. 358)	PPT 27-44 IRM Terminology Quiz IRM Exercise Quizzes A-D IRM Dictation and Comprehension Quiz, Vocabulary and Terminology IRM Spelling Quiz IRM Vocabulary Quiz Figure 10-12 Hematomas (p. 356) Figure 10-13 Positioning of a patient for spinal anesthesia (p. 359) Exercise N (p. 383) Review Sheet, Combining Forms (p. 394) Companion CD Exercise 10-2, 10-3 ▶ Discuss the relevance of learning combining forms and their roots. *Class Activity Divide the class into pairs. Have each pair create flash cards with definitions for the key terms in this section. Have the students quiz each other on the key terms.* *Class Activity Use a bingo card generator to help students test their knowledge of nervous system combining forms.*

10.2 Homework/Assignments:

10.2 Teacher's Notes:

LESSON 10.3

CRITICAL THINKING QUESTION

After suffering from vision problems, Anne, a 34-year-old woman, has been diagnosed with a meningioma in the cerebellum. She is scheduled for surgery and, understandably, she is concerned and wants to know what will happen. What can you tell Anne to help her cope?

Guidelines: You can tell Anne that although a brain tumor is something to be concerned about, meningiomas are usually benign. However, a meningeoma may cause compression and distortion in the brain, so it is important that it be removed. You should suggest Anne talk with her physician about the surgery and the possibility of radiotherapy and the use of steroids after surgery, so that she has a clearer understanding of the procedure and follow-up.

OBJECTIVES	CONTENT	TEACHING RESOURCES

Define several pathological conditions affecting the nervous system.	■ Pathological conditions (p. 361)
	  ☐ Congenital disorders (p. 361)
	  ☐ Degenerative, movement, and seizure disorders (p. 363)
	  ☐ Infectious disorders (p. 366)
	  ☐ Neoplastic disorders (p. 367)
	  ☐ Traumatic disorders (p. 367)
	  ☐ Vascular disorders (p. 368)
		PPT 46-51
		
		IRM Pathology Quiz
		
		IRM Exercise Quizzes E-H
		
		IRM Dictation and Comprehension Quiz, Pathology
		
		MTO Module 10, Section II, Lessons 1-5
		
		Figure 10-14 Spina bifida (p. 362)
		
		Figure 10-15 A, Alzheimer's disease; B, multiple sclerosis (p. 363)
		
		Figure 10-16 Multiple sclerosis (p. 365)
		
		Figure 10-17 Bell's palsy (p.365)
		
		Figure 10-18 A, CT scan of astrocytoma; B, glioblastoma multiforme (p. 367)
		
		Figure 10-19 Three types of strokes (p. 368)
		
		Figure 10-20 Cerebral aneurysm (p. 369)
		
		Exercises F-J (pp. 379-382)
		
		Study Section (p. 370)
		
		Class Activity Have students split into small groups and make lists of the effects of stroke and the steps of the recovery process.
		
		Class Activity Show the students several examples of EEGs. Distinguish between normal electrical activity and seizure activity. Ask students to describe some of the causes of seizure.
		
		Alternatively, ask students to make cards with a pathological condition on one, and its definition on the other. Have them shuffle the "deck" and match them correctly.

Chabner

OBJECTIVES	CONTENT	TEACHING RESOURCES
Describe some laboratory tests, clinical procedures, and abbreviations that pertain to the system.	■ Laboratory tests, clinical procedures, and abbreviations (p. 371) ☐ Laboratory tests (p. 371) ☐ Clinical procedures (p. 371) – X-rays (p. 371) – Magnetic imaging (p. 371) – Radionuclide study (p. 372) – Ultrasound (p. 372) – Other procedures (p. 372)	⊠▤ PPT 53 ⬢ IRM Laboratory Tests and Clinical Procedures Quiz ⬢ IRM Abbreviations Quiz ➤ MTO Module 10, Section III, Lessons 1-2 Figure 10-21 PET brain scan (p. 372) Figure 10-22 Lumbar puncture (p. 373) Figure 10-23 Stereotactic radiosurgery (p. 373) Exercises K, L (p. 382) ⬤ Companion CD Exercises 10-4, 10-5, 10-6, 10-7 ▶ Discuss the types of laboratory tests and clinical procedures associated with the nervous system. ***Class Activity** Discuss experiences that students or their family members may have had with a diagnosis that involved the nervous system. What tests were involved? What was the outcome?* ***Class Activity** Show the class x-rays and MRIs of the brain, as well as myelography images. Ask them to identify specific parts of the brain and spinal cord on the images and to describe their functions.* ***Class Activity** Have students practice the meanings of the definitions by writing the abbreviation on one side and its definition on the other. Have students work in pairs, with each using his or her own deck, which is shuffled and placed with the definition sides up. Students take turns giving the meaning of the card on top of a partner's deck. If they define it wrong, the card goes on the bottom of the deck. If right, it goes in a separate pile. The goal is for each student to finish the partner's pile before his or her own is finished.*
Apply your new knowledge to understanding medical terms in their proper contexts, such as medical reports and records.	■ Practical applications (p. 374) ■ Pronunciation of terms (p. 388) ☐ Vocabulary and combining forms terminology (p. 388) ☐ Pathological conditions, laboratory tests, and clinical procedures (p. 391)	⊠▤ PPT 53-66 ⬢ IRM Pronunciation Quiz ⬢ IRM Practical Applications ➤ MTO Module 10, Section V Figure 10-24 Common carotid arteries (p. 375)

OBJECTIVES	CONTENT	TEACHING RESOURCES
		Practical Applications (pp. 374-376)
		Exercises M, N (pp. 383-384)
		Pronunciation of terms, Vocabulary and Combining Forms and Terminology (pp. 388-391)
		Pronunciation of Terms, Pathological Conditions, Laboratory Tests, and Clinical Procedures (pp. 391-393)
		⊙ Companion CD Exercises 10-8, 10-9
		▣ iTerms Chapter 10
		▸ Discuss how to best handle patients who exhibit unusual behavior caused by nervous system pathologies.
		Class Activity Write each of the terms on pp. 375-380 on small slips of paper and place them in a "hat." Go around the room and have each student draw a slip of paper, give a definition of the term, and provide a context for its usage. Continue until all terms have been defined.
		Class Activity Using the Practical Applications Case Report X, read the report to the students and ask them to give definitions for the following abbreviations: EEG, MRA, MRI, CSF. Ask them to spell, analyze, define, and underline the accented syllable in the following terms: **hemiparesis, hemiplegic, cerebral, aphasia, hemiplegia, and anesthesia.**
Performance Evaluation		⊙ IRM Multiple Choice Quiz
		⊙ IRM Terminology Quiz
		⊙ IRM Pathology Quiz
		⊙ IRM Laboratory Tests and Clinical Procedures Quiz
		⊙ IRM Exercise Quiz
		⊙ IRM Dictation and Comprehension Quiz, Vocabulary and Terminology
		⊙ IRM Dictation and Comprehension Quiz, Pathology

OBJECTIVES	CONTENT	TEACHING RESOURCES
		IRM Spelling Quiz
		IRM Pronunciation Quiz
		IRM Abbreviations Quiz
		IRM Diagram Quiz
		IRM Vocabulary Quiz
		IRM Review Sheet Quiz
		IRM Medical Scramble
		IRM Crossword Puzzle
		IRM Practical Applications
		ESLR Body Spectrum Electronic Anatomy Coloring Book, Nervous
		ESLR Student Quiz, Chapter 10
		MTO Module 10, Sections I-III quizzes
		MTO Module 10 Exam.
		Companion CD Exercises 10-10, 10-11

10.3 Homework/Assignments:

10.3 Teacher's Notes:

Chabner

Slide 1

The Language Of Medicine

9th edition

Davi-Ellen Chabner

Slide 2

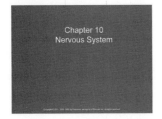

Chapter 10
Nervous System

Slide 3

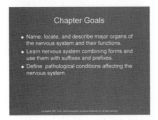

Chapter Goals

- Name, locate, and describe major organs of the nervous system and their functions.
- Learn nervous system combining forms and use them with suffixes and prefixes.
- Define pathological conditions affecting the nervous system.

Slide 4

Chapter Goals (cont'd)

- Describe laboratory tests, clinical procedures, and abbreviations that pertain to the system.
- Apply your new knowledge to understanding medical terms in the proper contexts, such as medical reports and records.

Slide 5

Chapter 10
Lesson 10.1

Chabner

Slide 6

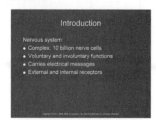

- What are external stimuli?
- How can internal chemicals be stimuli?
- What are some of the involuntary body functions controlled by the nervous system?

Slide 7

- Internal and external stimuli activate the cell membranes to release stored electrical energy called the nervous impulse.
- External and internal receptors receive and transmit these impulses to the brain and spinal cord (central nervous system).
- The central nervous system recognizes, interprets, and relays impulses to other nerve cells that extend through parts of the body, such as muscles, glands, and organs.
- What is the scope of influence nerve cells have on bodily function?

Slide 8

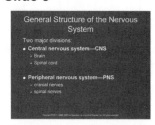

- Cranial nerves carry electrical impulses between the brain and the head and neck (except vagus nerve).
- Spinal nerves carry impulses between the spinal cord and the chest, abdomen, and extremities.
- Why is the 10th cranial nerve called the vagus nerve? What does it do?

Slide 9

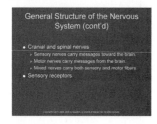

- What is the difference between voluntary and involuntary functioning?
- What are parasympathetic and sympathetic nerves?

Slide 10

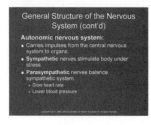

- The autonomic nervous system contains a large group of nerves that function automatically.
- It controls heart, blood vessels, glands, and involuntary muscles like intestines, and hollow organs such as stomach and urinary bladder.
- Why is the autonomic nervous system necessary?

Chabner

Slide 11

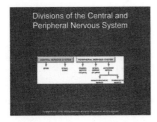

- How are stimuli processed by the nervous system?
- What are the parenchymal cells of the nervous system?

Slide 12

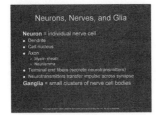

- What structure carries the nerve impulse away from the cell body?
- What substances are examples of neurotransmitters?
- What is the singular form of "ganglia"?

Slide 13

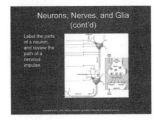

- Answers are on the next slide.
- What are the parts of the neurons shown in this slide?
- What structures comprise the parenchymal cells of the nervous system?

Slide 14

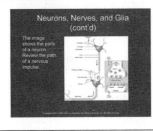

- What are the parts of the neurons shown in this slide?
- What structures comprise the parenchymal cells of the nervous system?

Slide 15

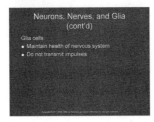

- How do the glia cells keep the nervous system healthy?

Chabner

Slide 16

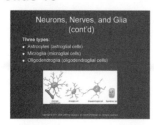

- These are the supportive, protective, and connective cells of the central nervous system.
- (**Recap**) What purpose does stromal tissue serve?

Slide 17

Slide 18

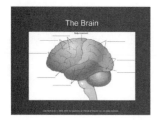

Slide 19

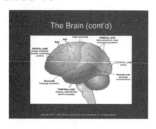

- The brain is divided into right and left hemispheres.
- The brain consists of four major lobes, including the frontal lobe, parietal lobe, temporal lobe, and occipital lobe.
- What are the parts of the left cerebral hemisphere as shown in the diagram?
- What primary functions are carried out by the different lobes of the brain?

Slide 20

- What is the purpose of the cerebral cortex?
- How many major divisions can be applied to the entire cerebral cortex?

Slide 21

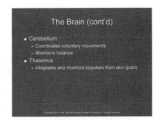

- What is the value of the ability to sense pain?

Slide 22

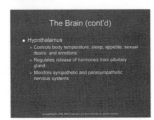

- How do messages travel from one side of the brain to another?

Slide 23

Slide 24

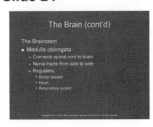

- How does the word "crossover" apply to a function of the medulla oblongata?

Slide 25

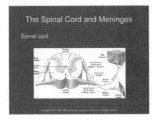

- The spinal cord is the column of nervous tissue from the medulla oblongata to second lumbar vertebra.

- It serves as a pathway for impulses to and from the brain.

- The inner section of the cross section of the spinal cord is gray matter.

- The outer section of the cross section of the spinal cord is white matter.

- What is the difference between efferent and afferent neurons?

Slide 26

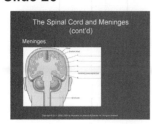

- Meninges are the three layers of connective tissue membranes that surround the brain and spinal cord.
- What is the function of the outer dura mater? (*It channels blood to brain tissue.*)
- What fluid lies between the arachnoid membrane and the subarachnoid space?
- The inner pia mater offers a rich supply of blood vessels.
- Where are the layers of the meninges in the figure?

Slide 27

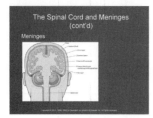

- Meninges are the three layers of connective tissue membranes that surround the brain and spinal cord.
- What is the function of the outer dura mater? (*It channels blood to brain tissue.*)
- What fluid lies between the arachnoid membrane and the subarachnoid space?
- The inner pia mater offers a rich supply of blood vessels.
- Where are the layers of the meninges in the figure?

Slide 28

Slide 29

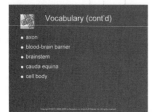

Slide 30

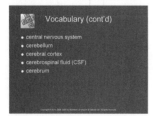

The Language of Medicine, 9th ed.

Chabner

Slide 31

Vocabulary (cont'd)

- dendrite
- dura mater
- ependymal cell
- efferent nerve
- ganglion/ganglia
- glial cell or neuroglial cell
- gyrus

Slide 32

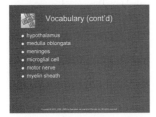

Vocabulary (cont'd)

- hypothalamus
- medulla oblongata
- meninges
- microglial cell
- motor nerve
- myelin sheath

Slide 33

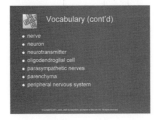

Vocabulary (cont'd)

- nerve
- neuron
- neurotransmitter
- oligodendroglial cell
- parasympathetic nerves
- parenchyma
- peripheral nervous system

Slide 34

Vocabulary (cont'd)

- pia mater
- plexus
- pons
- receptor
- sciatic nerve
- sensory nerve
- spinal nerves

Slide 35

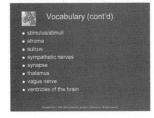

Vocabulary (cont'd)

- stimulus/stimuli
- stroma
- sulcus
- sympathetic nerves
- synapse
- thalamus
- vagus nerve
- ventricles of the brain

The Language of Medicine, 9th ed.

Chabner

Slide 36

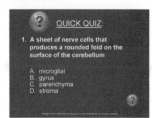

- Correct answer is B: gyrus

Slide 37

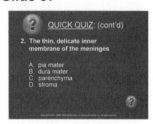

- Correct answer is A: pia mater

Slide 38

Slide 39

Slide 40

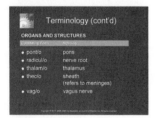

The Language of Medicine, 9th ed.

Chabner

Slide 41

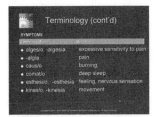

Slide 42

Slide 43

Slide 44

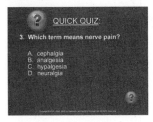

- Correct answer is D: neuralgia

Slide 45

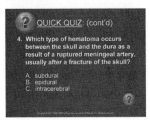

- Correct answer is B: epidural.

Slide 46

Chapter 10
Lesson 10.3

Slide 47

Pathology

Congenital Disorders
• Hydrocephalus
• Spina bifida
  › Spina bifida cystica
  › Spina bifida occulta

- How is hydrocephalus treated?
- What are the two types of spina bifida? Ask students to describe the differences between the two types.

Slide 48

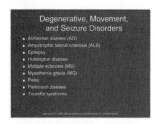

Degenerative, Movement, and Seizure Disorders

• Alzheimer disease (AD)
• Amyotrophic lateral sclerosis (ALS)
• Epilepsy
• Huntington disease
• Multiple sclerosis (MS)
• Myasthenia gravis (MG)
• Palsy
• Parkinson disease
• Tourette syndrome

- Which conditions are movement related?
- Which conditions are degenerative?

Slide 49

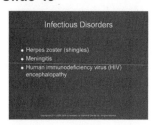

Infectious Disorders

• Herpes zoster (shingles)
• Meningitis
• Human immunodeficiency virus (HIV) encephalopathy

- What is a viral infection caused by chickenpox?
- What types of meningitis exist, and how is meningitis treated?
- What is the most malignant form of brain tumor?

Slide 50

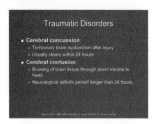

Traumatic Disorders

• **Cerebral concussion**
  › Temporary brain dysfunction after injury
  › Usually clears within 24 hours
• **Cerebral contusion**
  › Bruising of brain tissue through direct trauma to head
  › Neurological deficits persist longer than 24 hours

- What is the primary difference between a concussion and a contusion?

The Language of Medicine, 9th ed.

Chabner

Slide 51

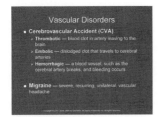

- What is the primary difference between a concussion and a contusion?

Slide 52

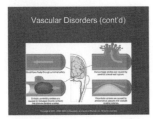

- There are three types of cerebrovascular accident (CVA): thrombotic, embolic, and hemorrhagic.

- What is another name for CVA?

- What causes a transient ischemic attack (TIA)?

Slide 53

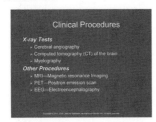

- Which x-ray uses a contrast medium?

Slide 54

- Which items are disorders or injuries, and which are procedures?

Slide 55

- Which items are pathologies, and which are tests?

- What is an EEG used to measure?

The Language of Medicine, 9th ed.

Chabner

Slide 56

• Which of the items listed above are pathologies? Describe them.

Slide 57

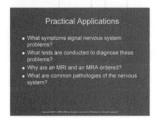

Slide 58

Slide 59

Slide 60

Slide 61

Review Sheet (cont'd)

COMBINING FORMS

Combining Form	Meaning
comat/o	deep sleep
crani/o	skull
cry/o	cold
dur/o	dura mater
encephal/o	brain
esthes/o	nervous sensation

Slide 62

Review Sheet (cont'd)

COMBINING FORMS

Combining Form	Meaning
gli/o	
hydr/o	
kines/o	
lept/o	
lex/o	
mening/o, meningi/o	
my/o	

Slide 63

Review Sheet (cont'd)

COMBINING FORMS

Combining Form	Meaning
gli/o	glue
hydr/o	water
kines/o	movement
lept/o	thin, slender
lex/o	word, phrase
mening/o, meningi/o	membranes, meninges
my/o	muscle

Slide 64

Review Sheet (cont'd)

COMBINING FORMS

Combining Form	Meaning
myel/o	
narc/o	
neur/o	
olig/o	
pont/o	
radicul/o	

Slide 65

Review Sheet (cont'd)

COMBINING FORMS

Combining Form	Meaning
myel/o	spinal cord
narc/o	sleep
neur/o	nerve
olig/o	scanty
pont/o	pons
radicul/o	nerve root

Slide 66

Slide 67

TEACHING FOCUS

Students will have the opportunity to understand the anatomy and physiology of the heart and accompanying blood vessels that comprise the cardiovascular system, which supplies the cells and tissues of the body with nutrients and oxygen. The student will become acquainted with the terminology used to describe the pathologic conditions that affect the heart and blood vessels and the clinical tests and laboratory procedures that facilitate the identification of these abnormalities. Ultimately, terminology will be presented that describes medical treatments for cardiovascular pathology.

MATERIALS AND RESOURCES

- ☐ Automatic blood pressure kit (Lesson 11.1)
- ☐ Bingo cards (Lesson 11.3)
- ☐ Cards of landmarks of the heart (Lesson 11.1)
- ☐ Cot (Lesson 11.1)
- ☐ Electrocardiography machine with electrodes and paper (ECG) (Lesson 11.1)

- ☐ Set of flash cards or index cards with one major step in the blood pathway on each card (Lesson 11.3)
- ☐ Pacemaker (Lesson 11.1)
- ☐ Sphygmomanometer (Lesson 11.1)
- ☐ Stethoscope (Lesson 11.1)
- ☐ Transparency of illustration of the heart (Lesson 11.1)

LESSON CHECKLIST

Preparations for this lesson include:

- Lecture
- Demonstrations: sphygmomanometer, automatic kit for checking blood pressure, portable ECG
- Picture cards with cardiac "landmarks"
- Heart model to show flow of blood and valves
- Student performance evaluation of all entry-level skills required for student comprehension and application of the terminology of the cardiovascular system, including:
  - ○ applying medical terms in the proper context
  - ○ using appropriate medical terminology in oral and written communication

KEY TERMS

Vocabulary (pp. 408-409)

aorta
arteriole
artery
atrioventricular bundle (bundle of His)
atrioventricular node (AV node)
atrium, atria
capillary
carbon dioxide (CO_2)
coronary arteries
deoxygenated blood
diastole
endocardium
endothelium
mitral valve
murmur
myocardium
normal sinus rhythm
oxygen
pacemaker

pericardium
pulmonary artery
pulmonary circulation
pulmonary valve
pulmonary vein
pulse
septum, septa
sinoatrial node (SA node)
sphygmomanometer
systemic circulation
systole
tricuspid valve
valve
vein
vena cava, venae cavae
ventricle
venule
Terminology (pp. 409-412)
angi/o
aort/o

ELSEVIER

arter/o
arteri/o
ather/o
atri/o
brachi/o
cardi/o
cholesterol/o
coron/o
cyan/o
myx/o
ox/o
pericardi/o
phleb/o
rrhythm/o
sphygm/o
steth/o
thromb/o
valvul/o
valv/o
vas/o
vascul/o
ven/o, ven/i
ventricul/o

Pathology:
The Heart and Blood Vessels (pp. 412-423)
arrhythmias
heart block (atrioventricular block)
flutter
fibrillation
congenital heart disease
coarctation of the aorta (CoA)
patent ductus arteriosus (PDA)
septal defects
tetralogy of Fallot
congestive heart failure
coronary artery disease
endocarditis
hypertensive heart disease
mitral valve prolapse (MVP)
murmur
pericarditis
rheumatic heart disease
aneurysm
hypertension (HTN)
peripheral arterial disease (PAD)
Raynaud's disease
varicose veins

Laboratory Tests and Clinical Procedures (pp. 425-431)
BNP test
cardiac biomarkers
lipid tests
lipoprotein electrophoresis
angiography
computed tomography angiography
digital subtraction angiography
electron beam computed tomography
Doppler ultrasound studies
echocardiography
positron emission tomography
technetium Tc 99m sestamibi scan
thallium 201 scan

cardiac MRI
cardiac catheterization
electrocardiography
Holter monitoring
stress test
catheter ablation
coronary artery bypass grafting
defibrillation
endarterectomy
extracorporeal circulation
heart transplantation
percutaneous coronary intervention
thrombolytic therapy

REFERENCE LIST
PowerPoint slides (CD, Evolve): 1-70

Legend

   CD
Companion
CD

   iTerms

   IRM
Instructor's
Resource Manual
available on CD
and Evolve

   Evolve
Evolve
Resources

   PPT
PowerPoint
Slides

   MTO
Medical
Terminology
Online

Class Activities are indicated in ***bold italic.***

ELSEVIER

Chabner

LESSON 11.1

PRETEST
IRM Exercise Quiz B

BACKGROUND ASSESSMENT
Question: How is pulmonary circulation different from systemic circulation?
Answer: Pulmonary circulation describes the flow of blood from the heart to the lungs and back to the heart; systemic circulation describes the flow of blood from the heart to the body, and back to the heart.

Question: After a patient's blood pressure is measured with a sphygmomanometer, it is reported in the form of a fraction (e.g., 120/80 mm Hg). What do these numbers represent?
Answer: Blood pressure is the force that blood exerts on the arterial walls. The upper number in the fraction represents the higher *systolic* blood pressure in the artery when the left ventricle is contracting to force the blood into the aorta and other arteries. The lower number represents the *diastolic* pressure, which is the pressure in the artery when the ventricles are relaxing and the heart is filling with blood from the venae cavae and pulmonary veins. The pressure that results when the cuff on the sphygmomanometer is blown up helps suppress the blood in an artery and block the sound of the pulse. As that pressure is slowly released, the first sound of the pulse is heard through a stethoscope. That is the systolic blood pressure reading. The sound continues to get louder as the artery fills. When the sound fades way, the diastolic pressure is read.

CRITICAL THINKING QUESTION
How does a blockage in a coronary artery cause a heart attack?
Guidelines: If a coronary artery is blocked, the heart muscle is deprived of its oxygen supply. Because tissue requires oxygen, that particular part of the muscle will die, resulting in a myocardial infarction, or heart attack.

OBJECTIVES	CONTENT	TEACHING RESOURCES
Name the parts of the heart and associated blood vessels and their functions in the circulation of blood.	■ Introduction (p. 398) ■ Blood vessels and the circulation of blood (p. 398) □ Blood vessels (p. 398)	PPT 5-9 IRM Dictation and Comprehension Quiz: Vocabulary and Terminology MTO Module 11, Lesson 3 Figure 11-1 Blood vessels (p. 398) Figure 11-2 Relationship and characteristics of blood vessels (p. 399) Exercise A (p. 435) ▶ Discuss the structure of blood vessels. Have students look up the process by which blood exits and enters the capillary. Make certain that students use terms such as *lymph* and *edema*. *Class Activity Divide the class into three groups and have them choose a "contestant" for a quiz show. Display a transparency of an illustration of the heart. Ask the three contestants to identify each of the numbered items in the illustration. The first contestant to give the correct answer wins a point for the team. If a contestant gives an incorrect answer, the team selects a new contestant.*

OBJECTIVES	CONTENT	TEACHING RESOURCES
		Class Activity Divide the class into three groups: arteries, veins, and capillaries. Have students use medical atlases or online sources to research examples of their vessels. Have each group explain to the class their vessel's functions using pictures and illustrations to assist them. (Students might opt to get electron micrographs of their vessels to help show how nutrients escape vessels, etc.) An additional group can present the three types of capillaries and why they are important to the body. Compare structural differences. *Alternatively, have students identify the singular and plural forms for each of the structures.*
Trace the pathway of blood through the heart.	☐ Circulation of blood (p. 400)	Figure 11-3 Schematic diagram of the pulmonary circulation (p. 400) Figure 11-4 The aorta and arteries (p. 401) Exercise B (p. 435) *Class Activity Give small groups a set of index cards or flash cards with one major step in the pathway of blood on each card. First, have each group arrange their cards in order. Then have the groups exchange tables to observe the other groups' work. Give all groups one last chance to correct their original pathways before revealing the correct answer. Have the students use either blue or red ink to identify when the blood is oxygenated or deoxygenated.* *Class Activity Create cards with pictures of "landmarks" of the heart, such as the mitral valve, pulmonary vein, and right atrium. Have students take on the "job" of a red blood cell. Their first job is to pick a card; this represents their starting point in the heart. They now must find their way out of the aorta, following the normal path of the blood through the heart and lungs. Points are given for mentioning correct landmarks on their path; points are subtracted for missed landmarks.*
Name the parts of the heart and associated blood vessels and their functions in the circulation of blood.	■ Anatomy of the heart (p. 402) ■ Physiology of the heart (p. 405) ☐ Heartbeat and heart sounds (p. 405)	PPT 10-21 IRM Diagram Quiz MTO Module 11, Section I, Lessons 1-2

OBJECTIVES	CONTENT	TEACHING RESOURCES
	☐ Conduction system of the heart (p. 405)	Figure 11-5 Structure of the heart (p. 403)
		Figure 11-6 The walls of the heart and pericardium (p. 404)
		Figure 11-7 Pathway of the blood through the heart (p.404)
		Figure 11-8 Phases of the heartbeat: diastole and systole (p. 405)
		Figure 11-9 Conduction system of the heart (p. 406)
		Exercise C (p. 436)
		💿 Companion CD Exercise 11-1
		*Class Activity **Have students use a diagram to follow the path of the electrical impulse in the heart from the sinoatrial node.***
		*Class Activity **Have students name and describe all of the valves in the heart and the blood vessels near the heart. Have groups explain the cardiac cycle, including when each valve is open or shut.***
Recognize the meaning of many laboratory tests, clinical procedures, and abbreviations pertaining to the cardiovascular system.	■ Blood pressure (p. 406)	PPT 22-25
		MTO Module 11, Section I, Lessons 4-5
		Figure 11-10 Electrocardiogram (p. 407)
		Figure 11-11 Measurement of blood pressure (p. 407)
		Exercise C questions 4, 7 (p. 436)
		Exercise E question 7 (p. 437)
		Exercise F question 6 (p. 437)
		Exercise H questions 7-8 (p. 439)
		Exercise O question 4 (p. 443)
		*Class Activity **Using the internet, locate sound files of the different heart sounds. Play them for the students twice, then ask them to identify them when you play them randomly.***
		*Class Activity **Have students make cards with the terms on one side and the definitions on the other. Divide them into pairs and have them practice defining the terms.***

ELSEVIER

The Language of Medicine, 9th ed.

Chabner

OBJECTIVES	CONTENT	TEACHING RESOURCES
Define combining forms that relate to the cardiovascular system.	■ Terminology (p. 409)	⊠ PPT 26-31 IRM Terminology Quiz Figure 11-12 Atherosclerosis (p. 410) Exercise D (pp. 436) Exercise O (pp. 443) 💿 Companion CD Exercises 11-2, 11-3, 11-4, 11-5 ***Class Activity** Form two or more competing teams. Using flash cards or transparencies, give the teams one of the combining forms and ask them to define it. The first team to answer correctly wins a point. For an extra point, have them provide a term that uses this combining form. The team with the most points wins the game.*

11.1 Homework/Assignments:

Using online sources and medical textbooks, have students write reports on abnormal heart sounds and present their findings to the class. Presentations should include the pathology that created the abnormal sound and why those pathologies emit certain sounds.

Instruct students to find an article from a newspaper, magazine, or medical journal and underline all of the combined forms and terminology associated with conditions of the heart. Have students exchange an article for that of a classmate.

11.1 Teacher's Notes:

ELSEVIER

LESSON 11.2

CRITICAL THINKING QUESTION

Why would a septal defect cause a patient to feel tired?

Guidelines: A septal defect allows the oxygenated and deoxygenated blood to mix, resulting in a patient never being able to get fully oxygenated blood.

OBJECTIVES	CONTENT	TEACHING RESOURCES
List the meanings of major pathologic conditions affecting the heart and blood vessels.	■ Pathology: the heart and blood vessels (p. 412) ☐ Heart (p. 412) – Arrhythmias (p. 412) – Congenital heart disease (p. 415) – Congestive heart failure (CHF) (p. 417) – Coronary artery disease (CAD) (p. 417) – Endocarditis (p. 420) – Hypertensive heart disease (p. 420) – Mitral valve prolapse (MVP) (p. 420) – Murmur (p. 420) – Pericarditis (p. 420) – Rheumatic heart disease (p. 421) ☐ Blood vessels (p. 421) – Aneurysm (p. 421) – Deep vein thrombosis (DVT) (p. 422) – Hypertension (HTN) (p. 422) – Peripheral arterial disease (PAD) (p. 422) – Raynaud's disease (p. 422) – Varicose veins (p. 423)	▣ PPT 33-41 ⊚ IRM Pathology Quiz ⊚ IRM Dictation and Comprehension Quiz, Pathology ⊚ IRM Practical Applications A ▶ MTO Module 11, Section II, Lessons 1-6 Figure 11-13 Pacemaker (p. 413) Figure 11-14 A, Coarctation of the aorta; B, patent ductus arteriosus (p. 415) Figure 11-15 A, Ventricular septal defect; B, tetralogy of Fallot (p. 416) Figure 11-16 Ischemia and infarction (p. 418) Figure 11-17 Acute myocardial infarction (MI) (p. 418) Figure 11-18 Acute coronary syndromes (p. 419) Figure 11-19 A, Acute rheumatic mitral valvulitis with chronic rheumatic heart disease; B, artificial heart valve; C, porcine xenograft valve (p. 420) Figure 11-20 A, Abdominal aortic aneurysm; B, bifurcated synthetic graft (p. 421) Figure 11-21 A, Valve function in normal and varicose veins; B, varicose veins; C, edema and pigmented skin (p. 423) Study Section (p. 424) Practical Applications questions 1-10 (p. 433) Exercises E (p. 437) ⊚ Companion CD Exercises 11-6, 11-7 ***Class Activity** Divide the class into four groups: congenital abnormalities of the heart, degenerative diseases of the heart resulting from diseases of blood vessels, heart disease*

OBJECTIVES	CONTENT	TEACHING RESOURCES
		resulting from infection, and electrical abnormalities. (There may be some overlap among groups.) What are common ailments and symptoms? What tests should be used to diagnose these ailments? Now, exchange ailments between groups. What are the appropriate treatments for ailments? Note: Limit the number of ailments to three.
		Class Activity *Have students spell, analyze, and define the following terms and underline the accented syllable: atherosclerosis, cardiomegaly, bradycardia, tachycardia, hypercholesterolemia, thrombophlebitis, and mitral valvulitis.*
		Have students list heart pathologies from least to most threatening. Have students pick two heart conditions (one that they believe poses a lesser threat and one that poses a greater threat) and have them compare their choices in class. Do students generally agree on the severity of the pathologies? Was it difficult to rank conditions? Why or why not?

11.2 Homework/Assignments:

Have students memorize the Study Section (p. 424) for the next lesson by creating flash cards for each term listed. Students should write the term on one side of the card and the definition on the other side.

11.2 Teacher's Notes:

The Language of Medicine, 9th ed.

Chabner

LESSON 11.3

CRITICAL THINKING QUESTION

How does a coronary artery bypass address the problem of a blocked artery? Why is it often not a permanent solution?

Guidelines: Coronary artery bypass grafts detour a blocked artery, providing a renewed blood supply to the heart tissue affected. The reason for the initial graft is often the same as for subsequent ones: hypercholesterolemia and new blockages in the coronary arteries.

OBJECTIVES	CONTENT	TEACHING RESOURCES
Recognize the meaning of many laboratory tests, clinical procedures, and abbreviations pertaining to the cardiovascular system.	■ Laboratory tests and clinical procedures (p. 425) □ Laboratory tests (p. 425) □ Clinical procedures: diagnostic (p. 425) – X-ray (p. 425) – Ultrasound (p. 427) – Nuclear cardiology (p. 427) – Magnetic resonance imaging (MRI) (p. 428) – Other diagnostic procedures (p. 428) □ Clinical procedures: treatment (p. 430)	PPT 43-51 IRM Laboratory Tests and Clinical Procedures Quiz IRM Exercise Quiz G IRM Abbreviations Quiz IRM Practical Applications B, C MTO Module 11, Section III, Lessons 1-4 Figure 11-22 A, Computed tomography angiography; B, Electron beam computed tomography (p. 426) Figure 11-23 A, Echocardiogram, B, Transe-sophageal schocardiography (p. 427) Figure 11-24 Left-sided cardiac catheterization (p. 428) Figure 11-25 ECG rhythm strips showing normal sinus rhythm and dysrhythmias (p. 429) Figure 11-26 Coronary artery bypass graft (CABG) surgery (p. 430) Figure 11-27 Placement of an intracoronary artery stent (p. 431) Exercises J-Q (pp. 440-444) Companion CD Exercise 11-8 ***Class Activity Using the Study Section, find a diagnostic test that would be associated with each of the terms (e.g., claudication–stress test). There will be several answers for many of these terms. Ask students, "Is there an overlap in possible procedures and treatments? Are you having difficulty in making diagnoses?"*** ***Class Activity Using Google Video, find a short demonstration of one of the procedures listed***

OBJECTIVES	CONTENT	TEACHING RESOURCES
		to the left. Show students the video and leave time for questions. *Class Activity Have the students take turns reading the sentences in Exercise Q. Where appropriate, ask them to either give the meaning of the abbreviation used, or analyze and define the term.* *Class Activity Display WebMD on a computer and show normal versus abnormal (atrial fibrillation) ECGs.*
Apply your new knowledge to understand medical terms in their proper context, such as in medical reports and records.	■ Abbreviations (p. 432)	PPT 52-69 IRM Abbreviations Quiz *Class Activity "Abbreviation Bingo." Create a set of bingo cards with a 5 x 5 grid and a different abbreviation in each box; vary the abbreviations and/or the order so cards are not all alike. Bingo card generators are available on the Internet. Create a list of terms related to the cardiovascular system and corresponding to the abbreviations on the bingo cards. Call out a term. Students must circle the correct abbreviation on the bingo card. The first student to complete bingo wins.*
Performance Evaluation		IRM Multiple Choice Quiz IRM Terminology Quiz IRM Pathology Quiz IRM Laboratory Tests and Clinical Procedures Quiz IRM Exercise Quiz IRM Dictation and Comprehension Quiz, Vocabulary and Terminology (IRM Dictation and Comprehension Quiz, Pathology IRM Spelling Quiz IRM Pronunciation Quiz IRM Abbreviations Quiz IRM Diagram Quiz

OBJECTIVES	CONTENT	TEACHING RESOURCES
		IRM Vocabulary Quiz
		IRM Review Sheet Quiz
		IRM Medical Scramble
		IRM Crossword Puzzle
		IRM Practical Applications
		ESLR Body Spectrum Electronic Anatomy Coloring Book, Circulatory
		ESLR Student Quiz Chapter 11
		MTO Module 11, Sections I-III quizzes
		MTO Module 11 Exam
		Companion CD Exercises 11-9, 11-10, 11-11, 11-12
		iTerms Chapter 11

11.3 Homework/Assignments:

11.3 Teacher's Notes:

Slide 1

The Language Of Medicine

9ᵗʰ edition

Davi-Ellen Chabner

Slide 2

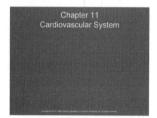

Chapter 11
Cardiovascular System

Slide 3

Chapter Goals

- Name the parts of the heart and associated blood vessels and their functions in the circulation of blood.
- Trace the pathway of blood through the heart.
- Identify and describe major pathologic conditions affecting the heart and blood vessels.

Slide 4

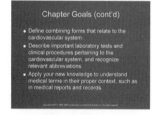

Chapter Goals (cont'd)

- Define combining forms that relate to the cardiovascular system.
- Describe important laboratory tests and clinical procedures pertaining to the cardiovascular system, and recognize relevant abbreviations.
- Apply your new knowledge to understand medical terms in their proper context, such as in medical reports and records.

Slide 5

Chapter 11
Lesson 11.1

Slide 6

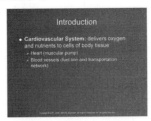

- What are three types of blood vessels in the body?
- What are the primary differences between them? (*See next slide.*)

Slide 7

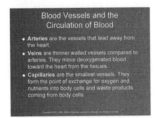

- What are smaller branches of arteries called? (*arterioles*)
- What are small veins that carry waste-filled blood back to the heart called? (*venules*)

Slide 8

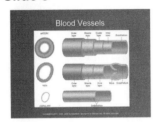

- Point out the discrete layers of each vessel.
- Compare and contrast the substructures of each type of vessel.
- Why is the muscle layer in an artery thicker than that of a vein?

Slide 9

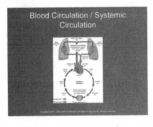

- Make sure students understand this basic flow in order to fully understand the pathology.
- The anatomic terminology here is often associated with any pathology.

Slide 10

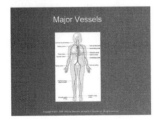

- The major pulse points should be considered. For example, the brachial artery is important because blood pressure is routinely measured at this junction.
- What symptoms are associated with potential blockage in these vessels?

Slide 11

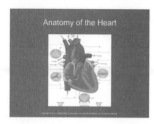

- Fill in the identified structures and mention their specific functions. Identify the major valves of the heart and important blood vessels.

- Which of the four chambers has the thickest walls and why? (*The left ventricle walls have three times the thickness of the right ventricle walls; it requires great force to pump blood throughout the body.*)

Slide 12

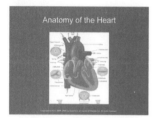

- Fill in the identified structures and mention their specific functions. Identify the major valves of the heart and important blood vessels.

- Which of the four chambers has the thickest walls and why? (*The left ventricle walls have three times the thickness of the right ventricle walls; it requires great force to pump blood throughout the body.*)

Slide 13

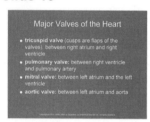

- Point these out on the diagram from the previous slide to reinforce.

Slide 14

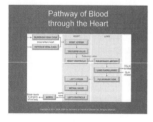

- Go through each step of how the blood travels through the heart.

Slide 15

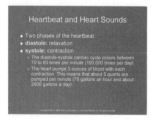

- Which valves open and which valves close during diastole? (The tricuspid and mitral valves open as blood passes from the right and left atria into the ventricles. The pulmonary and aortic valves close.)

Chabner

Slide 16

- Borrow a stethoscope to demonstrate.

- Audio recordings are also available online. Many also contain pathological sounds.

Slide 17

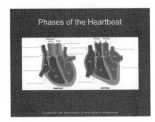

Slide 18

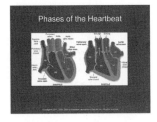

- Have students fill in the labels using this slide.

Slide 19

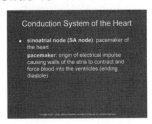

- Where in the heart is the SA node located? (in a small region of specialized muscle tissue in the posterior portion of the right atrium.)

Slide 20

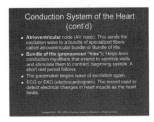

- Where is the AV node? (in the posterior portion of the interatrial septum)

- The normal ECG shows five waves (deflections) that represent the electrical changes as a wave of excitation spreads through the heart. What are the deflections called? (P, QRS, and T waves.)

Slide 21

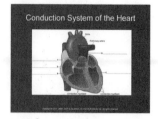

Slide 22

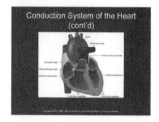

Slide 23

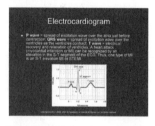

- The ECG diagnoses electrical problems in the heart, such as arrhythmias.

- Identify deflections on the ECG.

- What is happening in the heart with each wave complex?

Slide 24

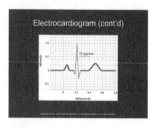

- The ECG diagnoses electrical problems in the heart, such as arrhythmias.

- Identify deflections on the ECG.

- What is happening in the heart with each wave complex?

Slide 25

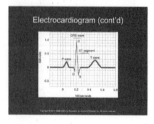

- The ECG diagnoses electrical problems in the heart, such as arrhythmias.

- Identify deflections on the ECG.

- What is happening in the heart with each wave complex?

The Language of Medicine, 9th ed.

Chabner

Slide 26

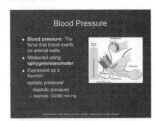

- How does the sphygmomanometer work?
- Compare this device to over-the-counter electronic monitors.
- What effect does exercise have on blood pressure measurements?
- What causes increases and decreases in blood pressure?

Slide 27

Slide 28

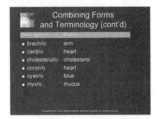

Slide 29

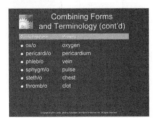

Slide 30

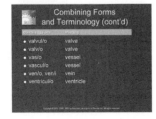

Slide 31

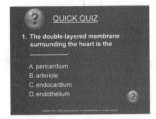

- Correct answer is A: pericardium

Slide 32

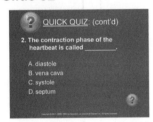

- Correct answer is C: systole.

Slide 33

Chapter 11
Cardiovascular System
Lesson 11.2

Slide 34

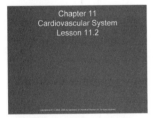

- What device establishes normal heart rhythm?
- What term describes the action of applying a defibrillator to give an electric shock to the heart?
- On the list, which terms are associated with "palpitations"?

Slide 35

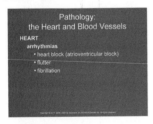

- What is a "blue baby"?
- In terms of septal defects, what are two recent procedures that serve as alternatives to traditional surgery? (*trans-catheter closure and minimally invasive heart surgery*)

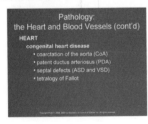

Chabner

Slide 36

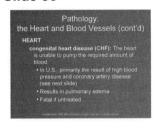

- What drugs improve the performance of the heart and its pumping activity? (*angiotensin-converting enzyme (ACE) inhibitors and beta-blockers*)

- What device do patients awaiting a transplant use to help assist the heart's pumping? (*a left ventricular assist device or LVAD*)

Slide 37

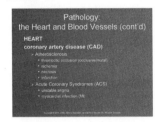

- What is atherosclerosis? (*the deposition of fatty compounds on the inner lining of the coronary arteries*)

- What is ACS? (*It describes the consequences after plaque rupture in coronary arteries.*)

- What is unstable angina? (*chest pain at rest or chest pain of increasing frequency*)

Slide 38

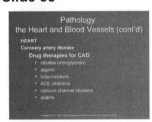

- What drug is given for acute attacks of angina? (*Nitroglycerin is given sublingually.*)

- This drug is one of several nitrates that is a powerful vasodilator that increases coronary blood flow and lowers blood pressure.

- What do statins do?

Slide 39

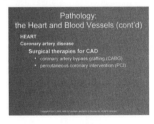

- What is CABG? (*an open heart operation to treat coronary artery disease by replacing clogged vessels*)

- What is PTCA? (*catheterization with balloons and stents opens clogged coronary arteries*)

- What is TMLR? (*a laser makes holes in the heart muscle to induce angiogenesis or growth of new blood vessels*)

Slide 40

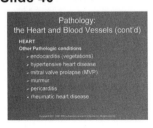

- What is endocarditis? (*inflammation of the inner lining of the heart caused by bacteria*)

- What is MVP? (*improper closure of the mitral valve*)

- What is rheumatic heart disease? (*heart disease caused by rheumatic fever*)

Chabner

Slide 41

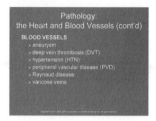

- What is PVD? (*blockage of blood vessels outside the heart*)
- A sign of PVD in the lower extremities is intermittent claudication, an absence of pain or discomfort in a leg at rest, but a recurrence of pain, tension, and weakness after walking has begun.
- What are the signs of Raynaud disease?

Slide 42

- Correct answer is A: fibrillation

Slide 43

Slide 44

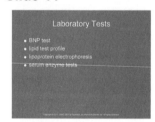

- What are lipid tests?
- What is lipoprotein electrophoresis? Why is this test ordered?
- What are serum enzyme tests? Why is this test ordered?

Slide 45

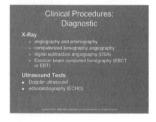

- What determines when each of these tests should be used?
- Differentiate between invasive and noninvasive diagnostic tests.

Slide 46

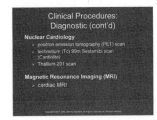

- Are there any risks or side effects from having these tests performed?

Slide 47

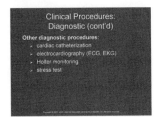

- What is the anticipated or theorized cardiac problem that leads a person to get a test?

- Be as specific as possible when describing the procedures. Find one unique thing about each test that makes it memorable. Have the students help you do this.

Slide 48

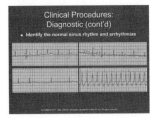

Slide 49

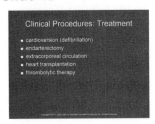

- Use photographs or online images to show some of the equipment used routinely to diagnose and treat the heart during acute abnormalities.

Slide 50

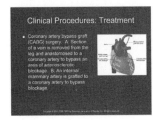

Slide 51

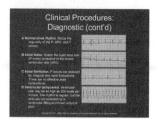

Slide 52

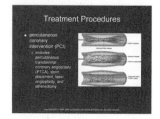

Slide 53

- Ask students to identify the terms associated with these abbreviations.

Slide 54

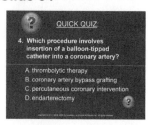

- Correct answer is C: percutaneous coronary intervention (also known as PCI) see text for more information.

Slide 55

Slide 56

Slide 57

Slide 58

Slide 59

Slide 60

Slide 61

Slide 62

Slide 63

Slide 64

Slide 65

Slide 66

Review Sheet (cont'd)

SUFFIXES

Suffix	Meaning
-meter	measure
-oma	tumor; mass; fluid collection
-osis	condition; usually abnormal
-plasty	surgical repair
-sclerosis	hardening
-stenosis	tightening; stricture
-tomy	process of cutting

Slide 67

Review Sheet (cont'd)

PREFIXES

Prefix	Meaning
a-, an-	
brady-	
de-	
dys-	
endo-	
hyper-	

Slide 68

Review Sheet (cont'd)

PREFIXES

Prefix	Meaning
a-, an-	no; not; without
brady-	slow
de-	lack of; down; less; removal of
dys-	bad; painful; difficult; abnormal
endo-	in; within
hyper-	above; excessive

Slide 69

Review Sheet (cont'd)

PREFIXES

Prefix	Meaning
hypo-	
inter-	
peri-	
tachy-	
tetra-	
tri-	

Slide 70

Review Sheet (cont'd)

PREFIXES

Prefix	Meaning
hypo-	deficient; below; under; less than normal
inter-	between
peri-	surrounding
tachy-	fast
tetra-	four
tri-	three

Chabner

12 Lesson Plan
Respiratory System

TEACHING FOCUS

Students will have the opportunity to learn the organs of the respiratory system and to [...]
locations, normal functions, and pathologies. Chapter material enables students to recog[...]
that pertain to respiration and to identify related procedures and abbreviations. In additio[...]
have the opportunity to apply terms in the context of medical records.

MATERIALS AND RESOURCES

- ☐ Chest x-rays (Lesson 12.3)
- ☐ Cigarette package (Lesson 12.2)
- ☐ Computer/Internet access (Lesson 12.1)
- ☐ Medical journals (Lesson 12.3)

- ☐ MRIs (Lesson 12.3)
- ☐ Stethoscopes (Lesson 12.1)
- ☐ ER videotape (Lesson 12.2)
- ☐ VCR (Lesson 12.2)

LESSON CHECKLIST

Preparations for this lesson include:

- Lecture
- Student performance evaluation of all entry-level skills required for student comprehension and application of the terminology of the respiratory system, including:
  - o applying medical terms in the proper context
  - o using appropriate medical terminology in oral and written communication

KEY TERMS

Vocabulary (pp. 462-463)

adenoids	larynx
alveolus	lobe
apex of the lung	mediastinum
base of the lung	oxygen (O_2)
bronchioles	palatine tonsil
bronchus	paranasal sinus
carbon dioxide (CO_2)	parietal pleura
cilia	pharynx
diaphragm	pleura
epiglottis	pleural cavity
expiration	pulmonary parenchyma
glottis	respiration
hilum (of lung)	trachea
inspiration	visceral pleura

Terminology (pp. 464-469)

adenoid/o	ox/o
alveol/o	pector/o
bronch/o	pharyng/o
bronchi/o	phon/o
bronchiol/o	phren/o
capn/o	pleur/o
coni/o	pneum/o
cyan/o	pneumon/o
epiglott/o	pulmon/o
laryng/o	rhin/o
lob/o	sinus/o
mediastin/o	spir/o
nas/o	tel/o
orth/o	thorac/o

Chabner

tonsil/o
trache/
-ema
-os

Pat

-pnea
-ptysis
-sphyxia
-thorax

emphysema
epistaxis
mesothelioma
pertussis
pleural effusion
pleurisy (pleuritis)
pneumoconiosis
pneumonia
pneumothorax
pulmonary abscess
pulmonary edema
pulmonary embolism (PE)
pulmonary fibrosis
sarcoidosis
tuberculosis (TB)

rcinoma (lung cancer)

hitis

osis

a

ical Procedures (pp. 476-481)

bronchoscopy
chest x-ray
computed tomography (CT) scan of the chest
endotracheal intubation
laryngoscopy
lung biopsy
magnetic resonance imaging (MRI) of the
    chest
mediastinoscopy
positron emission tomography (PET) scan of
    the lung

pulmonary angiography
pulmonary function tests (PFTs)
thoracentesis
thoracotomy
thorascopy
tracheostomy
tube thoracostomy
tuberculin test
ventilation-perfusion (V/Q) scan

REFERENCE LIST

PowerPoint slides (CD, Evolve): 1-55

Legend

 CD
Companion
CD

 iTerms

 IRM
Instructor's
Resource Manual
available on CD
and Evolve

 Evolve
Evolve
Resources

 PPT
PowerPoint
Slides

 MTO
Medical
Terminology
Online

Class Activities are indicated in ***bold italic***.

 ELSEVIER

The Language of Medicine, 9th ed.

Chabner

LESSON 12.1

PRETEST
IRM Exercise Quiz B questions 1-10

BACKGROUND ASSESSMENT
Question: What are the structures in the respiratory system?
Answer: Answers will vary, but students may mention the lungs, the bronchi, th
the nose.
e larynx, and
Question: Describe the mechanical process of breathing. Why is tissue elasticity—t
to an initial state following deformation—important for optimal functioning?
Answer: Breathing is the exchange of gases in the air between the lungs and the extern
f returning
enters the body via the nose. Air then passes through the nasal cavity, throat, trachea, bro
into the lungs. The lungs are located in the chest cavity, which is separated from the abdo
nt. Air
diaphragm. With each inhalation, the diaphragm contracts, increasing the size of the chest c
and
enabling the lungs to expand because of decreased air pressure. Air flows into the lungs to eq
y the
pressure. When the diaphragm relaxes, the space in the chest cavity decreases, and the pressure
Air is then exhaled from the lungs to equalize the pressure. Elasticity is important because it hel
lung capacity and an uninterrupted flow of air. Disorders that obstruct or make the lungs less elasu
airflow and reduce lung capacity, which results in less oxygen reaching the body.

CRITICAL THINKING QUESTION
**Question: Jackson, age 65, comes to the doctor's office complaining of a sharp pain in the right si
his chest. He says his chest hurts when he breathes deeply or coughs. This is a problem, he says,
because he has been coughing a lot, has difficulty drawing breath, and feels a tightness in the center
his chest. What condition or conditions might the doctor suspect? What methods of diagnosis would
the doctor use, and what specific signs would the doctor look for to pinpoint the cause?**
Guidelines: Jackson's symptoms indicate he may have both pneumonia and pleurisy, a probable
consequence of pneumonia. The doctor would perform ausculation (listening to Jackson's chest with a
stethoscope) and percussion (tapping the surface of the chest and dorsal cavities). Pleurisy would produce
friction rub, caused by pleura thickened from inflammation or scarring. Hearing crackles or rales during
inspiration indicates fluid or pus in the alveoli, a sign of pneumonia.

OBJECTIVES	CONTENT	TEACHING RESOURCES
Name the organs of the respiratory system and describe their location and function.	■ Introduction (p. 458) ■ Anatomy and physiology of respiration (p. 458)	⊠▪ PPT 5-12 IRM Multiple Choice Quiz questions 1-6 IRM Exercise Quiz A, B IRM Diagram Quiz MTO Module 12, Section I, Lessons 1-3 Figure 12-1 Organs of the respiratory system (p. 459) Figure 12-2 The larynx (p. 460) Figure 12-3 Position of the diaphragm during inspiration and expiration (p. 461) Figure 12-4 Pathway of air from the nose to the capillaries of the lungs (p. 462)

ELSEVIER

The Language of Medicine, 9th ed.

OBJECTIVES	CONTEN		TEACHING RESOURCES
			Exercise A, B (p. 485)
			⊙ Companion CD Exercise 12-1
			Class Activity Invite one or two students to volunteer to be scribes. These students will diagram the respiratory system on the board and trace the flow of air as directed by other students. The class should label and describe key body parts and functions.
			Class Activity Designate half of the class the oxygen (O_2) molecule team and the other half the carbon dioxide (CO_2) molecule team. Choose one student alternately from each team to draw a step in sequence that shows how gas molecules enter or leave the blood and gain access to the outside. The team with the fewest mistakes wins.

...ms .n to ɔn.	■ Vocabulary (p. 462)
	■ Terminology (p. 464)
	  □ Combining forms (p. 464)
	  □ Suffixes (p. 468)
			⊞ PPT 13-23
			
			IRM Multiple Choice Quiz
			
			IRM Terminology Quiz
			
			IRM Dictation and Comprehension Quiz, Vocabulary and Terminology
			
			Figure 12-5 Pulmonary resections (p. 465)
			
			Figure 12-6 Pneumothorax (p. 466)
			
			Figure 12-7 Two forms of atelectasis (p. 467)
			
			Figure 12-8 Man sleeping with nasal CPAP (p. 468)
			
			Exercise C (p. 486)
			
			⊙ Companion CD Exercises 12-2, 12-3, 12-4, 12-5
			
			Class Activity Divide the class into teams. In a timed session, call out the name of a combining form or suffix. Each team should create as many respiratory system medical terms from the combining form or suffix as it can in a 60-second period. After 60 seconds, announce another combining form or suffix. The team with the most terms wins.
			
			Class Activity Have students make flash cards with the combining forms for the structures in the respiratory system. Ask them to shuffle them, and then arrange them in order from the nose to the alveoli.

The Language of Medicine, 9th ed.

Chabner

12.1 Homework/Assignments:

12.1 Teacher's Notes:

Chabner

LESSON 12.2

CRITICAL THINKING QUESTION

Question: Robbie's mother calls a new pediatrician in a panic to report that her 5-year-old son has started a high-pitched, wheezing cough and cannot breathe. They have just moved from the Southwest to the Midwest, where they are renovating an old house. In the past, Robbie occasionally had slight coughs and tired easily, his mother say s, but this episode is more alarming. The doctor says Robbie should be taken to a hospital emergency room immediately. What respiratory conditions does the doctor suspect? What may have triggered it?

Guidelines: Robbie's high-pitched, wheezing cough and shortness of breath may indicate asthma, which is characterized by swelling and constriction of the bronchial tubes and by increased mucus production. Likely triggers in Robbie's case may be exposure to more and different pollens in a new part of the country and to dust and molds stirred up during the house renovation.

OBJECTIVES	CONTENT	TEACHING RESOURCES
Identify various pathological conditions that affect the system.	■ Pathology (p. 469) ☐ Diagnostic terms (p. 469) ☐ Upper Respiratory Disorders (p. 470) ☐ Bronchial disorders (p. 470) ☐ Lung disorders (p. 471) ☐ Pleural disorders (p. 475)	⊠▤ PPT 25-32 IRM Multiple Choice Quiz questions 8-20 IRM Pathology Quiz IRM Exercise Quiz questions C-G IRM Dictation and Comprehension Quiz, Pathology A, B IRM Pronunciation quiz A-C IRM Practical Application B ↖ MTO Module 12, Section II, Lessons 1-5 Figure 12-9 A, Normal lung tissue; B, Emphysema (p. 472) Figure 12-10 Lung cancer (p. 472) Figure 12-11 A, Anthracosis; B, lobar pneumonia (p.473) Figure 12-12 Pulmonary embolism (p. 474) Exercises D-F (pp. 486-487) Study Section (pp. 476) Exercise H (pp. 488-489) ▸ Discuss the short-term and long-term effects of smoking, including the issue of secondhand smoke. ▸ Discuss the ramifications of laws that prohibit smoking in restaurants. ▸ Discuss pneumoconiosis and its connection to 9/11/01.

ELSEVIER

The Language of Medicine, 9th ed.

Chabner

OBJECTIVES	CONTENT	TEACHING RESOURCES
		Class Activity Ask students to write each pathologic condition on a card with the definition on the back. Have them divided into upper and lower respiratory system disorders.
		Class Activity Use an Internet Web site to demonstrate normal and abnormal respiratory sounds. Have students use stethoscopes to listen to each other's respiratory sounds. Students should describe what they hear and point out anything that sounds like an abnormality. Ask for volunteers with known noncontagious conditions in which respiration is not typical, such as asthma or allergies.
		Class Activity Have students watch an episode of ER at home or on a video in class. Have students write down each respiratory term they hear. With the class, define each term and discuss in the context of the show scenarios.

12.2 Homework/Assignments:

Divide students into four groups, one for each disorder type: upper respiratory, bronchial tube, lung, and pleural. Each group should select one specific disorder to research and report on. Guide groups so that different primary contributing factors are represented, i.e., infection, environmental insult, heredity, or mutation. In addition to describing causes, symptoms, treatments, and prevention, reports should include a brief historical timeline with key events noted. Focus on trends in morbidity and mortality and identify contributing factors such as detection, treatment, and exposure.

12.2 Teacher's Notes:

ELSEVIER

LESSON 12.3

CRITICAL THINKING QUESTION

Question: Pulmonary function tests (PFTs) can measure many different aspects of lung function. How can PFTs help to distinguish whether a lung disease is obstructive, restrictive, or both?

Guidelines: Obstructive lung disease is marked by a decrease in expiratory flow rate. Airways are typically narrowed, which results in a reduced forced expiratory volume in the first second and resistance to airflow during breathing. Restrictive lung disease is typically marked by decreased total lung capacity due to chest wall, pleura, or lung tissue diseases that limit lung expansion. As a result, the lung becomes less elastic, or fibrotic, leading to lower compliance. PFTs also can identify diaphragm weakness or paralysis, which are restrictive conditions due to neuromuscular disease.

OBJECTIVES	CONTENT	TEACHING RESOURCES
Identify clinical procedures and abbreviations related to the system.	■ Clinical procedures and abbreviations (p. 476) ☐ Clinical procedures (p. 476) – X-rays (p. 476) – Magnetic imaging (p. 477) – Radioactive test (p. 477) ☐ Other procedures (p. 478) ☐ Abbreviations (p. 482)	PPT 34-42 IRM Multiple Choice Quiz questions 21-25 IRM Clinical Procedures Quiz IRM Exercise Quiz H, I IRM Abbreviations Quiz IRM Crossword Puzzle IRM Practical Application A IRM Practical Applications C MTO Module 12, Section III, Lessons 1-3 Figure 12-13 Normal chest x-ray and pneumonia (p. 477) Figure 12-14 A, Fiberoptic bronchoscopy; B, Bronchoscope (p. 478) Figure 12-15 Endotracheal intubation (p. 479) Figure 12-16 Thoracentesis, A and B (p. 480) Figure 12-17 A, Tracheostomy; B, Healed tracheostomy (p. 480) Figure 12-18 Thoracostomy (p. 481) Exercises G, I-K (pp. 488-490) ▸ Discuss point of view, right and left views, and dorsal and ventral views shown in Figure 12-13. Point out the landmarks used by technicians for people reading the images. ***Class Activity Have students obtain copies of x-rays, CT scans, and MRI images of respiratory disorders from medical textbooks,***

OBJECTIVES	CONTENT	TEACHING RESOURCES
		journal articles, and online sources. Have students divide the images into categories based on pathologic condition. Discuss the type of information about a respiratory disorder the physician can obtain from each category of image.
		Class Activity *Chapter Bingo: Have students make bingo cards with all the abbreviations in the text. Rotate callers so that students get a chance to practice acronyms and pronunciation. If you want to make more or bigger cards, students can use combining forms on the cards as well.*
		Class Activity *Using Figure 12-6, have students determine in what context a surgeon might use each type of resection. Divide the class into four groups, and assign each group one type of resection for a report to the class.*
		Class Activity *Have students look at the clinical procedures that have been discussed in class. Have them group the procedures into invasive versus noninvasive procedures. Ask them to explain what determines if a procedure is invasive.*
Apply your new knowledge to understanding medical terms in their proper contexts, such as medical reports and records.	▪ Practical applications (p. 483)	⊠ PPT 43-54 IRM Spelling Quiz A, B IRM Practical Application ↖ MTO Module 12, Section V Exercise L (p. 491) ⊙ Companion CD Exercises 12-6, 12-7, 12-8 **Class Activity** *Terminology Exchange: Have students obtain an article from a newspaper or medical journal that describes a respiratory dysfunction. Students should underline several terms (up to 10). Then have students exchange articles with one another. The second student defines each term, describes it in context, and presents the information to the class.* **Class Activity** *Have students take turns reading the sentences in Exercise L. Ask them to define any definitions and analyze and spell the other terms. Have them underline the accented syllable.*

OBJECTIVES	CONTENT	TEACHING RESOURCES
Performance Evaluation		IRM Multiple Choice Quiz
		IRM Terminology Quiz
		IRM Pathology Quiz
		IRM Clinical Procedures Quiz
		IRM Exercise Quiz
		IRM Dictation and Comprehension Quizzes
		IRM Spelling Quiz
		IRM Pronunciation Quiz
		IRM Abbreviations Quiz
		IRM Diagram Quiz
		IRM Vocabulary Quiz
		IRM Review Sheet Quiz
		IRM Medical Scramble
		IRM Crossword Puzzle
		IRM Practical Applications
		ESLR Body Spectrum Electronic Anatomy Coloring Book, Respiratory
		ESLR Student Quiz Chapter 12
		MTO Module 12, Sections I-III quizzes
		MTO, Module 12 Exam
		Companion CD Exercises 12-9, 12-10, 12-11, 12-12
		iTerms Chapter 12

Chabner

12.3 Homework/Assignments:

12.3 Teacher's Notes:

Chabner

Slide 1

The Language Of Medicine
9th edition
Davi-Ellen Chabner

Slide 2

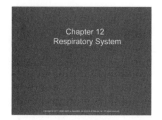

Chapter 12
Respiratory System

Slide 3

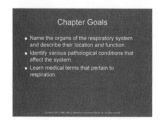

Chapter Goals

- Name the organs of the respiratory system and describe their location and function.
- Identify various pathological conditions that affect the system.
- Learn medical terms that pertain to respiration.

Slide 4

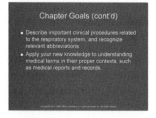

Chapter Goals (cont'd)

- Describe important clinical procedures related to the respiratory system, and recognize relevant abbreviations.
- Apply your new knowledge to understanding medical terms in their proper contexts, such as medical reports and records.

Slide 5

Chapter 12
Lesson 12.1

Chabner

Slide 6

- What percent of oxygen does inhaled air contain? (*about 21%*)
- What percent of oxygen does exhaled air contain? (*about 16%*)
- What is the medical term for air sacs?

Slide 7

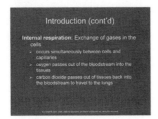

Slide 8

- What is the singular form of bronchi? (*bronchus*)
- Which lung is larger? (*right*)
- How many lobes does each lung have? (*right: three, left: two*)

Slide 9

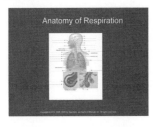

- Engage the class to identify the organs of the respiratory system.
- Trace the path of a breath of air.

Slide 10

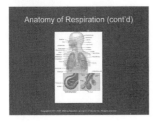

- Engage the class to identify the organs of the respiratory system.
- Trace the path of a breath of air.

Slide 11

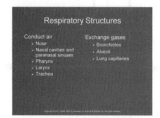

Slide 12

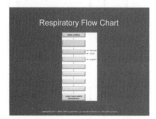

- Trace the flow, and then conduct the class activity in the lesson plan by dividing the class into two groups and assigning each a gas. (see LP 12.1)

Slide 13

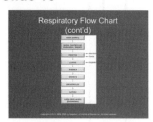

- Trace the flow, and then conduct the class activity in the lesson plan by dividing the class into two groups and assigning each a gas. (see LP 12.1)

Slide 14

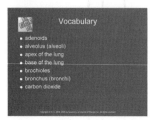

- Reference pp. 260-262 for definitions of vocabulary terms

Slide 15

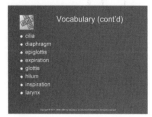

- Reference pp. 260-262 for definitions of vocabulary terms

Chabner

Slide 16

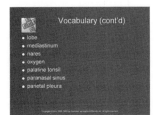

- Reference pp. 260-262 for definitions of vocabulary terms

Slide 17

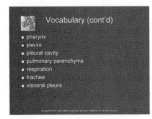

- Reference pp. 260-262 for definitions of vocabulary terms

Slide 18

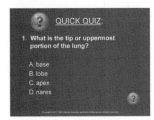

- Correct answer is C: apex

Slide 19

Slide 20

Slide 21

Slide 22

Slide 23

Slide 24

Slide 25

The Language of Medicine, 9th ed.

Chabner

Slide 26

- Many of these terms are ways to help identify respiratory abnormalities that can be heard.

- Discuss the fact that auscultation, though not high tech, is still a very effective way to uncover disease.

Slide 27

- Distinguish between disorders arising from infectious agents, trauma, neoplasms, or genetic disorders. Which are most often caused by smoking?

- Epistaxis is also known as rhinorrhagia, but epistaxis is the more commonly used term for nosebleed.

Slide 28

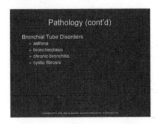

- Distinguish between disorders arising from infectious agents, trauma, neoplasms, or genetic disorders. Which are most often caused by smoking?

- Epistaxis is also known as rhinorrhagia, but epistaxis is the more commonly used term for nosebleed.

Slide 29

- Distinguish between disorders arising from infectious agents, trauma, neoplasms, or genetic disorders.

- What are the types of pneumoconiosis?

Slide 30

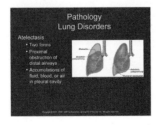

- Distinguish between atelectasis and pneumothorax.

ELSEVIER

The Language of Medicine, 9th ed.
Chabner

Slide 31

- Distinguish between disorders arising from infectious agents, trauma, neoplasms, or genetic disorders.

- Use slides to discuss definitions, context, spelling, and derivations.

Slide 32

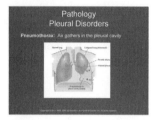

- Explain collapsed lung.

- What conditions may cause a lung to collapse?

- What are some examples of trauma- and disease-induced collapsed lung?

Slide 33

- Distinguish between disorders arising from infectious agents, trauma, neoplasms or genetic disorders.

Slide 34

Slide 35

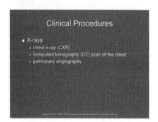

- Briefly discuss the technology of each type of x-ray.

- For what kinds of information (hard tissues, soft tissue, etc.) and which conditions is each type best suited?

Slide 36

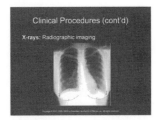

- Use this slide to discuss point of view, right and left, dorsal and ventral, and landmarks.

Slide 37

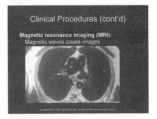

Slide 38

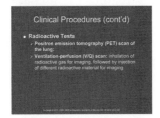

Slide 39

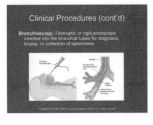

- Why would a physician recommend this invasive diagnostic procedure?

- What are the pros and cons?

- What can the physician expect to learn?

Slide 40

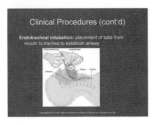

- Watch an episode of ER and count how many times they do this procedure in the ER.

- Why do many people coming into the emergency room need this procedure?

- Why is this done for surgical patients?

Chabner

Slide 41

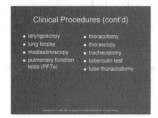

- Why do many of these procedures start with "thor"?
- What is the difference between laryngoscopy, mediastinoscopy, and thorascopy?

Slide 42

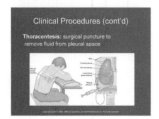

Slide 43

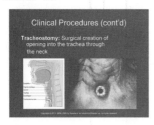

- Under what conditions would a physician perform this invasive procedure?
- Explain advantages and disadvantages.

Slide 44

Slide 45

Slide 46

Slide 47

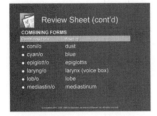

Slide 48

Slide 49

Slide 50

Slide 51

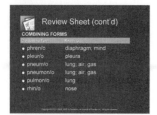

Review Sheet (cont'd)

COMBINING FORMS

Combining Form	Meaning
phren/o	diaphragm; mind
pleur/o	pleura
pneum/o	lung; air, gas
pneumon/o	lung; air, gas
pulmon/o	lung
rhin/o	nose

Slide 52

Review Sheet (cont'd)

COMBINING FORMS

Combining Form	Meaning
sinus/o	
spir/o	
tel/o	
thorac/o	
tonsill/o	
trache/o	

Slide 53

Review Sheet (cont'd)

COMBINING FORMS

Combining Form	Meaning
sinus/o	sinus
spir/o	to breathe
tel/o	complete
thorac/o	chest
tonsill/o	tonsil
trache/o	trachea (windpipe)

Slide 54

Review Sheer (cont'd)

SUFFIXES

Suffix	Meaning
-ema	
-osmia	
-pnea	
-ptysis	
-sphyxia	
-thorax	

Slide 55

Review Sheet (cont'd)

SUFFIXES

Suffix	Meaning
-ema	condition
-osmia	smell
-pnea	breathing
-ptysis	spitting
-sphyxia	pulse
-thorax	chest; pleural cavity

TEACHING FOCUS

Students will have the opportunity to learn about the various functions of blood. Students will be exposed to blood formation and composition, including different cell types and whole blood samples; identification of blood types; blood transfusion therapy; diseases of the blood; and laboratory tests, clinical procedures, and abbreviations associated with diagnosis and treatment of blood abnormalities. Students also will be exposed to medical terminology in the proper context of medical reports and records.

MATERIALS AND RESOURCES

- ☐ Bingo cards (Lesson 13.1)
- ☐ Electron micrographs of red blood cell (Lesson 13.1)
- ☐ Glass cover slips (Lesson 13.1)
- ☐ Glass slides (Lesson 13.1)
- ☐ Light microscopes (Lesson 13.1)
- ☐ Medical journals (Lesson 13.3)
- ☐ Permount (Lesson 13.1)
- ☐ Stain for whole blood smears (Lesson 13.1)
- ☐ Sterile blood-drawing device (Lesson 13.1)

LESSON CHECKLIST

Preparations for this lesson include:

- Lecture
- Demonstration
- Student performance evaluation of all entry-level skills required for student comprehension and application of principles of the blood system, including:
  o identification of terms relating to blood and blood clotting
  o application of abbreviations in medical reports and records
  o differentiation of blood types
  o application of pathological conditions affecting blood

KEY TERMS

Vocabulary (pp. 512-513)

albumin	immune reaction
antibody	immunoglobulin
antigen	leukocyte
basophil	lymphocyte
bilirubin	macrophage
coagulation	megakaryocyte
colony-stimulating factor (CSF)	monocyte
differentiation	mononuclear
electrophoresis	neutrophil
eosinophil	plasma
erythrocyte	plasmapheresis
erythropoietin (EPO)	platelet
fibrin	prothrombin
fibrinogen	reticulocyte
globulin	Rh factor
granulocyte	serum
hemoglobin	stem cell
hemolysis	thrombin
heparin	thrombocyte

Terminology (pp. 514-516)

bas/o	poikil/o
chrom/o	sider/o
coagul/o	spher/o
cyt/o	thromb/o
eosin/o	-apharesis
erythr/o	-blast
granul/o	-cytosis
hem/o	-emia
hemat/o	-globin
hemoglobin/o	-globulin
is/o	-lytic
kary/o	-oid
leuk/o	-osis
mon/o	-penia
morph/o	-phage
myel/o	-philia
neutr/o	-phoresis
nucle/o	-poiesis
phag/o	-stasis

Pathology (pp. 517-522)

anemia	mononucleosis
aplastic anemia	multiple myeloma
granulocytosis	pernicious anemia
hemochromatosis	polycythemia vera
hemolytic anemia	purpura
hemophilia	sickle cell anemia
leukemia	thalassemia

Laboratory Tests and Clinical Procedures (pp. 522-525)

antiglobulin test (Coombs test)	prothrombin time (PT)
bleeding time	red blood cell count (RBC)
coagulation time	red blood cell morphology
complete blood count (CBC)	white blood cell count (WBC)
erythrocyte sedimentation rate (ESR or sed rate)	white blood cell differential
	apharesis
hematocrit (Hct)	blood transfusion
hemoglobin test (H, Hg, HGB)	bone marrow biopsy
partial thromboplastin time (PTT)	hematopoietic stem cell transplant
platelet count	

REFERENCE LIST

PowerPoint slides (CD, Evolve): 1-44

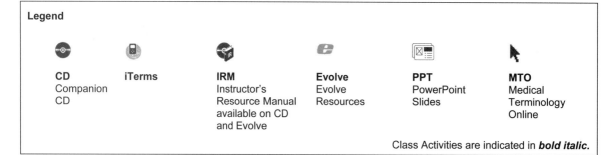

Legend

CD	iTerms	IRM	Evolve	PPT	MTO
Companion CD		Instructor's Resource Manual available on CD and Evolve	Evolve Resources	PowerPoint Slides	Medical Terminology Online

Class Activities are indicated in ***bold italic.***

The Language of Medicine, 9th ed.

Chabner

LESSON 13.1

PRETEST
IRM Exercise Quiz A, B

BACKGROUND ASSESSMENT

Question: Red and white blood cells develop from a common hematopoietic stem cell, which is large and nucleated. After cell differentiation and maturation, red cells no longer have nuclei and are very small, and white cells are nucleated, often large, filled with granules, and are capable of phagocytosis. Why do mature red blood cells look so different from their white counterparts?

Answer: Mature red blood cells are designed to squeeze in and out of the bone marrow and capillaries and have a large surface area to carry and deliver gases to cells and tissues in the body. They shed their nuclei during maturation after they make protein called hemoglobin. Hemoglobin molecules allow red blood cells to carry oxygen in the form of oxy-hemoglobin, a molecule that produces the bright red color. Without nuclei, red blood cells are incapable of reproducing themselves. Instead, after 120 days they are destroyed by macrophages, which are cells in the spleen, liver, and bone marrow.

Question: What is the term for white blood cells? How many types are there and what does each one do? What is an easy way to remember the names of the different types?

Answer: White blood cells are called leukocytes. There are three granulocytes and two mononuclear leukocytes. The granulocytes include eosinophils, which are active and elevated in allergic conditions such as asthma; basophils, which play a role in inflammation; and neutrophils, which are disease-fighting cells. Within the mononuclear leukocytes there are lymphocytes, which fight disease by producing antibodies and destroying foreign cells and monocytes, which engulf and destroy cellular debris, after neutrophils have attacked foreign cells. An easy way to remember the names of the five leukocytes is **N**ever (neutrophil) **L**et (lymphocyte) **M**onkeys (monocyte) **E**at (eosinophil) **B**ananas (basophil).

CRITICAL THINKING QUESTION

Susan finally visits her physician after feeling tired, dizzy, nauseous, and feverish for a long time. During her physical, the doctor draws whole blood to do a complete blood count and white cell differential. How might this help in making a diagnosis?

Guidelines: The white cell differential breaks down cellular components of peripheral whole blood. In a normal differential, the percentage of leukocytes in the blood includes 0% to 1% basophils, 1% to 4% eosinophils, 50% to 70% neutrophils, 20% to 40% lymphocytes, and 3% to 8% monocytes. Susan may be fighting an infection if her lymphocyte count is elevated, or she may have a parasitic infection if her eosinophil count is elevated. The doctor may find an unusually high percentage of a particular cell type or more immature cells that are overcrowding other cell types. This may indicate blood dyscrasia of the bone marrow or acute leukemia. If her red blood cells are showing changes in their morphology, this could indicate a reduction in cells that transport oxygen to the tissues.

OBJECTIVES	CONTENT	TEACHING RESOURCES
Identify terms relating to the composition, formation, and function of blood	■ Introduction (p. 504) ■ Composition and formation of blood (p. 504) □ Cells (p. 504) □ Erythrocytes (p. 504) □ Leukocytes (p. 507) □ Platelets (p. 508) □ Plasma (p. 509)	PPT 5-11 IRM Multiple Choice Quiz questions 1, 3, 5, 6 IRM Exercise Quiz D IRM Diagram Quiz IRM Practical Application A MTO Module 13, Section I, Lessons 1-4

OBJECTIVES	CONTENT	TEACHING RESOURCES
		Figure 13-1 Stages in blood cell development (p. 505)
		Figure 13-2 Erythrocytes (p.505)
		Figure 13-3 The breakdown of hemoglobin (p. 506)
		Figure 13-4 Normal leukocytes (p. 506)
		Figure 13-5 Phagocytosis (p. 507)
		Table 13-1 Leukocytes (p. 508)
		Figure 13-6 A, Megokaryocyte; B, Platelets (p. 508)
		Figure 13-7 The composition of blood (p. 509)
		Exercises A-C (pp. 528-529)
		Companion CD Exercises 13-1, 13-2
		***Class Activity** Have students make flash cards using the names, abbreviations, and combining forms for blood. Have them practice the definitions in pairs.*
		***Class Activity** Read the terms for the formation, composition, and functions of the blood. Ask students to correctly spell, analyze, and define them.*
Differentiate among the different types of blood groups.	■ Blood types (p. 510)	PPT 12
		▶ MTO Module 13, Section I, Lesson 5
		Table 13-2 Blood types (p. 510)
		Exercise D (p. 529)
		***Class Activity** Ask students to use the Internet to answer the following questions: What is the distribution of blood types among the general U.S. population? World population? Does it differ by race or ethnicity? If so, why? Have them report their results to the class.*
		***Class Activity** Divide students into the four different blood types by taping a specific type to their backs. Ask them to find their particular type by playing a form of Twenty Questions. They are allowed to ask "Am I type __?" only once. If wrong, they must sit down. At the end of the exercise, have all students who can donate to each type gather together. Then ask all who can receive from a specific type to gather together. Ask students*

OBJECTIVES	CONTENT	TEACHING RESOURCES
		to sit, and then discuss the problem of inadequate blood donation in the United States and what can be done to address the need.
Identify terms related to blood clotting.	■ Blood clotting (p. 510)	PPT 13 IRM Multiple Choice Quiz questions 2, 7 MTO Module 13, Section I, Lesson 6 Figure 13-8 The usual sequence of events in blood clotting (p. 511) Figure 13-9 A red blood cell enmeshed in threads of fibrin (p. 511) Exercises E, F (pp. 530) *Class Activity Ask groups of three to develop a description of the process of blood clotting. Ask that this be a visual display that can be drawn on the board or displayed on a transparency. Pick a group to present their description to the class. Have the class offer improvements.*
Apply your new knowledge to understanding medical terms in their proper contexts, such as medical reports and records.	■ Vocabulary (p. 512)	PPT 14-15 IRM Multiple Choice Quiz question 4 IRM Vocabulary Quiz *Class Activity Divide the class into two teams. Call out definitions and see which team names the most correct terms. Assign points to determine the winner.* *Class Activity Alternatively, read exercise A to students, asking them to spell, analyze, and underline the accented syllable in the terms that fit the definitions read.*
Build words and recognize combining forms used in the blood system terminology.	■ Terminology (p. 514)	PPT 16-20 IRM Multiple Choice Quiz questions 8-12 IRM Terminology Quiz IRM Exercise C IRM Dictation and Comprehension: Vocabulary A, B Companion CD Exercises 13-3, 13-4, 13-5

ELSEVIER

The Language of Medicine, 9th ed.

Chabner

OBJECTIVES	CONTENT	TEACHING RESOURCES
		Class Activity Create a set of bingo cards with a different combining form in each box (5 x 5); vary the combining forms and/or the order so cards are not all alike. Bingo card generators are available online. Create a list of definitions related to the blood system and corresponding to the combining forms on the bingo cards. Call out a definition. Students must circle the correct combining form on the bingo card. Award a point to the first student to complete bingo. If a student claims to have bingo and is incorrect, he or she is disqualified from that round.

13.1 Homework/Assignments:

13.1 Teacher's Notes:

The Language of Medicine, 9th ed.

Chabner

LESSON 13.2

CRITICAL THINKING QUESTION

Anemia is characterized by generalized fatigue because of a deficiency in erythrocytes or hemoglobin. What are different types of anemia and their deficiencies?

Guidelines: Anemia can be produced by a deficiency of normal red blood cells, and abnormal red cell formation can produce symptoms. With sickle cell anemia, for example, the crescent or sickle shapes of erythrocytes cause difficulty with normal passage through small blood vessels, leading to thrombosis and infarction (dead tissue). The condition is caused by an abnormal type of hemoglobin, a genetic defect prevalent in persons of African or African-American ancestry. Hemolytic anemia is the reduction of red cells resulting from a destruction of fragile red cells of abnormal spheroidal shape. Aplastic anemia is the reduction of red blood cells caused by the failure of stem cells in the marrow to produce cells. Thalassemia is an inherited defect, usually in people of Mediterranean background, in which hemoglobin content in red cells is diminished.

OBJECTIVES	CONTENT	TEACHING RESOURCES
Describe various pathological conditions affecting blood.	■ Pathology (p. 517) □ Diseases of red blood cells (p. 517) □ Disorders of blood clotting (p. 519) □ Diseases of white blood cells (p. 520) □ Diseases of the bone marrow (p. 522)	⊞ PPT 22-31 IRM Multiple Choice Quiz Questions 13-20 IRM Pathology Quiz IRM Exercise F IRM Dictation and Comprehension Quiz, Pathology and Tests A, B IRM Practical Applications, Case Report B questions 1-4 ↖ MTO Module 13, Section II, Lessons 1-3 Figure 13-10 A, Normal red blood cells; B, iron deficiency anemia (p. 517) Figure 13-11 Normal red blood cells and the abnormal cells in several types of anemia (p. 518) Figure 13-12 A, Petechiae; B, Ecchymoses (p. 520) Figure 13-13 Acute leukemia; A, Acute myeloblastic leukemia; B, Acute lymphoblastic leukemia (p. 521) Exercises G-I (pp. 531-532) ◉ Companion CD Exercise 13-7 ***Class Activity Divide students into four groups with each group reporting on one type of anemia. Have students explain the underlying cause of the anemia, potential therapies, and***

OBJECTIVES	CONTENT	TEACHING RESOURCES
		general prognosis. With regard to genetic abnormalities, have students explain which groups are most affected and why abnormalities are prevalent among certain groups.
		Class Activity *Discuss the various types of leukemia and the age groups most affected. Divide students into groups and have each group report on current therapies and the general prognosis for each type of leukemia.*

13.2 Homework/Assignments:

13.2 Teacher's Notes:

LESSON 13.3

CRITICAL THINKING QUESTION

Question: People who need blood transfusions after injury are blood-typed before being transfused. Both recipients and donors are tested to be certain their blood is compatible. This is especially important for the recipient. Why?

Answer: Blood-group antigens and antibodies in blood determine blood type. Type A blood contains A antigen and anti-B antibody, and Type B blood contains B antigen and anti-A antibody. The problem with transfusing from a type A donor into a type B recipient is that A antigens will react adversely with the anti-A antibodies in the recipient's type B bloodstream. The accidental adverse reaction is hemolysis, or breakdown of blood cells. Intravascular hemolysis may lead to disseminated intravascular coagulation, which is a serious coagulopathy.

OBJECTIVES	CONTENT	TEACHING RESOURCES
Differentiate among various laboratory tests, clinical procedures, and abbreviations used in connection with the blood system.	■ Laboratory tests, clinical procedures, and abbreviations (p. 522) □ Laboratory tests (p. 522) □ Clinical procedures (p. 524)	PPT 33-35 IRM Multiple Choice Quiz questions 21-25 IRM Laboratory Tests and Clinical Procedures Quiz IRM Exercise H MTO Module 13, Section III, Lessons 1-2 Figure 13-14 Leukapheresis (p. 524) Practical Applications (pp. 526-527) Exercises J, K (pp. 532-533) Companion CD Exercises 13-6, 13-8, 13-9 *Class Activity **Divide the class into four groups. Their mission: to determine the appropriate lab tests for certain conditions. Have students create cards with a different lab test and its definition written on each one. When the teacher describes a symptom or condition being tested, each group holds up the card with the proper blood test. There may be several right answers. Discuss which tests should be performed and why. Give points for correct answers; deduct points if test names or medical conditions are mispronounced.*** *Class Activity **Have four student groups create crossword puzzles relating to terms about transplant or transfusion therapy. Have groups exchange puzzles.***

OBJECTIVES	CONTENT	TEACHING RESOURCES
Apply your new knowledge to understanding medical terms in their proper contexts, such as medical reports and records.	■ Practical Applications (p. 526)	⊠ PPT 36-43 ➤ MTO Module 13, Section V Practical Applications (pp. 526-527) ***Class Activity Read the case report and ask students to write the answers to the questions. Ask them to spell out all abbreviation and analyze and define terms used in the answers.***
Differentiate among various laboratory tests, clinical procedures, and abbreviations used in connection with the blood system.	■ Abbreviations (p. 525)	🔲 IRM Abbreviations Quiz Exercise L (p. 533) ***Class Activity Blood Terminology Bingo: Create bingo cards with blood terminology abbreviations and acronyms. To play, the meanings of terms are called out. Switch callers.***
Define combining forms for blood system and the meaning of related terminology using these words.	■ Pronunciation of terms (p. 538) ☐ Vocabulary and terminology (p. 538) ☐ Pathological conditions, laboratory tests, and clinical procedures (p. 540)	🔲 IRM Pronunciation Quiz Pronunciation of Terms (pp. 538-541) Review Sheet (pp. 542-543) ⊙ Companion CD Exercise 13-10 💾 iTerms Chapter 13 ***Class Activity Word Component Terminology Bingo: Create bingo cards with word components that are presented in this chapter. To play, the meanings of terms are called out. The first winner becomes the next caller.*** ***Class Activity Spell a medical term to the class. Ask students to copy the term, underlining the accented syllable and analyzing the terms. Ask students to pronounce the word. Repeat this for 10 to 20 terms.*** ***Class Activity Divide the class into teams of two. Have one student practice pronouncing half of the list of terms while the other student keeps track of the correct and incorrect pronunciations. Have the students switch sides for the second half of the list of terms.***
Performance Evaluation		🔲 IRM Multiple Choice Quiz 🔲 IRM Terminology Quiz 🔲 IRM Pathology Quiz

OBJECTIVES	CONTENT	TEACHING RESOURCES
		IRM Laboratory Tests and Clinical Procedures Quiz
		IRM Exercise Quiz
		IRM Dictation and Comprehension Quiz
		IRM Spelling Quiz
		IRM Pronunciation Quiz A-C
		IRM Abbreviations Quiz
		IRM Diagram Quiz
		IRM Vocabulary Quiz
		IRM Review Sheet Quiz
		IRM Medical Scramble
		IRM Crossword Puzzle
		IRM Practical Applications
		ESLR Student Quiz Chapter 13
		MTO Module 13, Sections I-III quizzes
		MTO Module 13 Exam
		Companion CD Exercises 13-11, 13-12

13.3 Homework/Assignments:

Have students find articles from medical journals, newspapers, or periodicals that include terminology associated with the blood system. Students should underline about 15 to 25 terms. In class, have students exchange articles and together identify meanings of the underlined terms.

13.3 Teacher's Notes:

The Language of Medicine, 9th ed.
Chabner

Slide 1

The Language Of Medicine
9th edition
Davi-Ellen Chabner

Slide 2

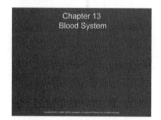

Chapter 13
Blood System

Slide 3

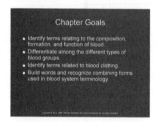

Chapter Goals

- Identify terms relating to the composition, formation, and function of blood.
- Differentiate among the different types of blood groups.
- Identify terms related to blood clotting.
- Build words and recognize combining forms used in blood system terminology.

Slide 4

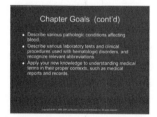

Chapter Goals (cont'd)

- Describe various pathologic conditions affecting blood.
- Describe various laboratory tests and clinical procedures used with hematologic disorders, and recognize relevant abbreviations.
- Apply your new knowledge to understanding medical terms in their proper contexts, such as medical reports and records.

Slide 5

Chapter 13
Lesson 13.1

Slide 6

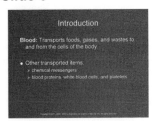

- What are chemical messengers called? (*hormones*)
- What do white blood cells do? (*Fight infection*)
- What do platelets do? (*help the blood clot*)
- What is the medical term for WBC? (*leukocyte*)
- What is the medical term for platelet? (*thrombocyte*)

Slide 7

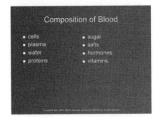

- What are cells? (*Formed elements, suspended in a clear, straw-colored liquid called plasma.*) What percentage of blood volume do cells constitute? (*45%. The other 55% are items listed here.*)

Slide 8

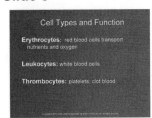

- What is an immature red blood cell called? (*erythroblast*)
- Where do erythrocytes originate? (*In bone marrow*)
- What are cells in the spleen, liver, and bone marrow that destroy worn-out erythrocytes? (*macrophages*)
- What is a phagocyte?
- See next slide. Review a normal differential of these cell types in a smear of whole peripheral blood.

Slide 9

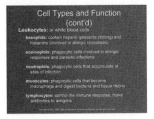

Slide 10

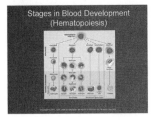

- Explain phagocytosis.

The Language of Medicine, 9th ed.

Chabner

Slide 11

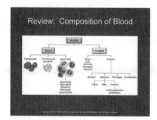

- Describe each section of the chart.

Slide 12

- What are fibrinogen and prothrombin? (*Clotting proteins*)

- What does albumin do? (*Maintains the proper proportion and concentration of water in the blood*)

- What are globulins? (*Another part of the blood containing plasma proteins: alpha, beta, and gamma globulins*)

- What are immunoglobulins? (*Antibodies that bind to and sometimes destroy antigens or foreign substances, ie., IgG, IgA*)

Slide 13

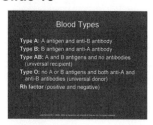

- Why is blood type matching important for transfusions?

- What is Rh factor? What is the difference between Rh-positive and Rh-negative?

- Why is blood type matching important for identification of pregnancy? (*Most people are Rh positive so problem arises with Rh negative mother with Rh positive fetus.*)

Slide 14

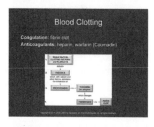

- What is blood clotting or coagulation?

- The final result (usually taking less than 15 minutes) is the formation of a fibrin clot from the plasma protein fibrinogen.

- Why are platelets important in the beginning of the process following injury to tissues or blood vessels?

Slide 15

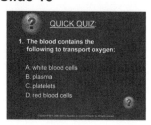

- Correct answer is D: red blood cells

Slide 16

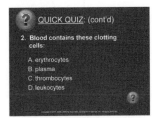

- Correct answer is C: thrombocytes

Slide 17

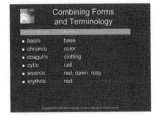

Slide 18

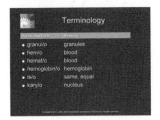

Slide 19

Slide 20

Slide 21

- Ask meanings and examples of terms.
- What is thrombolytic therapy? (*Used to dissolve clots*)
- What is plasmapheresis? (*A centrifuge spins blood to remove plasma from the other parts of the blood.*)

Slide 22

Slide 23

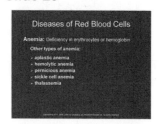

- What is the most common type of anemia? (*Iron-deficiency anemia*)
- What is an example of hemolytic anemia? (*Congenital spherocytic anemia*)

Slide 24

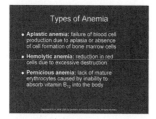

Slide 25

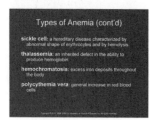

- Persons of what background are prone to thalassemia? (*Mediterranean*)
- Sickle cell is prevalent among which group? (*Black people of African or African-American ancestry*) Why? (*Sickling is a genetic response to malaria.*)
- What treatment is used for polycythemia vera? How is this similar to doping?

Chabner

Slide 26

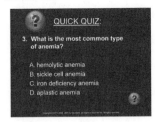

- Correct answer is C: iron deficiency anemia (see p. 498 of text)

Slide 27

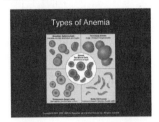

Slide 28

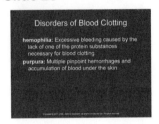

- What is a treatment for hemophilia? (*Administration of the deficient factor*)
- What is autoimmune thrombocytopenic purpura? (*A condition in which a patient's body makes an antibody that destroys platelets*)

Slide 29

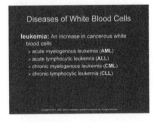

- What are characteristics of acute leukemia?
- What form of leukemia is most often in children and adolescents? (*ALL*)
- What form of leukemia usually occurs in the elderly and follows a slowly progressive course? (*CLL*)

Slide 30

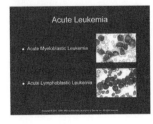

- The terms acute and chronic discriminate between leukemias of primarily immature and mature leukocytes.

Chabner

Slide 31

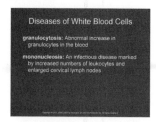

- How is mononucleosis usually transmitted? (*By oral contact*)
- Is treatment necessary for EBV infections? (*No*)
- What is eosinophilia? (*An increase in eosinophilic granulocytes, seen in certain allergic conditions*)

Slide 32

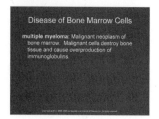

- The malignant cells destroy bone tissue and cause the overproduction of immunoglobulins, including Bence Jones protein. What is Bence Jones protein? (*An immunoglobulin fragment found in urine*)
- How is this treated?

Slide 33

Slide 34

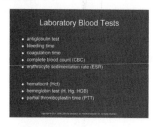

- What is a normal coagulation time? (*Less than 15 minutes*)
- What is the speed at which erythrocytes settle out of plasma? (*ESR or sed rate*)
- What test finds the total amount of hemoglobin in a sample of peripheral blood? (*hemoglobin test*)

Slide 35

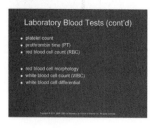

- What is the number of leukocytes per cubic millimeter or microliter? (*WBC*)
- What determines the percentage of the total WBC made up by different types of leukocytes? (*White blood cell differential*)

Slide 36

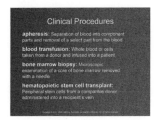

- What is plasma exchange? (*A procedure in which plasma is removed from the patient and fresh plasma is given*)

- What is autologous transfusion? (*The collection and later reinfusion of a patient's own blood or blood components*)

- What is a bone marrow aspirate? (*When bone marrow is removed by brief suction produced by a syringe*)

Slide 37

Slide 38

Slide 39

Slide 40

Slide 41

Slide 42

Slide 43

Slide 44

TEACHING FOCUS

Students will have the opportunity to learn about the structure and function of the immune and lymph vascular systems. The text presents terminology associated with the pathological conditions affecting the lymphatic and immune systems, so that the student can become familiar with laboratory tests, clinical procedures, and abbreviations that are pertinent to these systems. The student will then have the opportunity to apply knowledge and understanding of medical terms in context.

MATERIALS AND RESOURCES

- ☐ Flash cards (Lesson 14.1)
- ☐ Index cards (Lesson 14.2)
- ☐ Medical journals (Lesson 14.1)
- ☐ Photocopies of a relevant journal article (Lesson 14.2)

LESSON CHECKLIST

Preparations for this lesson include:

- Lecture
- Flash cards
- Student performance evaluation of entry-level skills required for student comprehension and application of knowledge about the lymphatic and immune systems, including:
  - o recognizing terms related to structure, function, pathology, and clinical procedures
  - o obtaining and recording patient history
  - o preparing patient for and assisting with examinations, procedures, and treatments

KEY TERMS

Vocabulary (pp. 554-555)

acquired immunity
adenoids
antibody
antigen
axillary node
B cell
cervical node
complement system
cytokine
cytotoxic cell
dendritic cell
helper T cell
immunity
immunoglobulins
immunotherapy
inguinal node
interferons
interleukins
interstitial fluid
lymph

lymph capillaries
lymphoid organs
lymph node
lymph vessel
macrophage
mediastinal node
monoclonal antibody
natural immunity
plasma cell
right lymphatic duct
spleen
suppressor T cell
T cell
tolerance
thoracic duct
thymus gland
tonsils
toxin
vaccination
vaccine

Terminology (pp. 556-557)

immun/o

lymph/o

lymphaden/o

splen/o

thym/o

tox/o

ana-

inter-

Pathology (pp. 558-561)

acquired immune deficiency syndrome (AIDS)

allergy

lymphoma

multiple myeloma

thymoma

Laboratory Tests and Clinical Procedures (pp. 562-563)

CD4$^+$ cell count

CT scan

ELISA

immunoelectrophoresis

viral load test

REFERENCE LIST

PowerPoint slides (CD, Evolve): 1-51

Legend

CD
Companion CD

iTerms

IRM
Instructor's Resource Manual available on CD and Evolve

Evolve
Evolve Resources

PPT
PowerPoint Slides

MTO
Medical Terminology Online

Class Activities are indicated in **bold italic**.

LESSON 14.1

PRETEST
IRM Exercise Quiz A

BACKGROUND ASSESSMENT
Question: When a cancerous lesion is surgically removed from the breast, axillary lymph nodes are often removed as well. Why is removal of axillary lymph nodes thought to be important?
Answer: Sampling the lymph nodes can give the surgeon information about metastatic spread of the cancer in the breast. Lymph vessels drain interstitial fluid that has come out of the blood and courses through the tissues of the body. This fluid drains into specialized thin-walled vessels called lymph capillaries. The fluid in these vessels, now called lymph, passes through larger lymphatic vessels and through deposits of lymph tissues called lymph nodes. Ultimately the lymph fluid reenters the bloodstream. Because the axillary nodes drain the areas of the breast, malignant cells could easily enter the lymph and end up in the nodes in the axilla.

Question: What type of immunity does a vaccination during childhood provide? What is the advantage of receiving a vaccination?
Answer: Immunity is the body's ability to resist foreign organisms and toxins that damage the tissues. A childhood vaccination makes the body immune to a disease-causing organism by exposing the body to a modified pathogen that stimulates lymphocytes to produce antibodies. The antibodies remain ready to mount an attack if the body is exposed to the foreign organism years later. A person either will not become ill or may contract a milder form of the disease. A person also may acquire immunity after contracting a disease because the body produces antibodies that repel future attacks. However, if the disease is contracted without having had a vaccination, it probably will be more severe and may have other serious side effects.

CRITICAL THINKING QUESTION
Rosa has been diagnosed with systemic lupus erythematosus (SLE). She recognizes that this is one of the disorders that is referred to as an autoimmune disorder. What could you tell her that describes these diseases?
Autoimmune disorders result when the lymphocytes fail to accept the body's own antigens as "self" or friendly. The cause is currently unknown, but other autoimmune disorders are multiple sclerosis and rheumatoid arthritis.

OBJECTIVES	CONTENT	TEACHING RESOURCES

Identify the structures and analyze terms related to the lymphatic system.	■ Introduction (p. 546)
	
	■ Lymphatic system (p. 548)
	
	  □ Anatomy (p. 548)
	
	  □ Spleen and thymus gland (p. 550)
		⊠ PPT 5-18
		
		IRM Diagram Quiz
		
		IRM Multiple Choice Quiz questions 1-12
		
		MTO Module 14, Section I, Lessons 1-2
		
		Figure 14-1 Interstitial fluid and lymph capillaries (p. 547)
		
		Figure 14-2 Relationship between the circulatory systems of blood and lymph (p. 547)
		
		Figure 14-3 Lymphatic system (p. 548)
		
		Figure 14-4 A lymph node (p. 549)
		
		Figure 14-5 A, Spleen; B, thymus gland (p. 550)

Chabner

OBJECTIVES	CONTENT	TEACHING RESOURCES
		Exercises A, B (p. 566)
		⊙ Companion CD Exercise 14-1
		▸ Discuss the function of the lymphatic system. Review the names and locations of tissues and organs.
		▸ Discuss the flow of lymph and blood through the spleen. Ask students to describe what happens if the spleen or thymus is removed.
		Class Activity Divide students into two groups to do additional research on the flow of lymph and blood through the spleen. Have one group report to the class on the "open system" theory and the other group report on the "closed system" theory. Discuss with the class which theory is preferred today and why.

Learn terms to describe basic elements of the immune system.	■ Immune system (p. 551)
	
	■ Terminology (p. 556)
	
	   □ Combining forms (p. 556)
	
	   □ Prefixes (p. 557)
		⊠ PPT 19-28
		
		IRM Multiple Choice Quiz questions 13-15
		
		IRM Terminology Quiz
		
		IRM Exercise Quiz G
		
		↖ MTO Module 14, Section I, Lessons 3-4
		
		Figure 14-6 Types of immunity (p. 551)
		
		Figure 14-7 B call, plasma cell, and immunoglobulins (p. 552)
		
		Figure 14-8 Types of T cells (p. 552)
		
		Figure 14-9 Functions of B-cell (humoral immunity) and T-cell lymphocytes (cell-mediated immunity) (p. 553)
		
		Figure 14-10 Lymphedema (p. 556)
		
		Exercises C-E (pp. 567-568)
		
		Review Sheet (p. 575)
		
		⊙ Companion CD Exercises 14-2, 14-3
		
		▸ Discuss basic elements of the immune system.
		
		Class Activity Divide the class into three groups, each one focusing on a different type of immunity, natural, active acquired, or passive acquired. Have each group describe

OBJECTIVES	CONTENT	TEACHING RESOURCES
		the type and present at least three examples of real conditions in which that type is the body's primary or secondary response.
		Class Activity *Make flash cards, or have students make them, with key vocabulary terms on one side and short definitions on the other. Divide the class into three groups and distribute one third of the cards to each group. Have members of each group quiz each other. Then, rotate the cards among groups until each group has worked with all the cards.*
		Class Activity *Divide the students into teams. During a timed session, call out the name of a combining form. Each team needs to create as many lymphatic and immune system medical terms from the combining form as it can in a 60-second period. After 60 seconds, announce another combining form.*

14.1 Homework/Assignments:

14.1 Teacher's Notes:

LESSON 14.2

CRITICAL THINKING QUESTION

What are opportunistic infections? What specific immunodeficiency leads to the development of opportunistic infections in AIDS patients?

Guidelines: Potentially invasive organisms normally contained by the immune system can produce opportunistic infections. These include yeast-like fungi, bacteria, parasites, and viral organisms normally present in the mouth, skin, intestinal tract, respiratory tract, and elsewhere. The AIDS virus specifically destroys T-cell helper lymphocytes, which promote antibody production by B cells and stimulate cytotoxic T cells that act directly on antigens to destroy them.

OBJECTIVES	CONTENT	TEACHING RESOURCES
Recognize terms that describe various pathological conditions affecting the lymphatic and immune systems.	■ Pathology (p. 558) ☐ Immunodeficiency (p. 558) – Acquired immunodeficiency syndrome (AIDS) (p. 558) ☐ Hypersensitivity (p. 560) – Allergy (p. 560) ☐ Malignancy (p. 560) – Lymphoma (p. 560) – Multiple myeloma (p. 561) – Thymoma (p. 561)	PPT 30-36 IRM Multiple Choice Quiz questions 16-25 IRM Pathology Quiz MTO Module 14, Section II, Lessons 1-4 Table 14-1 Opportunistic infections with AIDS (p. 558) Figure 14-11 A, Kaposi sarcoma; B, Wasting syndrome (p. 559) Table 14-2 Common routes of transmission (p. 559) Figure 14-12 Atopic dermatitis (p. 560) Figure 14-13 Staging of Hodgkin's disease (p. 561) Exercises G-I (pp. 568-569) *Class Activity Pass out photocopies of a medical journal article pertaining to an immune system dysfunction. Have students trade articles and underline terms related to immune function. Then pair off students and have the pairs identify and define 25 terms related to immune system dysfunction in their articles.* *Class Activity Alternatively, ask the students to make flash cards for the conditions with definitions on the back. In pairs, have them shuffle their cards and quiz one other. After 10 minutes, have one pair compete against another to see who can identify the most terms correctly.*

OBJECTIVES	CONTENT	TEACHING RESOURCES
Identify laboratory tests, clinical procedures, and abbreviations that are pertinent to the lymphatic and immune systems.	■ Laboratory tests, clinical procedures, and abbreviations (p. 562) □ Laboratory tests (p. 562) – CD4+ cell count (p. 562) – ELISA test (p. 562) – Immunoelectrophoresis (p. 563) – Viral load tests (p. 563) □ Clinical procedures (p. 563) – CT scan (p. 563) □ Abbreviations (p. 563)	PPT 37-48 IRM Laboratory Tests and Clinical Procedures Quiz IRM Exercise Quiz F-H IRM Abbreviations Quiz MTO Module 14, Section III, Lessons 1-2 Study Section (p. 562) Companion CD Exercises 14-4, 14-5, 14-6 *Class Activity Play medical terminology bingo. Have half the students make lists of abbreviations and half make lists of medical terms related to the lymphatic and immune systems. Put the components on index cards. Have the class switch the cards between groups and then put the meanings on the backs. Then shuffle the cards and make bingo place cards. Have the meanings called by rotating callers and play bingo.*
Apply your new knowledge to understanding medical terms in their proper contexts, such as medical reports and records.	□ Abbreviations (p. 563)	IRM Dictation and Comprehension Quiz IRM Abbreviations Quiz IRM Practical Applications *Class Activity Have students take turns reading Exercise J to the class. Ask that the student who is reading the question pronounce, analyze, define, and underline the accented syllable in the correct answer.*
Performance Evaluation		IRM Multiple Choice Quiz IRM Terminology Quiz IRM Pathology Quiz IRM Laboratory Tests and Clinical Procedures Quiz IRM Exercise Quiz IRM Dictation and Comprehension Quiz IRM Spelling Quiz

OBJECTIVES	CONTENT	TEACHING RESOURCES
		IRM Pronunciation Quiz
		IRM Abbreviations Quiz
		IRM Diagram Quiz
		IRM Vocabulary Quiz
		IRM Review Sheet Quiz
		IRM Opportunistic Infections Quiz
		IRM Medical Scramble
		IRM Crossword Puzzle
		IRM Practical Applications
		ESLR Body Spectrum Electronic Anatomy Coloring Book, Lymphatic
		ESLR Student Quiz Chapter 14
		MTO Module 14, Sections I-III quizzes
		MTO Module 14 Exam
		Companion CD Exercises 14-7, 14-8, 14-9
		iTerms Chapter 14

14.2 Homework/Assignments:

Have students research the types of laboratory tests that might be performed to identify allergies. Have students make brief oral reports to the class.

14.2 Teacher's Notes:

Slide 1

The Language Of
Medicine
9th edition
Davi-Ellen Chabner

Slide 2

Chapter 14
Lymphatic and Immune Systems

Slide 3

Chapter Goals

- Identify the structures and analyze terms related to the lymphatic and immune systems.

- Learn basic terminology, combining forms and other word parts related to these systems.

Slide 4

Chapter Goals (cont'd)

- Identify laboratory tests, clinical procedures, and abbreviations.
- Apply your new knowledge to understanding medical terms in their proper contexts, such as medical reports and records.

Slide 5

Chapter 14
Lesson 14.1

Slide 6

- Tonsils are aggregate lymphatic organs.
- Lymphocytes and monocytes in lymph organs protect the body from foreign invaders.
- What are the three functions of the lymphatic system?

Slide 7

- Tonsils are aggregate lymphatic organs.
- Lymphocytes and monocytes in lymph organs protect the body from foreign invaders.
- What are the three functions of the lymphatic system?

Slide 8

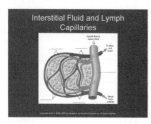

- Have students label the figure .or use the next figure, which has the labels in place.
- Review the circulation of blood in blood vessels.
- Compare and contrast with lymph in lymph capillaries.
- How do the blood and lymph systems complement each other?
- How are the structures of lymph vessels and veins similar? (valves, no pump)

Slide 9

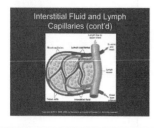

- Review the circulation of blood in blood vessels.
- Compare and contrast with lymph in lymph capillaries.
- How do the blood and lymph systems complement each other?
- How are the structures of lymph vessels and veins similar? (valves, no pump)

Slide 10

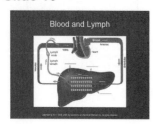

- Use this slide to continue your discussion from previous slide.
- What happens in situations such as edema?

Chabner

Slide 11

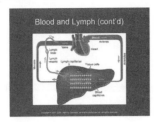

- Use this slide to continue your discussion from previous slide.
- What happens in situations such as edema?

Slide 12

- What are lymph capillaries and lymph vessels?
- What does each do?
- Describe lymph nodes and what they do.

Slide 13

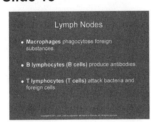

- What happens in a lymph node?
- How do T cells act to attack foreign cells?

Slide 14

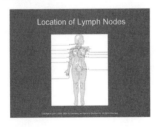

- Ask students to fill in the names and locations of the major areas of the body occupied by lymph nodes.

Slide 15

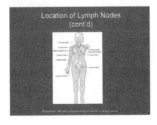

- Ask students to fill in the names and locations of the major areas of the body occupied by lymph nodes.

Chabner

Slide 16

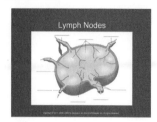

- Point out and discuss elements and functions of each part in this figure

Slide 17

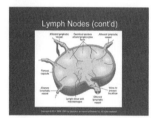

- Point out and discuss elements and functions of each part in this figure

Slide 18

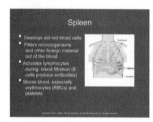

- The spleen and thymus gland are composed of lymph tissue.
- Note their locations.
- What are the functions of the spleen?
- Is the thymus proportionately larger in infants or adults? Why?

Slide 19

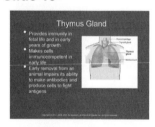

- The spleen and thymus gland are composed of lymph tissue.
- Note their locations.
- What are the functions of the spleen?
- Is the thymus proportionately larger in infants or adults? Why?

Slide 20

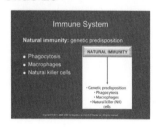

- Why is it important for infants to possess natural immunity at birth?
- What is an example of genetic predisposition? (Humans cannot contract feline leukemia.)

Chabner

Slide 21

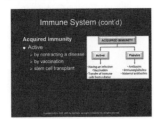

- Ask students to provide an example for each method of acquiring active immunity.

- Ask students what vaccinations they have had.

Slide 22

Slide 23

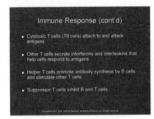

- T-cell lymphocytes originate from bone marrow stem cells. They are processed in the thymus gland.

Slide 24

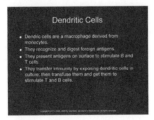

- Some of the dendritic cell work (sensitizing them in a culture) is under investigation in clinical studies used to treat tumors and tumor antigens, thus getting the patient's own immune system to attack the tumor.

Slide 25

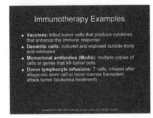

Slide 26

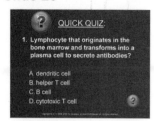

- Correct answer is B: helper T cell..

Slide 27

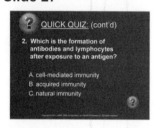

- Correct answer is B: acquired immunity

Slide 28

Slide 29

Slide 30

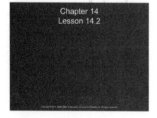

Chabner

Slide 31

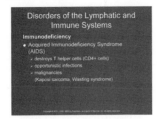

Slide 32

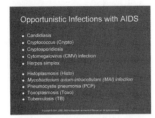

- Ask students to provide symptoms for the opportunistic infections listed.

Slide 33

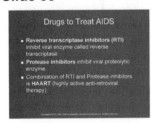

- HIV needs protease at a later stage than it needs RT to make viral parts that will spread throughout the body.

Slide 34

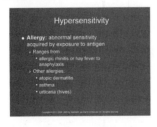

- Review examples of hypersensitivity reactions. Discuss reactions that students have had.
- What is anaphylaxis? Why is it dangerous?
- What is the common name for urticaria?

Slide 35

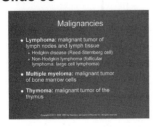

- Ask students to define associated terms:
  - Splenomegaly
  - Lymphadenopathy
  - Radiotherapy

Slide 36

- Ask students to define associated terms, and reuse them correctly in another context:
  - Mediastinum
  - Extranodal
  - Extralymphatic
  - Splenectomy

Slide 37

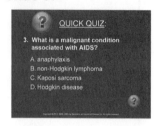

- Correct answer is C: Kaposi sarcoma.

Slide 38

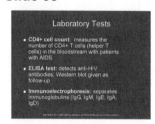

- ELISA is an acronym that stands for what? (<u>e</u>nzyme-<u>l</u>inked <u>i</u>mmuno<u>s</u>orbent <u>a</u>ssay)
- For what conditions is immunoelectrophoresis utilized?

Slide 39

Slide 40

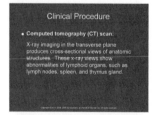

Slide 41

Slide 42

Slide 43

Slide 44

Slide 45

Slide 46

Slide 47

Slide 48

Slide 49

Slide 50

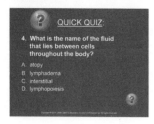

- Correct answer is C: interstitial fluid.

Chabner

Slide 51

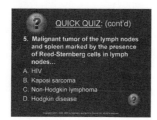

- Correct answer is D: Hodgkin disease

15 Musculoskeletal System

TEACHING FOCUS

Students will have the opportunity to learn about the musculoskeletal system, which includes the bones, muscles, and joints of the body. Students will be introduced to the structure and function of the major supports and protection for internal organs. They will have the opportunity to learn the location of the major bones, joints, and muscles of the body and understand how movement and flexibility of both internal and external structures depends on these tissues and organ systems, including parts of the viscera and blood vessels. Students will have the opportunity to gain an understanding of the terms related to musculoskeletal disease and bone fracture and the important laboratory tests and clinical procedures used for the diagnosis and treatment of disorders in this system. Students will be shown how to apply their new knowledge to understanding medical terms in their proper contexts of medical reports and records.

MATERIALS AND RESOURCES

- ☐ Human skeleton (Lesson 15.1)
- ☐ Medical atlas of histology (Lesson 15.3)
- ☐ Medical journals (Lesson 15.1)
- ☐ Slips of paper with written terms (Lesson 15.1)

LESSON CHECKLIST

Preparations for this lesson include:

- Lecture
- Method of student evaluation of comprehension and application of terminology relating to the musculoskeletal system, including:
  - o anatomical terminology for bones, joints, and muscles
  - o pathology of the musculoskeletal system
  - o combining forms, prefixes, and suffixes
  - o knowledge of lab tests and clinical procedures to support patient education

KEY TERMS

Vocabulary – Bones (pp. 592-593)

acetabulum	medullary cavity
acromion	metaphysis
articular cartilage	olecranon
bone	osseous tissue
calcium	ossification
cancellous bone	osteoblast
cartilage	osteoclast
collagen	periosteum
compact bone	phosphorus
condyle	pubic symphysis
cranial bones	red bone marrow
diaphysis	ribs
disk (disc)	sella turcica
epiphyseal plate	sinus
epiphysis	styloid process
facial bones	suture
fissure	temporomandibular joint
fontanelle	trabeculae
foramen	trochanter
fossa	tubercle
haversian canals	tuberosity
malleolus	vertebra
manubrium	xiphoid process
mastoid process	yellow bone marrow

Terminology – Bones (pp. 594-598)

acetabul/o

calc/o, calci/o

calcane/o

carp/o

clavicul/o

cost/o

crani/o

femor/o

fibul/o

humer/o

ili/o

isch/o

kyph/o

lamin/o

lord/o

lumb/o

malleol/o

mandibul/o

maxill/o

metacarp/o

metatars/o

myel/o

olecran/o

orth/o

oste/o

patell/o

pelv/i

perone/o

phalang/o

pub/o

radi/o

scapula/o

scoli/o

spondyl/o

stern/o

tars/o

tibi/o

uln/o

vertebr/o

-blast

-clast

-listhesis

-malacia

-physis

-porosis

-tome

Pathology – Bones (pp. 598-601)

Ewing sarcoma

exostosis

fracture

osteogenic sarcoma

osteomalacia

osteomyelitis

osteoporosis

talipes

Vocabulary – Joints (p. 603)

articular cartilage

articulation

bursa, bursae

ligament

suture joint

synovial cavity

synovial fluid

synovial joint

synovial membrane

tendon

Terminology – Joints (pp. 604-605)

ankyl/o

arthr/o

articul/o

burs/o

chondr/o

ligament/o

rheumat/o

synov/o

ten/o

tendin/o

-desis

-stenosis

Pathology – Joints (pp. 606-610)

ankylosing spondylitis

arthritis

bunion

carpal tunnel syndrome (CTS)

dislocation

ganglion

gouty arthritis

herniation of an intervertebral disk

Lyme disease

osteoarthritis

rheumatoid arthritis

sprain

systemic lupus erythematosus (SLE)

ELSEVIER

The Language of Medicine, 9th ed.

Chabner

Vocabulary – Muscles (p. 614)

abduction

adduction

dorsiflexion

extension

fascia

flexion

insertion of a muscle

origin of a muscle

plantar flexion

pronation

rotation

skeletal muscle

smooth muscle

striated muscle

supination

visceral muscle

Terminology – Muscles (pp. 614-615)

fasci/o

fibr/o

leiomy/o

my/o

myocardi/o

myos/o

plant/o

rhabdomy/o

sarc/o

-asthenia

-trophy

ab-

ad-

dorsi-

poly-

Pathology – Muscles (p. 616)

muscular dystrophy

polymyositis

Laboratory Tests and Clinical Procedures (pp. 616-619)

antinuclear antibody test (ANA)

erythrocyte sedimentation rate (ESR)

rheumatoid factor test (RF)

serum calcium (Ca)

serum creatine kinase (CK)

uric acid test

arthrocentesis

arthrography

arthroplasty

arthroscopy

bone density test

bone scan

computed tomography

diskography

electromyography

magnetic resonance imaging (MRI)

muscle biopsy

REFERENCE LIST

PowerPoint slides (CD, Evolve): 1-77

Legend					
CD Companion CD	**iTerms**	**IRM** Instructor's Resource Manual available on CD and Evolve	**Evolve** Evolve Resources	**PPT** PowerPoint Slides	**MTO** Medical Terminology Online

Class Activities are indicated in ***bold italic.***

Chabner

LESSON 15.1

PRETEST
IRM Exercise Quiz B

BACKGROUND ASSESSMENT

Question: Many of the bones of the body have an English name as well as a medical name. How many of these bones can you currently name?

Answer: Students may answer as follows: skull (cranium), thigh (femur), shinbone (tibia), hand bones (metacarpals), finger bones (phalanges), pelvis (pelvis: ilium, ischium, pubis), backbones (vertebrae), collarbones (clavicles), shoulder blades (clavicles), and so forth.

Question: Many different types of fractures occur in bones. One of the most typical occurs when a person uses his or her hand to block a fall before hitting the pavement. What is the name of this sort of fracture, where does it occur, and what are the correct terms used for the process that fixes it?

Answer: When a person uses his or her hand to break a fall, usually the hand is bent backward in a dorsiflexed position, absorbing the pressure of nearly all of the body's weight. The radius breaks around the area of the wrist joint at the lower end, usually in the area of the metaphysis. This is called a Colles fracture. The physician must treat the fracture by first doing a "reduction," which is a procedure to restore the bone to its normal position. Then the physician must cast the region (sometimes over the elbow) to keep the joint immobile and keep the hand from pronating, dorsiflexing, and supinating.

CRITICAL THINKING QUESTION

Sarah is a freshman high school student who is also holding down a 20-hour-a-week job. She drinks diet cola several times a day to keep her energized without adding calories, and she has given up all dairy products as part of her newly embraced vegan diet. At a routine check up, her physician warned against excessive soda consumption and recommended that she add more sources of calcium to her diet. Why?

As a teenager, Sarah is still growing and her bones are still developing. A lack of calcium in her diet will lead to weakened bones, along with the potential for harm to her nervous, muscular, and cardiovascular systems. Sarah does not have to eat dairy products for her calcium requirements, but can substitute other foods, such as dark green leafy vegetables and calcium-fortified soy products.

OBJECTIVES	CONTENT	TEACHING RESOURCES
Define terms relating to the structure and function of bones, joints, and muscles.	■ Introduction (p. 578)	PPT 6-7 IRM Exercise Quiz A Part I MTO Module 15, Section I, Lesson 1 ▶ Discuss the IRM Diagram Quiz. Fill out labels of the diagram as a class. *Class Activity Have a member of the class borrow a human skeleton from a local medical or dental school, or some facility that uses skeletons to teach. Students may even be able to purchase their own models inexpensively in the weeks before Halloween, when skeletons are plentiful. Go over the bones of the body regions that will be discussed in future segments of this chapter. Be certain to take advantage of access to processes and depressions that are easy to*

OBJECTIVES	CONTENT	TEACHING RESOURCES
		palpate on the 3-dimensional skeleton. You might try to obtain a human skull if you cannot find the whole skeleton. A small toy or Halloween skeleton from a store may also be useful. *Class Activity Alternatively, have students use sticky notes to identify the bones on the skeleton. If more than one skeleton is available, stations can be set up to address different bones and structures. Have students rotate through the stations.*
Describe the process of bone formation and growth.	■ Bones (p. 578) ☐ Formation and structure (p. 578) – Formation (p. 578) – Structure (p. 579)	PPT 8-10 IRM Multiple Choice Quiz questions 1, 8 IRM Exercise Quiz questions 1-16 IRM Dictation Quiz questions 1-20 MTO Module 15, Section I, Lessons 2-3 Figure 15-1 A, Divisions of long bone and interior bone structure; B, Composition of compact bone (p. 580) Exercise A (pp. 624) *Class Activity In small groups, have students draw charts outlining the formation of bones. They should begin with a fetus and show how bones form from cartilaginous tissue and grow to become adult bones. Have students present their charts to the class for discussion.*
Define terms relating to the structure and function of bones, joints, and muscles.	☐ Processes and depressions in bone (p. 581) ☐ Cranial bones (p. 582) ☐ Facial bones (p. 584) ☐ Vertebral column and structure of vertebrae (p. 586) ☐ Bones of the thorax, pelvis, and extremities (p. 588) ■ Vocabulary (p. 592)	PPT 11-34 IRM Multiple Choice Quiz questions 2-7, 14-16 IRM Comprehension Quiz Exercise B MTO Module 15, Section I, Lessons 4-7 Figure 15-2 Bone process on the femur and humerus (p. 581) Figure 15-3 Cranial bones, lateral view (p. 582) Figure 15-4 Cranial bones (p. 583) Figure 15-5 Facial bones (p. 585) Figure 15-6 Sinuses of the skull (p. 585)

OBJECTIVES	CONTENT	TEACHING RESOURCES
		Figure 15-7 Vertebral column (p. 586)
		Figure 15-8 (A) General structure of a vertebra; (B) Series of vertebrae (p. 587)
		Figure 15-9 Bones of the thorax, pelvis, and extremities (p. 588)
		Figure 15-10 Scapula and rib cage (p. 589)
		Figure 15-11 Bones of the foot (p. 590)
		Table 15-1 Bones or processes and their common names (p. 591)
		Exercises B-H (pp. 624-627)
		⊙ Companion CD Exercises 15-1, 15-2, 15-3, 15-4
		Class Activity Prepare bone flash cards for use in a Password game. Have students make flash cards including the bones of the body. On the back of each card, list the major function of the bone and its location. Divide the class into groups of four. Have students in each group of four pair off. Each pair plays against another pair as in the game Password. The student trying to extract the word only has to give the definition on the card. If the answering student does not answer correctly from the definition, it goes to the other team. If they both do not answer correctly, the student can start to give one-word hints as in the real Password game. Each incorrect answer subtracts one of 10 possible points per round.
		Class Activity Ask students to research the processes and depressions in bones that are palpable directly or indirectly during a physical examination. Have them demonstrate these to the class.
		Class Activity Make a crossword puzzle for the vocabulary list in the text. Ask them to work in pairs to complete the puzzle.
		Class Activity Read the definitions of the vocabulary terms in the text. Ask them to spell and underline the accented syllable in each of the terms.

OBJECTIVES	CONTENT	TEACHING RESOURCES
Analyze the combining forms, prefixes, and suffixes used to describe bones, joints, and muscles.	☐ Terminology - Bones (p. 594) – General terms, combining forms (p. 594) – Suffixes (p. 596) – Terms related to specific bones, combining forms (p. 596)	PPT 35-42 IRM Terminology - Bones Quiz IRM Pronunciation Quiz C Figure 15-12 Kyphosis and lordosis (p. 594) Figure 15-13 Moderate thoracic idiopathic adolescent scoliosis (p. 595) Exercise I (p. 627) Review Sheet (pp. 646-647) Companion CD Exercise 15-5 *Class Activity Write the combining forms, prefixes, and suffixes on small slips of paper and place them in a "hat." Go around the room and have each student draw a slip of paper and give the meaning, use it in a medical term, and use the term in a sentence. Continue until all terms have been covered.* *Class Activity Use the terms listed in the text. Pronounce the term, and ask the students to spell, analyze, define, and underline the accented syllable in each term.* *Class Activity Have students play "Twenty Questions" for bones. Divide students into pairs and have them each write down a bone in the body. Using their knowledge of the organization of the skeleton, have them ask yes/no questions to discover the bone chosen by their opponent. Beginning questions may include "Am I part of the appendicular skeleton?" or "Am I a long bone?"*
Explain various musculoskeletal disease conditions and terms related to bone fractures.	☐ Pathology - Bones (p. 598)	PPT 43-45 IRM Multiple Choice Quiz questions 8-12, 17-19 IRM Pathology – Bones Quiz IRM Exercise Quiz questions 35-50 IRM Dictation and Comprehension Quiz IRM Spelling Quiz A MTO Module 15, Section II, Lesson 4

ELSEVIER

The Language of Medicine, 9th ed.

Chabner

OBJECTIVES	CONTENT	TEACHING RESOURCES
		Figure 15-14 Types of fractures (p. 599)
		Figure 15-15 Osteosarcoma (p. 599)
		Figure 15-16 Scanning electron micrograph (p. 600)
		Figure 15-17 Kyphosis (p. 601)
		Exercises J-L (pp. 628-629)
		Practical Applications (pp. 621-623)
		Class Activity Write out the names of each of the eight pathological conditions and fractures on flash cards. Have students draw a card and see if they can describe the condition and its treatment. If the student cannot, have other class members help out.
		Class Activity Have students write a quick paragraph describing the circumstances surrounding one of the fractures described and its treatment. At least 4 of the terms describing fractures must be used. Have them read their paragraphs to the class.

15.1 Homework/Assignments:

For each pathological condition of the bones, have students research the types of treatments that are used to alleviate the condition or treat the discomfort. Do this exercise for joints and muscle conditions as well, when you reach those lessons.

15.1 Teacher's Notes:

LESSON 15.2

CRITICAL THINKING QUESTION

Kathy has been a secretary for many years and is an excellent typist with a record number of words per minute. She has recently been complaining about a burning sensation in her middle finger that sometimes extends to her elbow. Her doctor gave her a splint to wear on her wrist to immobilize it while she types. What condition is he attempting to treat?

Guidelines: Kathy is likely suffering from carpal tunnel syndrome. This condition is due to compression of the median nerve as it passes between the ligament and the bones and tendons of the wrist. This nerve innervates the thumb, pointer, and middle finger and the medial side of the ring finger. Excessive supination, pronation, and dorsiflexion of the wrist during typing can cause swelling and pressure on the median nerve. Immobilizing the wrist, using antiinflammatory medications, and injecting cortisone into the carpal tunnel can help; surgical release of the carpal ligament might also be therapeutic.

OBJECTIVES	CONTENT	TEACHING RESOURCES
Define terms relating to the structure and function of bones, joints, and muscles.	■ Joints (p. 602) □ Types of joints (p. 602) □ Bursae (p. 602)	PPT 47-51 IRM Multiple Choice Quiz questions 20-23 IRM Exercise Quiz questions 1-6 IRM Dictation and Comprehension Quiz MTO Module 15, Section I, Lesson 9 Figure 15-18 Structure of synovial joint (p. 602) Figure 15-19 Sagittal section of the knee with bursae (p. 603) Exercise M (p. 629) *Class Activity Have students list sports injuries related to joints, then have students check the daily newspapers and extract all articles related to these types of injuries. Ask students who find such articles to report to the class.*
Analyze the combining forms, prefixes, and suffixes used to describe bones, joints, and muscles.	■ Vocabulary (p. 603) □ Terminology - Joints (p. 604) – Combining forms (p. 604) – Suffixes (p. 605)	PPT 52-54 IRM Terminology - Joints Quiz IRM Exercise Quiz questions 7-15 IRM Pronunciation Quiz C Exercise I (p. 627) Review Sheet (pp. 646-647) *Class Activity Divide the class into groups of three to five. Have each group write and perform a skit involving an allied health*

ELSEVIER

The Language of Medicine, 9th ed.

Chabner

OBJECTIVES	CONTENT	TEACHING RESOURCES
		professional and a patient. Students may add additional roles, however, they must use all the combining forms and suffixes.
		Class Activity Divide students into groups of three to five and give each a combining form or a suffix. Ask them to come up with as many terms related to the musculoskeletal system as possible, then report their results to the class. The use of dictionaries may help students check their answers and expand their knowledge beyond what is covered in the text.
Explain various musculoskeletal disease conditions and terms related to joints.	■ Pathology - Joints (p. 606)	▣ PPT 55-60
		📦 IRM Pathology – Joints Quiz
		📦 IRM Exercise Quiz questions 16-20
		📦 IRM Pronunciation Quiz C questions 1-9
		📦 IRM Practical Applications A questions 1-4 and B questions 1-2
		➤ MTO Module 15, Section II, Lessons 2-3
		Figure 15-20 Spinal stenosis (p. 605)
		Figure 15-21 Osteoarthritis and rheumatoid arthritis (p. 607)
		Figure 15-22 Carpal tunnel syndrome (p. 608)
		Figure 15-23 Protrusion of an intervertebral disk (p. 609)
		Figure 15-24 Butterfly rash (p. 610)
		Exercises N-P (pp. 629-631)
		◉ Companion CD Exercise 15-6
		Class Activity Have students work in groups to collect illustrations of the pathological conditions described in the text. Divide the conditions between the groups, so that all are covered. Each group member must provide at least 1 new illustration that shows the process of the disease and one new illustration that shows the appearance of the disease. Have students display their findings to the class.
		Class Activity Divide the class into four groups. Assign each group three pathological conditions, excluding arthritis. Have students create posters explaining what the conditions

OBJECTIVES	CONTENT	TEACHING RESOURCES
		are and how they are treated. They should also draw pictures illustrating the conditions. Have students present their posters to the class.

15.2 Homework/Assignments:

Ask students to do a report on the history and spread of Lyme disease in the United States.

Ask students to research the current choices of therapy for herniation of an intervertebral disk. How have these treatments progressed over time? Determine which treatments are considered invasive versus those that are not.

Ask students to prepare a report on bursitis. Ask them to try to discover how common it is, who is likely to suffer from it, how long bouts last, how it is treated, whether it can be prevented, and whether there is a cure.

15.2 Teacher's Notes:

LESSON 15.3

CRITICAL THINKING QUESTION

The types of muscle that make up each third of the esophagus (from pharynx to stomach) are characterized in the following way: upper third is skeletal muscle, middle third is mixed skeletal and smooth muscle, and lower third is smooth muscle. What do you think might be true of esophagus function that could help you to remember this histological "floor plan"?

Guidelines: Skeletal muscle is voluntary muscle and smooth muscle is involuntary. When one looks at the top of the esophagus, one realizes it lies close to the pharynx. Movement of the pharynx is voluntary and as you move your food around in your mouth and decide to swallow, you have voluntary (skeletal) muscle to help you accomplish that function. Once the food is making its way down the esophagus (after swallowing), you no longer have control of its destiny. Gradually, the esophagus gives way to involuntary muscle (final third), after a brief region (middle third) where there is a combination of both types of muscle in a "transition" zone.

OBJECTIVES	CONTENT	TEACHING RESOURCES
Define terms relating to the structure and function of bones, joints, and muscles.	■ Muscles (p. 611) ☐ Types of muscles (p. 611) ☐ Actions of skeletal muscle (p. 612)	PPT 62-69 IRM Multiple Choice Quiz questions 24, 25 IRM Exercise Quiz questions 21-39 IRM Dictation and Comprehension Quiz A, B MTO Module 15, Section I, Lessons 8-9 Figure 15-25 Types of muscles (p. 611) Figure 15-26 Selected muscles of the head, neck, torso, arm and their functions (p. 612) Figure 15-27 Origin and insertion of the biceps in the arm (p. 612) Figure 15-28 Types of muscular actions (p. 613) Exercises Q, R (pp. 631-632) *Class Activity Using a medical atlas, compare and contrast the differences between the three types of muscle. Have three student groups determine how the structure of the various muscle types supports their individual function. Use both electron and light micrographs to make the comparisons.*
Analyze the comining forms, prefixes, and suffixes used to describe bones, joints, and muscles.	■ Vocabulary (p. 614) ☐ Terminology - Muscles (p. 614) – Combining forms (p. 614) – Suffixes (p. 615)	PPT 70-73 IRM Terminology – Muscles Quiz IRM Exercise Quiz questions 7-15

ELSEVIER

The Language of Medicine, 9th ed.

Chabner

OBJECTIVES	CONTENT	TEACHING RESOURCES
	– Prefixes (p. 615)	***Class Activity** Ask students to obtain an article from a periodical or medical journal and underline at least 25 terms related to the musculoskeletal system. Ask students to exchange articles with one other and define the terms.* ***Class Activity** Read the terms in Exercise S to the students. Ask them to spell, analyze, define, and underline the accented syllable.*
Explain various musculoskeletal disease conditions and terms related to muscle.	☐ Pathology - Muscles (p. 616)	⊞ PPT 74 IRM Exercise Quiz questions 40-50 IRM Dictation and Comprehension Quiz A, B MTO Module 15, Section II, Lesson 1 Exercise S (p. 632) ***Class Activity** In pairs, have students role-play a medical assistant or a physician and a patient. They can be as creative as they like, but they must use at least five combining forms, suffixes, and prefixes (total) and one pathological condition. Have students perform their skits for the class.*
Identify important laboratory tests, clinical procedures, and abbreviations relating to the musculoskeletal system.	■ Laboratory tests, clinical procedures, and abbreviations (p. 616) ☐ Laboratory tests (p. 616) ☐ Clinical procedures (p. 616) ■ Abbreviations (p. 620)	⊞ PPT 75-76 IRM Laboratory Tests and Clinical Procedures Quiz IRM Abbreviations Quiz MTO Module 15, Section III, Lessons 1-3 Figure 15-29 Acetabular and femoral components of a total hip arthroplasty (p. 617) Figure 15-30 Knee replacement prosthesis (p. 617) Figure 15-31 Arthroscopy of the knee (p. 618) Figure 15-32 Bone density test (p. 618) Figure 15-33 Bone scan of skeleton (p. 619) Exercises S-W (pp. 632-635) Pronunciation of terms (pp. 639-645) Companion CD Exercise 15-7

ELSEVIER

OBJECTIVES	CONTENT	TEACHING RESOURCES
		Class Activity Terminology bingo: Make bingo cards with terminology about the musculoskeletal system. Have students act as rotating callers using the definitions to practice pronunciation. *Class Activity Play Alpha Quest with the class. Beginning with the letter A, ask the first student to name a term (or word component) that is associated with the musculoskeletal system. The next student is assigned the letter B, etc. If a student cannot think of a term, he/ she passes, and the next person tries. Students will get a workout with all of the terms for the system*
Apply your knowledge to understanding medical terms in their proper contexts, such as medical reports and records.	■ Practical Applications (p. 621)	IRM Practical Applications MTO, Module 15, Section V *Class Activity Divide students into two or three teams, depending on class size. Play a game in which you call out a combining term, prefix, suffix, disease, or other characteristic and the students identify whether it relates to bones, joints, or muscles. The game ends when the first team reaches 10 or 15 points.* *Class Activity Read the sentences in Exercise U to the class (or have students take turns reading them). Have them choose the correct answer, and spell, analyze, and underline the accented syllable.*
Performance Evaluation		IRM Multiple Choice Quiz IRM Terminology Quiz IRM Pathology Quiz IRM Laboratory Tests and Clinical Procedures Quiz IRM Exercise Quiz IRM Dictation and Comprehension Quiz IRM Spelling Quiz IRM Pronunciation Quiz IRM Abbreviations Quiz

OBJECTIVES	CONTENT	TEACHING RESOURCES
		IRM Diagram Quiz
		IRM Vocabulary Quiz
		IRM Review Sheet Quiz
		IRM Medical Scramble
		IRM Crossword Puzzle
		IRM Practical Applications
		ESLR Student Quiz Chapter 15
		MTO Module 15, Sections I-III quizzes
		MTO Module 15 Exam
		Companion CD Exercises 15-8, 15-9, 15-10
		iTerms Chapter 15

15.3 Homework/Assignments:

Have students do a report comparing the medical approach versus the yoga approach of treatment for any ailment. Have students explore the varieties of healthcare professionals that treat disorders of the musculoskeletal system. Include alternative therapies, such as yoga and massage therapy, as well as occupational therapy, physical therapy, chiropractic, etc.

15.3 Teacher's Notes:

ELSEVIER

Chabner

Slide 1

The Language Of Medicine
9th edition
Davi-Ellen Chabner

Slide 2

Chapter 15
Musculoskeletal System

Slide 3

Chapter Goals

- Define terms relating to the structure and function of bones, joints, and muscles.
- Describe the process of bone formation and growth.
- Locate and name the major bones of the body.

Slide 4

Chapter Goals (cont'd)

- Analyze the combining forms, prefixes, and suffixes used to describe bones, joints, and muscles.
- Explain various musculoskeletal disease conditions and terms related to bone fractures.

Slide 5

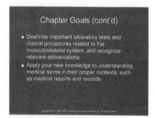

Chapter Goals (cont'd)

- Describe important laboratory tests and clinical procedures related to the musculoskeletal system, and recognize relevant abbreviations.
- Apply your new knowledge to understanding medical terms in their proper contexts, such as medical reports and records.

ELSEVIER

Slide 6

Slide 7

- Which bones are located in the face?
- Which bones support and protect the internal organs of the body?
- Which muscles are most often used when an athlete is in training to run in a marathon?
- What are common joint injuries?

Slide 8

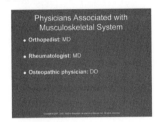

- Ask students who have had a broken bone to report to the class about the situation. Which bone was broken? How long did it take to heal? What was the treatment? Were any tests or procedures given prior to the diagnosis?

Slide 9

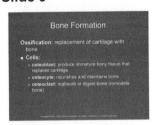

- Discuss bone formation and remodeling throughout life.
- What steps can people take to help with bone formation?
- Calcium: what role does it play? How much is enough? Where can you find it?
- How does phosphorous affect bones?
- Why is Vitamin D so valuable to the bones?

Slide 10

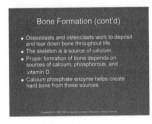

- Which foods provide Vitamin D? How does Vitamin D affect bones?
- How much Vitamin D do you need per day?

The Language of Medicine, 9th ed.
Chabner

Slide 11

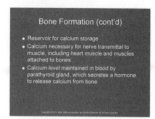

- Where is the parathyroid gland located and how does it function?
- What happens when you have too much calcium?
- What happens if you have too little calcium?

Slide 12

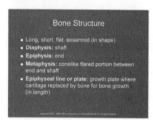

- What minerals and vitamins help with bone formation?
- What happens if a bone is incorrectly formed?

Slide 13

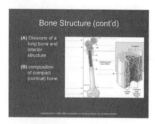

- Fill in the correct names where the numbers are located using the text.

Slide 14

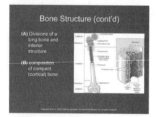

Slide 15

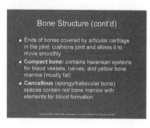

- Which of these bones is porous? How does this occur?
- As a child ages, what happens to the red bone marrow? Where is it located in young children?

ELSEVIER

The Language of Medicine, 9th ed.

Chabner

Slide 16

- What is the function of bone marrow?

Slide 17

- What are the major named processes and depressions?

Slide 18

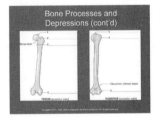

Slide 19

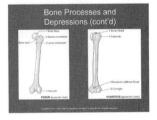

Slide 20

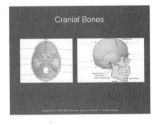

- What are the important bones of the skull?
- How do they correspond to the brain?
- Why do newborn babies need to have their heads well protected?
- What happens when a baby is severely shaken?

Slide 21

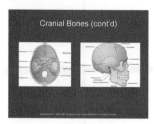

- What are the important bones of the skull?
- How do they correspond to the brain?
- Why do newborn babies need to have their heads well protected?
- What happens when a baby is severely shaken?

Slide 22

- Which bones aid in chewing, seeing, and breathing?

Slide 23

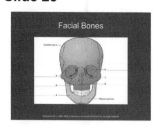

- Ask students to insert correct names of bones in the numbered diagram.

Slide 24

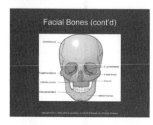

- Ask students to review correct names of bones in the numbered diagram.

Slide 25

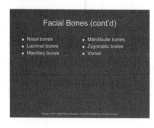

- Which bones contain fossae for lacrimal gland and canals for duct?
- What condition occurs if the maxillary bones do not separate at birth? (*cleft palate*)
- Which bones might be adjusted during rhinoplasty?
- What are the "cheek bones"?

ELSEVIER

Chabner

Slide 26

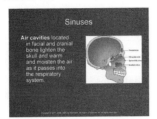

Slide 27

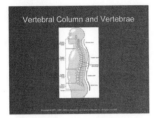

- Why is the human vertebral column subject to injury?

Slide 28

- What are the 4 vertebral regions?
- How many bones are there in each region?
- Way to help students remember the numbers:
  - Cervical 7 am breakfast
  - Thoracic 12 pm lunch
  - Lumbar 5 pm dinner

Slide 29

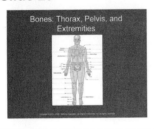

- Ask students to insert names on diagram with class.

Slide 30

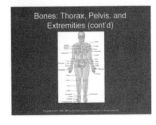

- Ask students to insert names on diagram with class.

Slide 31

- Ask students to close their textbooks and then identify the bones listed on their own bodies.
- Which are the true ribs? How are they connected to the sternum?
- Which are false ribs? Why are they so designated?
- Which are the proximal, middle, and distal phalanges?

Slide 32

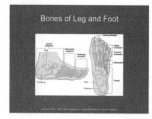

- There are seven bones of the leg and foot.
- Have students identify bones shown in the figure.

Slide 33

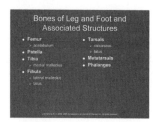

- Which are the bones of the foot?
- What happens if you wear shoes that are too small?
- Which is the largest bone in the body?

Slide 34

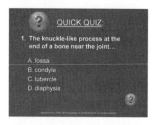

- Correct answer is B: condyle

Slide 35

- Correct answer is B: ossification

Slide 36

Slide 37

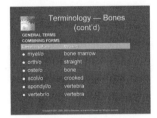

Slide 38

Slide 39

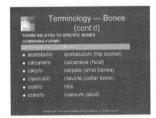

Slide 40

Slide 41

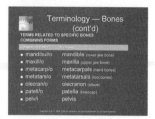

Slide 42

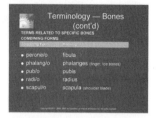

Slide 43

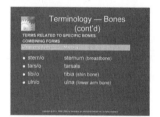

Slide 44

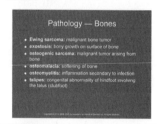

- Ask students to describe a Ewing sarcoma. How old are people who suffer from this condition? What treatment can be given?

- Is there any treatment for clubfoot?

- What is the difference between osteogenic sarcoma and bone cancer that has metastasized from the breast cancer or prostate?

- How does a broken leg with internal fixation increase the chance of osteomyelitis?

Slide 45

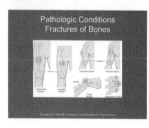

- What is the definition of a fracture?

- What are the common names used for specific types of fractures?

- What does reduction mean as it pertains to fractures?

Slide 46

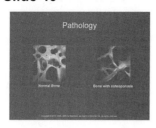

- Image A: normal bone
- Image B: bone with osteoporosis
- What is osteoporosis? (decrease in bone density; thinning and weakening of bone)
- How often should women get a bone density test?

Slide 47

Slide 48

- What are some examples of places on the body with joints?

Slide 49

Slide 50

- Name examples of bursae, such as elbow, knee and shoulder joints.
- Which sports injuries are related to this topic?
- Which bursae are associated with the knee and elbow?

The Language of Medicine, 9th ed.

Chabner

Slide 51

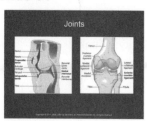

- Give the students examples of joints that look like the ones depicted in these figures.

Slide 52

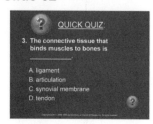

- Correct answer is D: tendon

Slide 53

Slide 54

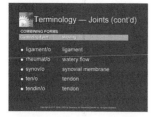

Slide 55

Chabner

Slide 56

- Can young people suffer from arthritis?
- What is the most common complaint of older individuals?
- What treatments are available for people who suffer from osteoarthritis? Rheumatoid arthritis?
- What is commonly known as degenerative joint disease?

Slide 57

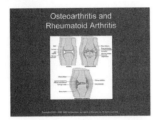

- Why do osteoarthritis and rheumatoid arthritis occur?
- What are the differences between the two types of arthritis?

Slide 58

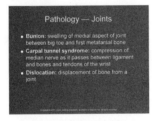

- Why do women get bunions more often than men?

Slide 59

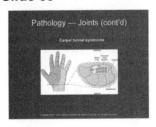

- Why is carpal tunnel syndrome considered a repetitive stress injury?
- What can be done to alleviate carpal tunnel syndrome?
- Ask students if they have suffered from carpal tunnel syndrome, and if so, what treatment was applied?
- Ganglion: fluid filled cyst arising from joint capsule or tendon in the wrist

Slide 60

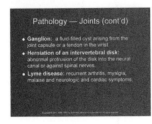

- How is sciatica related to herniated nucleus pulposus (*HNP*)?
- What is the cause of Lyme disease?
- What is the main carrier of Lyme disease in the United States (*deer tick*)
- Define the term "vector".

ELSEVIER

The Language of Medicine, 9th ed.

Chabner

Slide 61

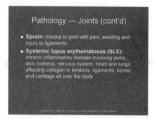

- Ask the students if they have ever had a sprain to an ankle or knee.
- Systemic lupus erythematosus (SLE), commonly called "lupus," is believed to be an autoimmune disease. What is the accepted treatment?
- Why does a rheumatologist treat a lupus patient? (*arthritis*)

Slide 62

Slide 63

- Which muscles are striated in appearance, smooth in character?

Slide 64

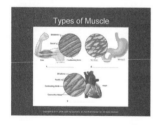

- Go over the figure with students, pointing to the parts of the arm where they are most likely to notice striations.
- Ask the students to describe smooth muscles.

Slide 65

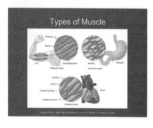

- Go over the figure with students, pointing to the parts of the arm where they are most likely to notice striations.
- Ask the students to describe smooth muscles.

ELSEVIER

The Language of Medicine, 9th ed.

Chabner

Slide 66

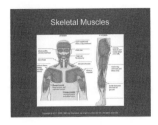

- Go over the figure with the students. Ask them to add labels to the figure.
- Students who exercise or are in weight training may be familiar with various muscle groups.
- Can students name some muscle groups that are not pictured here? (e.g., latissimus dorsii, abductors, adductors)

Slide 67

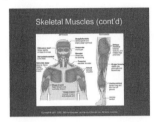

- Go over the figure with the students.
- Students who exercise or are in weight training may be familiar with various muscle groups.
- Can students name some muscle groups that are not pictured here? (e.g., latissimus dorsii, abductors, adductors)

Slide 68

- Go over these definitions and demonstrate the movement on individuals.

Slide 69

Slide 70

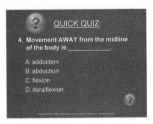

- Correct answer is B: adduction

Slide 71

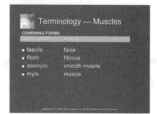

Slide 72

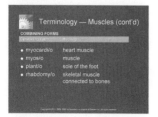

Slide 73

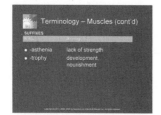

Slide 74

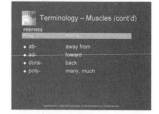

Slide 75

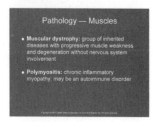

- Muscular dystrophy typically affects children.

The Language of Medicine, 9th ed.

Chabner

Slide 76

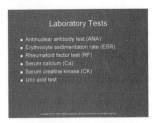

- For what conditions might an ESR be requested?

- For what conditions would CK be indicated?

- What is a uric acid test used to diagnose? (*gout*)

Slide 77

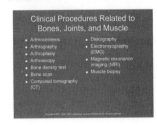

- If there are tests that students have seen before, discuss why they are appropriate for use in muscle-related disorders.

- If they are new, discuss how they are uniquely able to diagnose and treat conditions pertaining to muscle.

Chabner

TEACHING FOCUS

Students will have an opportunity to learn about skin, the largest organ in the body. Skin functions include thermoregulation, protection from foreign antigens, protection from desiccation, and sensation of the environment for pain, temperature, pressure, and touch. The student will become familiar with terms associated with the medical specialty of dermatology. The student will be introduced to pathological conditions of the skin and the laboratory procedures used for diagnosis and treatment of these abnormalities. Finally, the student will apply gained knowledge to understanding medical terms in the context of medical reports and records related to skin (also known as integument).

MATERIALS AND RESOURCES

- ☐ Bingo cards (Lesson 16.3)
- ☐ Dermatology journals (all Lessons)
- ☐ Flash cards or transparencies (Lessons 16.1, 16.3)
- ☐ Medical pathology textbooks (all Lessons)
- ☐ Transparency or PowerPoint slide of unlabeled, numbered illustration of the skin (Figure 16-1) (Lesson 16.1)
- ☐ Word-building game board and tiles (Lesson 16.3)

LESSON CHECKLIST

Preparations for this lesson include:
- Lecture
- Method of student performance evaluation for entry-level knowledge of the structure and function of the integumentary system, including:
  - o terminology associated with skin structures
  - o lesions, symptoms, and pathological conditions relating to the skin
  - o identification of laboratory tests, clinical procedures, and abbreviations

KEY TERMS

Vocabulary (pp. 655)

adipocyte	lunula
albino	melanin
apocrine sweat gland	paronychium
basal layer	pore
collagen	sebaceous gland
cuticle	sebum
dermis	squamous epithelium
epidermis	stratified
epithelium	stratum, strata
hair follicle	stratum corneum
integumentary system	subcutaneous layer
keratin	

Terminology (pp. 656-660)

adip/o	ichthy/o
albin/o	kerat/o
caus/o	leuk/o
cauter/o	lip/o
cutane/o	melan/o
derm/o	myc/o
dermat/o	onych/o
diaphor/o	phyt/o
erythem/o	pil/o
erythemat/o	py/o
hidr/o	rhytid/o

Chabner

seb/o
squam/o
steat/o
trich/o

ungu/o
xanth/o
xer/o

Cutaneous Lesions (pp. 662-663)

crust
cyst
erosion
fissure
macule
nodule

papule
polyp
pustule
ulcer
vesicle
wheal

Signs and Symptoms (pp. 664-665)

alopecia
ecchymosis, ecchymoses
petechia, petechiae
pruritis
urticaria (hives)

Abnormal Conditions (pp. 665-669)

acne
burns
cellulitis
eczema
exanthematous viral diseases
gangrene
impetigo

psoriasis
scabies
scleroderma
systemic lupus erythematosus (SLE)
tinea
vitiligo

Skin Neoplasms (pp. 669-672)

basal cell carcinoma
callus
Kaposi sarcoma
keloid
keratosis

leukoplakia
malignant melanoma
nevus, nevi
squamous cell carcinoma
verruca

Laboratory Tests and Clinical Procedures (p. 672)

bacterial analyses
cryosurgery
curettage
eletrodesiccation

fungal tests
Mohs surgery
skin biopsy
skin test

REFERENCE LIST

PowerPoint slides (CD, Evolve): 1-63

Legend

CD
Companion
CD

iTerms

IRM
Instructor's
Resource Manual
available on CD
and Evolve

Evolve
Evolve
Resources

PPT
PowerPoint
Slides

MTO
Medical
Terminology
Online

Class Activities are indicated in ***bold italic***.

ELSEVIER

The Language of Medicine, 9th ed.

Chabner

LESSON 16.1

PRETEST
IRM Exercise Quiz A

BACKGROUND ASSESSMENT

Question: What are the structures in the skin and its accessory organs?
Answer: The epidermis, dermis, and subcutaneous tissue; the sebaceous glands, the sudoriferous glands, hair, and nails.

Question: Are you familiar with any skin disorders?
Answer: Answers may vary, but students may identify acne, eczema, psoriasis, warts, and skin cancer.

Question: What types of glands in the skin are responsible for the condition called acne? Where are these glands located, and how do they produce acne?
Answer: Sebaceous glands are located in the dermal layer of the skin where there are hair follicles. They are not located on the palms of the hand or the soles of the feet. They secrete an oily substance called sebum. Their ducts open into hair follicles, and they lubricate the hair and the skin. They are influenced by sex hormones, and during puberty they are very active. If the sebum builds up in the pores of the skin, it can block the pores and cause blackheads or whiteheads. Bacteria break down the sebum and cause inflammation. Together these two occurrences lead to acne.

Question: Which component of the skin is responsible for the stretch marks that pregnant women get when their bellies become very large?
Answer: The extensibility and elasticity of skin results from connective tissue fibers in the dermis made of elastin and collagen. These are protein materials with different degrees of flexibility. These fibers are highly flexible in children and are loosely interwoven. As a person ages, the fibers get tougher. When a woman's abdominal skin stretches during pregnancy, overstretching of the skin occurs and breaks the elastic fibers, resulting in linear marks called striae, or stretch marks.

CRITICAL THINKING QUESTION

How does the function of melanin explain not only the variety of skin colors but susceptibility to skin cancer?
Guidelines: Deep in the basal layer of the epidermis there are cells called melanocytes. Melanocytes contain a brown-black pigment called melanin that is actually transferred to other epidermal cells to produce skin color. The number of these cells in the individual is not any different between races, but the amount of melanin contained by each cell accounts for racial differences in skin color. Melanin is critically important for protection from ultraviolet (UV) radiation. It is produced more with exposure to the sun, which actually protects an individual from effects such as wrinkles, permanent pigment changes, and cancer. When the melanin cannot absorb large amounts of UV radiation, skin gets burned. People who have more melanin and can produce more with sun exposure are less likely to get skin cancers because the UV rays do not damage their skin as readily.

OBJECTIVES	CONTENT	TEACHING RESOURCES
Identify the layers of the skin and the accessory structures associated with the skin.	■ Introduction (p. 650) ■ Anatomy of the skin (p. 650) □ Epidermis (p. 650) □ Dermis (corium) (p. 652) □ Subcutaneous layer (p. 652) ■ Accessory structures of the skin (p. 653)	PPT 5-15 IRM Multiple Choice Quiz questions 1-6 IRM Exercises Quiz A, B MTO Module 16, Section I, Lessons 1-2 Exercise A, B (p. 651) Exercise C questions 1, 2, 5-8 (p. 652)

ELSEVIER

Chabner

OBJECTIVES	CONTENT	TEACHING RESOURCES
	☐ Hair (p. 653) ☐ Nails (p. 653) ☐ Glands (p. 654) ■ Vocabulary (p. 655)	Figure 16-1 The skin (p. 651) Figure 16-2 Hair follicle (p. 652) Figure 16-3 (A) Anatomic structure of a nail; (B) Onycholysis (p. 653) Figure 16-4 Sebaceous gland, eccrine sweat gland, and apocrine sweat gland (p. 654) ⊙ Companion CD Exercises 16-1, 16-2 *Class Activity Show a transparency or PowerPoint slide of an unlabeled, numbered illustration of the skin (Figure 16-1, p. 631). Call out a number and ask students to name the structure. Students who answer correctly may take turns calling out the numbers on the diagram.*
Build medical words using the combining forms that are related to the specialty of dermatology.	■ Terminology (p. 656) ☐ Combining forms (p. 656)	▣ PPT 16-23 🗑 IRM Multiple Choice Quiz questions 5-12 🗑 IRM Terminology Quiz 🗑 IRM Dictation and Comprehension Quizzes Table 16-1 Colors (p. 656) Figure 16-5 A, Atrophic dermatitis; B, Erythema infectiosum (p. 657) Figure 16-6 A, Ichthyosis; B, Leukoplakia (p. 658) Figure 16-7 A, Athlete's Foot; B, Acute paronychia (p. 659) Figure 16-8 A, Impetigo; B, Xanthelasmas (p. 661) Exercise B-E (pp. 675-677) Review Sheet (pp. 690-691) ⊙ Companion CD Exercises 16-3, 16-4 *Class Activity Divide the class into three groups and have each choose a contestant for a game show. Using dermatology flash cards or transparencies, show the contestants a variety of combining forms one at a time. Ask them to define each word element correctly and give an example of its use in a term. Award a point to the first contestant to answer*

OBJECTIVES	CONTENT	TEACHING RESOURCES
		correctly. When a contestant answers incorrectly, the team chooses a new contestant. **Class Activity** *Ask students to divide into pairs to use flash cards to practice the word components.*

16.1 Homework/Assignments:

Ask the students to write short reports on how conditions of the hair, nails, and glands can help diagnose other diseases. Then have them report these findings to the class.

16.1 Teacher's Notes:

LESSON 16.2

CRITICAL THINKING QUESTION

How does a decubitus ulcer develop and why is it a serious condition?

Guidelines: Decubiti are also called pressure ulcers, because they develop over time when pressure is exerted on the skin. The constant pressure causes the skin to break down and unless it is addressed, it can cause the tissue to deteriorate until the bone is exposed. Because the skin is in the first line of defense for the immune system, any breakdown allows pathogens into the body.

OBJECTIVES	CONTENT	TEACHING RESOURCES
Describe lesions, symptoms, and pathological conditions that relate to the skin.	■ Pathology (p. 662) ☐ Cutaneous lesions (p. 662) ☐ Signs and symptoms (p. 664) ☐ Abnormal conditions (p. 641)	PPT 25-37 IRM Multiple Choice Quiz IRM Pathology Quiz IRM Exercise Quiz D-G IRM Dictation and Comprehension Quiz: Lesions, Symptoms, Abnormal Conditions, and Neoplasms IRM Spelling Quiz IRM Pronunciation Quiz IRM Diagram Quiz IRM Practical Applications MTO Module 16, Section II, Lessons 1-5 Figure 16-9 Cutaneous lesions (p. 663) Figure 16-10 A, Alopecia areata; B, Ecchymosis; C, Petechiae; D, Urticaria (p. 664) Figure 16-11 A, Blackhead formation; B, Acne vulgaris (p. 665) Figure 16-12 A, Second-degree burn; B, Third-degree burn (p. 666) Figure 16-13 Cellulitis (p. 666) Figure 16-14 Psoriasis (p. 667) Figure 16-15 A, Tinea corporis; B, Tinia unguium (p. 668) Figure 16-16 Vitiligo (p. 669) Practical Applications (pp. 673-674) Exercises F-L (pp. 678-681)

ELSEVIER

Chabner

OBJECTIVES	CONTENT	TEACHING RESOURCES
		Companion CD Exercises 16-5, 16-6
		Class Activity Have students research the various skin disorders listed and find an illustration of each. Arrange a class display to view their findings.
		Class Activity Have students cut out newspaper articles or advertisements for therapies that address signs and symptoms of skin disease. Have each student underline 25 (or fewer) terms in this context. Have students exchange articles and define the terms in a classmate's article. Then ask each student to present the list to the class.
		Class Activity Students should divide pathological skin conditions into a list of those that are caused from the "outside" (e.g., contact dermatitis) and those that are caused by a systemic disease or genetic disorder or both. Have students explain how they determined their classification schemes. Which types occur more often? Do treatments differ depending on the etiology?

16.2 Homework/Assignments:

16.2 Teacher's Notes:

Chabner

LESSON 16.3

CRITICAL THINKING QUESTION

Question: Mary is suspicious that her recent headaches and sinus drip result from allergies. Her doctor has told her that she needs to come in for some skin tests to help him determine what allergies she might have. Why does Mary's doctor want to do skin tests when her allergies do not seem to affect her skin?

Guidelines: Skin tests can be used to see the body's reaction to a substance by observing the results after injecting it intradermally or by applying it topically to the skin. In a patch test, an allergen-treated piece of gauze or filter paper is applied to the skin. If the skin becomes red or swollen, it is considered a positive test. In a scratch test, many scratches are made in the skin and a very small amount of potential allergens are inserted into the scratches. Again, a positive reaction results when the area becomes inflamed or swollen.

OBJECTIVES	CONTENT	TEACHING RESOURCES
Describe lesions, symptoms, and pathological conditions that relate to the skin.	☐ Skin neoplasms (p. 669) – Benign neoplasms (p. 669) – Cancerous lesions (p. 670)	PPT 39-44 IRM Multiple Choice Quiz questions 19, 23 IRM Exercise Quiz G question 58; Quiz H question 64 IRM Dictation and Comprehension Quiz MTO Module 16, Section II, Lessons 6-7 Figure 16-17 A, Callus; B, keloid (p. 669) Figure 16-18 A, Actinic keratosis; B, Verruca vulgaris (p. 670) Figure 16-19 A, Basal cell carcinoma; B, Squamous cell carcinoma (p. 671) Figure 16-20 The ABCDEs of melanoma (p. 671) Exercises H-L (pp. 679-681) *Class Activity Have students look up therapies for the abnormal conditions of the skin that they have been studying. Use the therapies and applicable descriptions to create a "skin" crossword puzzle. Divide the class into four groups for this exercise and create four puzzles. Have groups exchange puzzles and do them as a group exercise.* *Class Activity Create a set of bingo cards with a different skin-related term from the chapter in each box (5 x 5); vary the terms and/or the order so cards are not all alike. Create a list of definitions corresponding to the terms on the bingo cards. Call out a definition.*

The Language of Medicine, 9th ed.

Chabner

OBJECTIVES	CONTENT	TEACHING RESOURCES
		Students must circle the correct term on the bingo card. The first student to complete bingo wins. If a student claims to have bingo and is incorrect, he or she is disqualified from that round. *Class Activity Use terms from all three lesson plans and throughout the chapter. Have students create flash cards containing the terms from the chapter on one side and the meanings on the other. Abbreviations are permitted as well. Take the cards and create place cards for bingo. The caller can use the flash cards to play "skin terms bingo."*
Identify laboratory tests, clinical procedures, and abbreviations that pertain to the skin.	■ Laboratory tests and clinical procedures (p. 672) 　□ Laboratory tests (p. 672) 　□ Clinical procedures (p. 672) ■ Abbreviations (p. 673)	⊠ PPT 45-48 🎁 IRM Multiple Choice Quiz question 25 🎁 IRM Laboratory Tests and Clinical Procedures Quiz 🔺 MTO Module 16, Section III, Lessons 1-2 Exercises M, N (pp. 682-683) *Class Activity Divide students into groups and have them use a crossword puzzle generator to develop puzzles for the laboratory tests, clinical procedures, and abbreviations. Have them copy their puzzles and trade with another group. Have them complete the other team's puzzle.*
Apply your new knowledge to understanding medical terms in their proper contexts, such as medical reports and records.	■ Practical applications (p. 673)	⊠ PPT 49-62 🎁 IRM Practical Applications 🔺 MTO Module 16, Section V *Class Activity Divide the class into two competing teams. Give each team a set of different flash cards with terms related to the skin. The teams take turns showing a card to the opponent, who must define the term. Award a point for each correct answer. However, the presenting team loses a point for accepting an incorrect answer or rejecting a correct answer.* *Class Activity Read the sentences (or ask students to take turns reading them) in Exercise N of the text. Ask students to choose the correct answer, spell, analyze, define, and underline the accented syllable.*

OBJECTIVES	CONTENT	TEACHING RESOURCES
		Class Activity Have students play Alpha Quest, naming a condition or a structure for each letter of the alphabet. Ask them to work in teams. The team that wins is the one that has identified the most terms.
Performance Evaluation		IRM Multiple Choice Quiz
		IRM Terminology Quiz
		IRM Pathology Quiz
		IRM Laboratory Tests and Clinical Procedures Quiz
		IRM Exercise Quiz
		IRM Dictation and Comprehension Quiz
		IRM Spelling Quiz
		IRM Pronunciation Quiz
		IRM Diagram Quiz
		IRM Vocabulary Quiz
		IRM Review Sheet Quiz
		IRM Medical Scramble
		IRM Crossword Puzzle
		IRM Practical Applications
		ESLR Body Spectrum Electronic Anatomy Coloring Book, Integumentary
		ESLR Student Quiz, Chapter 16
		MTO Module 16, Sections I-III quizzes
		MTO Module 16 Exam
		Companion CD Exercises 16-7, 16-8, 16-9
		iTerms Chapter 16

Chabner

16.3 Homework/Assignments:

Have each student research one skin-related clinical procedure. Using medical textbooks and the Internet, have them show pictures of the results of each procedure (e.g., a picture of a skin biopsy) and then prepare a report. Each student should provide a 200-word abstract of the clinical report associated with the procedure. Give all students copies of the abstracts. Have students find combining forms within the abstracts and underline them.

16.3 Teacher's Notes:

Slide 1

The Language Of Medicine
9th edition
Davi-Ellen Chabner

Slide 2

Chapter 16
Skin

Slide 3

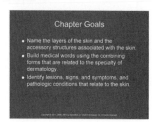

Chapter Goals

- Name the layers of the skin and the accessory structures associated with the skin.
- Build medical words using the combining forms that are related to the specialty of dermatology.
- Identify lesions, signs, and symptoms, and pathologic conditions that relate to the skin.

Slide 4

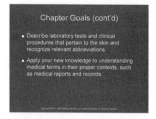

Chapter Goals (cont'd)

- Describe laboratory tests and clinical procedures that pertain to the skin and recognize relevant abbreviations.
- Apply your new knowledge to understanding medical terms in their proper contexts, such as medical reports and records.

Slide 5

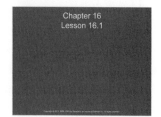

Chapter 16
Lesson 16.1

Slide 6

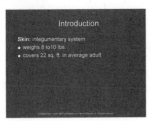

- What tissues can you predict will be integrated into this organ system?
- What are the unique qualities of epithelium that make it a suitable tissue for covering the body?
- How is the epithelium on the "outside" (part of the skin) similar to that on the inside of the body?

Slide 7

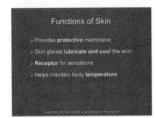

- Have students define *desiccation*. Ask them to list three ways that skin guards against desiccation.
- How does skin guard against acidic secretions?

Slide 8

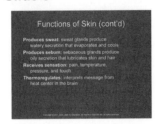

- Ask the students to define the word *thermoregulate*. How does the skin thermoregulate?
- There are multiple mechanisms for thermal control. Describe at least three or four.

Slide 9

- What does the epidermis lack? Ask the students to describe what it is dependent upon.
- What is the dermis composed of? Ask the students to describe what supports this layer.
- Ask the students what lipocytes are and where they are found.

Slide 10

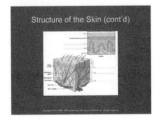

- In the inset of this picture (B) you can see what are called dermal papillae. They look like wavy folds. What is the advantage of this kind of tissue architecture?
- The dermis appears to be pushing up folds into the epidermis. Why?
- Is the epithelium vascular? Why is that an advantage or disadvantage?

Slide 11

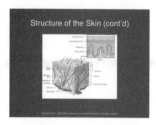

- In the inset of this picture (B) you can see what are called dermal papillae. They look like wavy folds. What is the advantage of this kind of tissue architecture?

- The dermis appears to be pushing up folds into the epidermis. Why?

- Is the epithelium vascular? Why is that an advantage or disadvantage?

Slide 12

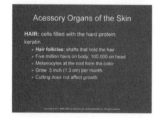

- Ask the students to describe melanocytes and where they can be found.

- What functions does hair have? (*sensory, thermoregulation*)

Slide 13

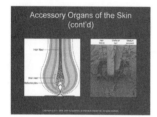

Slide 14

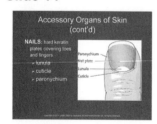

- How are hair, nails, and epidermis alike?

- How do these structures grow and slough off cells?

Slide 15

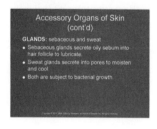

- Why do people have so many sweat glands?

- Could people live without sweat glands?

- Do sebaceous glands make hair feel oily?

Chabner

Slide 16

- Why do people have so many sweat glands?
- Could people live without sweat glands?
- Do sebaceous glands make hair feel oily?

Slide 17

Slide 18

Slide 19

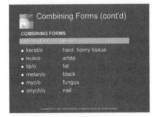

Slide 20

Chabner

Slide 21

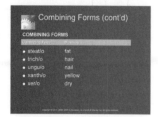

Slide 22

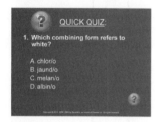

- Correct answer is D: albin/o means white as in albinism

Slide 23

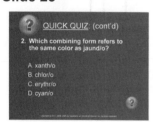

- Correct answer is A: xanth/o means yellow as in xanthoma

Slide 24

Slide 25

Slide 26

- What is the definition of a lesion?
- Which of these lesions are similar but are differentiated by size?
- Which lesions involve the dermis layer?

Slide 27

- What is the definition of a lesion?
- Which of these lesions are similar but are differentiated by size?
- Which lesions involve the dermis layer?

Slide 28

- What are some causes of alopecia?
- Are there any treatments for baldness? Are they successful?
- Another form of alopecia is a result of trichotillomania, or obsessive hair-pulling.

Slide 29

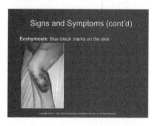

- What can cause ecchymosis?
- What is the treatment?

Slide 30

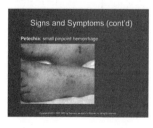

- Use the pictures as examples. Ask students whether they have ever been diagnosed with any of the skin conditions mentioned.
- What diseases are associated with these symptoms?
- What is pruritus?
- What is purpura?

ELSEVIER

The Language of Medicine, 9th ed.

Chabner

Slide 31

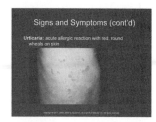

- What is the common term for urticaria?
- Have students discuss their experiences (or that of someone they know) with hives.
- What causes hives? How long do they last?

Slide 32

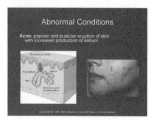

- What is the medical term for a blackhead?
- Why are adolescents so prone to acne? Myths and reality.
- Are over-the-counter treatments effective?

Slide 33

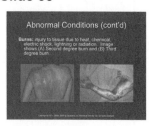

- Go over the different degrees of burns and use a chart with the layers of the skin to demonstrate how deep the burns go.
- What percentage of body burn results in death? Why?

Slide 34

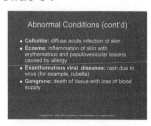

- Which of these diseases is/are common in children? Why?
- What are other diseases that are similar to eczema? Are they all treated in the same way?

Slide 35

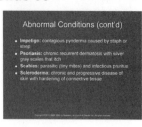

- Which of these diseases are NOT contagious?
- Which disease may worsen if the patient experiences anxiety?

The Language of Medicine, 9th ed.

Chabner

Slide 36

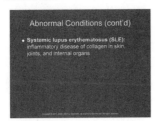

- What are the current thoughts about the origin of SLE? How is it treated?
- Where have we discussed it before because of other organ systems it affects?

Slide 37

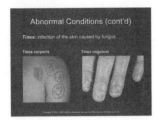

- What is tinea? (*fungal infection of skin or nails, that is, ringworm, athlete's foot*)

Slide 38

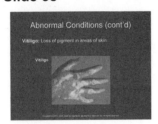

- What is vitiligo? (*loss of pigment in areas of skin causing milk-white patches*)

Slide 39

Slide 40

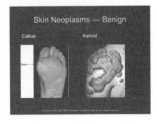

- What is a callus? (*increased growth of cells in keratin layer of epidermis due to friction against skin*)
- What is a keloid? (*hypertrophied, thickened scar after trauma or surgery*)
- Ask for student examples of places that commonly develop calluses. Why?
- Some people who are prone to keloids are discouraged from having their ears pierced.

Slide 41

- Have students find images for abnormalities not shown in the text. Images are very useful for remembering these conditions.

Slide 42

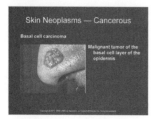

- Refer back to the chapter that included AIDS.

- Why are AIDS patients susceptible to this condition?

- Why does it rarely occur in the rest of the population?

Slide 43

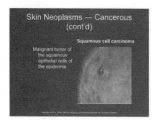

- Refer back to the chapter that included AIDS.

- Why are AIDS patients susceptible to this condition?

- Why does it rarely occur in the rest of the population?

Slide 44

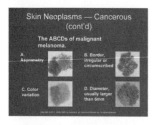

- These skin tumors often metastasize to the lung, liver, bone, and brain. What is the current treatment for this type of cancer?

- Squamous cells can grow wherever there is squamous epithelium (internal or external). Common places include the mouth, larynx, bladder, esophagus, and lungs. Some are cigarette-related.

- Why are healthy organs lined with squamous cells in the first place? What about this tissue makes it appropriate for those particular organ systems?

Slide 45

- Refer back to the chapter that included AIDS.

- Why are AIDS patients susceptible to this condition?

- Why does it rarely occur in the rest of the population?

Chabner

Slide 46

Slide 47

- For what conditions is electrodesiccation recommended?

Slide 48

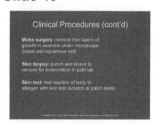

- Discuss how some of the surgeries are for both diagnosis and treatment. Removal is done whether or not the physician knows that the lesion is cancerous.
- All suspicious-looking tissues removed from the body are sent to the pathology lab for analysis. Why?

Slide 49

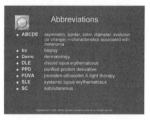

- Ask students to provide the full terms for these abbreviations.

Slide 50

Chabner

Slide 51

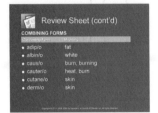

Review Sheet (cont'd)

COMBINING FORMS

Combining Form	Meaning
adip/o	fat
albin/o	white
caus/o	burn, burning
cauter/o	heat, burn
cutane/o	skin
derm/o	skin

Slide 52

Review Sheet (cont'd)

COMBINING FORMS

Combining Form	Meaning
dermat/o	
diaphor/o	
erythem/o	
erythemat/o	
hidr/o	
ichthy/o	

Slide 53

Review Sheet (cont'd)

COMBINING FORMS

Combining Form	Meaning
dermat/o	skin
diaphor/o	profuse sweating
erythem/o	redness
erythemat/o	redness
hidr/o	sweat
ichthy/o	scaly, dry

Slide 54

Review Sheet (cont'd)

COMBINING FORMS

Combining Form	Meaning
kerat/o	
leuk/o	
lip/o	
melan/o	
myc/o	
onych/o	

Slide 55

Review Sheet (cont'd)

COMBINING FORMS

Combining Form	Meaning
kerat/o	hard, horny tissue
leuk/o	white
lip/o	fat
melan/o	black
myc/o	fungus
onych/o	nail

The Language of Medicine, 9th ed.

Chabner

Slide 56

Slide 57

Slide 58

Slide 59

Slide 60

ELSEVIER

The Language of Medicine, 9th ed.
Chabner

Slide 61

Slide 62

Slide 63

Chabner

TEACHING FOCUS

Students will have the opportunity to learn the anatomy and physiology of two key sense organs: the eye and the ear. Students will have the opportunity to learn symptoms and pathologies, as well as common medical procedures, associated with these organs. Finally, the chapter provides an overview of combining forms, suffixes, and terminology related to these sense organs and how they can be properly applied in the context of medical reports and records.

MATERIALS AND RESOURCES

- ☐ Copies of articles from ophthalmology journals (Lesson 17.1)
- ☐ Diagrams of eyes with errors of refraction (Lesson 17.1)
- ☐ Aural thermometer (Lesson 17.3)
- ☐ Key term bingo cards (Lesson 17.1)

- ☐ Otoscope (Lesson 17.3)
- ☐ Snellen eye chart (Lesson 17.2)
- ☐ Transparency or PowerPoint slide of the eye and the ear (Lesson 17.1)
- ☐ Tuning fork (Lesson 17.3)
- ☐ Visual pathway chart (Lesson 17.1)

LESSON CHECKLIST

Preparations for this lesson include:

- Lecture
- Demonstration
- Student performance evaluation of all entry-level skills required for student comprehension and application of eye and ear terminology, including:
  - o anatomy and physiology of the eye and ear
  - o abbreviations, prefixes, suffixes, combining forms, and other eye and ear terminology
  - o appropriate clinical procedures
  - o symptoms and pathologies associated with the eye and ear

KEY TERMS

Vocabulary (Eye) (pp. 699-700)

accommodation
anterior chamber
aqueous humor
biconvex
choroid
ciliary body
cone
conjunctiva
cornea
fovea centralis
fundus of the eye
iris
lens
macula
optic chiasm
optic disc
optic nerve
pupil
refraction
retina
rod
sclera

thalamus
vitreous humor
Terminology (pp. 700-704)

aque/o
blephar/o
conjunctiv/o
cor/o
corne/o
cycl/o
dacry/o
ir/o
irid/o
kerat/o
lacrim/o
ocul/o
ophthalm/o
opt/o
optic/o
palpebr/o
papill/o
phac/o, phak/o
pupill/o
retin/o
scler/o

ELSEVIER

uve/o
vitre/o
ambly/o
dipl/o
glauc/o
mi/o
mydr/o
nyct/o
phot/o
presby/o
scot/o
xer/o
-opia
-opsia
-tropia

Errors of Refraction (pp. 704-706)
astigmatism
hyperopia (hypermetropia)
myopia
presbyopia

Pathology – The Eye (pp. 706-710)
cataract
chalazion
diabetic retinopathy
glaucoma
hordeolum
macular degeneration
nystagmus
retinal detachment
strabismus

Clinical Procedures (pp. 710-714)
fluorescein angiography
ophthalmoscopy
slit lamp microscopy
visual acuity test
visual field test
enucleation
keratoplasty
laser photocoagulation
LASIK
phacoemulsification
scleral buckle
vitrectomy

Vocabulary (Ear) (p. 717)
auditory canal
auditory meatus
auditory nerve fibers
auditory tube
auricle

cerumen
cochlea
endolymph
eustachian tube
incus
labyrinth
malleus
organ of Corti
ossicle
oval window
perilymph
pinna
semicircular canals
stapes
tympanic membrane
vestibule

Terminology – The Ear (pp. 718-719)
acous/o
audi/o
audit/o
aur/o
auricul/o
cochle/o
mastoid/o
myring/o
ossicul/o
ot/o
salping/o
staped/o
tympan/o
vestibul/o
-acusis or -cusis
-otia

Pathology – The Ear (pp. 720-721)
acoustic neuroma
cholesteatoma
deafness
Ménière disease
otitis media
otosclerosis
tinnitus
vertigo

Clinical Procedures (pp. 722-723)
audiometry
cochlear implant
ear thermometry
otoscopy
tuning fork test

REFERENCE LIST
PowerPoint slides (CD, Evolve): 1-70

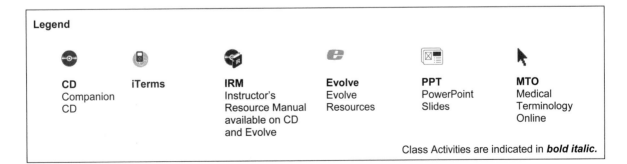

Legend

CD	iTerms	IRM	Evolve	PPT	MTO
Companion CD		Instructor's Resource Manual available on CD and Evolve	Evolve Resources	PowerPoint Slides	Medical Terminology Online

Class Activities are indicated in **bold italic.**

ELSEVIER

The Language of Medicine, 9th ed.

Chabner

LESSON 17.1

PRETEST
IRM Exercise Quiz B

BACKGROUND ASSESSMENT

Question: What is the error of refraction called that occurs in most people as they age, impairing their ability to see close objects? Why does this condition tend to occur with aging?

Answer: The typical impairment of vision as a result of aging is called presbyopia. It is due to the loss of elasticity of the ciliary body. The ciliary muscles and responding fibers normally adjust the thickness of the lens to accommodate for near vision. However, as the ciliary body loses elasticity, the lens cannot get fat enough to bend the light rays from near objects and focus them on the retina. For treatment, a correcting convex lens can refract the rays coming from objects closer than 20 feet and cause them to fall back onto the retina instead of behind. These convex lenses are often worn as reading glasses or in bifocals.

Question: What happens when you are on an airplane and you feel your ears start to "pop" or have a plugged-up feeling that is somewhat relieved when you swallow? Why does this feeling of the eardrum occur, and why does swallowing relieve the symptoms?

Answer: Air is present on both sides of the eardrum. Normally, the pressure of air in the middle ear is equal to the pressure of air in the external environment. When you go up in an airplane, the pressure in the outer ear, like that of the atmosphere, drops, while the pressure in the middle ear remains the same (greater than that in the outer ear). This causes the eardrum to bulge outward, resulting in a feeling of pressure. Swallowing can often relieve this pressure because it opens the eustachian tube, a canal leading from the middle ear to the pharynx that is normally closed. This allows air to leave the middle ear and enter the throat, balancing atmospheric and middle ear air pressures.

CRITICAL THINKING QUESTION

Claude Monet was an artist who was known for his impressionist paintings. Later in life, the choices of colors in his paintings changed. These color choices were the result of a visual disorder. What is the visual disorder and why did it affect his choice of colors?

Guidelines: Monet developed cataracts, which changed his perception of color. His particular type of cataracts caused him to perceive more yellow in what he saw, and fewer blues and greens.

OBJECTIVES	CONTENT	TEACHING RESOURCES
Identify locations and functions of the major parts of the eye and ear.	■ Introduction (p. 694) ■ The eye (p. 694) ☐ Anatomy and physiology (p. 694)	🖥 PPT 5-8 🎲 IRM Exercise Quizzes A, B 🎲 IRM Diagram Quiz ↖ MTO Module 17, Section I, Lessons 1-3 Figure 17-1 Pattern of events in the stimulation of a sense organ (p. 694) Figure 17-2 Structure of the eye (p. 695) Figure 17-3 Posterior, inner part (fundus) of the eye (p. 696) Exercises A, B (pp. 725-726) 💿 Companion CD Exercise 17-1 ▸ Discuss how light travels through the different parts of the eye on its path to the

ELSEVIER

OBJECTIVES	CONTENT	TEACHING RESOURCES
		cerebral cortex. Refer to Figure 17-4 (p. 697) and Figure 17-5 (p. 698) as necessary.
		Class Activity Divide the class into two competing teams. Show a transparency or PowerPoint slide of the eye and then the ear. Call out a number and ask students to name the unlabeled part. Award a point to the first team to answer correctly.
		Class Activity Have students label a blank diagram themselves. After reviewing the labeling of the structures, ask them to save the diagrams to label with the appropriate combining forms.
Name the combining forms, prefixes, and suffixes most commonly used to describe these organs and their parts.	☐ Vocabulary (p. 699) ☐ Terminology – The Eye (p. 700) – Structures and fluids (p. 700) – Conditions (p. 703) – Suffixes (p. 704)	PPT 9-11 IRM Terminology - Eye Quiz IRM Exercise Quizzes D, E Figure 17-6 A, Blepharitis; B, Acute bacterial conjunctivitis (p. 700) Figure 17-7 Lacrimal (tear) gland and ducts (p. 701) Companion CD Exercise 17-4 *Class Activity Pass out copies of various articles from ophthalmology journals to students. Ask students to search the articles to locate, underline, and define all terminology, combining forms, and suffixes related to the eye. Each student should define as many of the words as possible in a 5-minute period.*
Describe the pathological conditions that may affect the eye and ear.	☐ Errors of refraction (p. 704) ☐ Pathology (p. 706)	PPT 12-19 IRM Pathology - Eye Quiz IRM Exercise Quizzes F, G MTO Module 17, Section II, Lessons 1-4 Figure 17-8 Errors of refraction (p. 705) Figure 17-9 Cataract (p. 706) Figure 17-10 Chalazion (p. 706) Figure 17-11 Glaucoma and circulation of aqueous humor (p. 707) Figure 17-12 A, Normal vision; B, Macular degeneration (p. 709)

ELSEVIER

OBJECTIVES	CONTENT	TEACHING RESOURCES
		Table 17-1 Eyelid abnormalities (p. 708)
		Exercises C-J (pp. 726-730)
		◉ Companion CD Exercise 17-3
		▸ Discuss pathological conditions of the eye. Which are age-related conditions? What are potential treatments?
		Class Activity Provide students with unlabeled diagrams of eyes with various errors of refraction, similar to those in Figure 17-8. Ask students to label each diagram for the type of error portrayed, as well as the lens necessary to correct the problem.

17.1 Homework/Assignments:

17.1 Teacher's Notes:

LESSON 17.2

CRITICAL THINKING QUESTION

Roberta is considering laser surgery for her eyes. She has worn corrective lenses for years, with contact lenses for the past 7 years. What kinds of questions should she ask her doctor?

Guidelines: Roberta should realize that laser eye surgery is still not foolproof. Patients with uncontrolled vascular diseases, autoimmune disorders, and pregnant women should not have the procedure. It is a costly procedure, generally not covered by insurance, and although the results are quick and problem free for many people, others have complications such as halo effects and infection.

OBJECTIVES	CONTENT	TEACHING RESOURCES
Identify clinical procedures that pertain to ophthalmology and otology.	☐ Clinical procedures and abbreviations (p. 710) – Diagnostic (p. 710) – Treatment (p. 712)	▦ PPT 21-27 IRM Clinical Procedures - Eye Quiz IRM Exercise Quiz H IRM Dictation and Comprehension Quiz: Eye IRM Practical Applications: Chart Note ↖ MTO Module 17, Section III, Lessons 1-2 Figure 17-13 Normal fluorescein angiogram (p. 710) Figure 17-14 Ophthalmoscopy (p. 710) Figure 17-15 Slit lamp examination (p. 711) Figure 17-16 A, Snellen chart; B, Visual fields (p. 711) Figure 17-17 Eye after keratoplasty (p. 712) Figure 17-18 LASIK (p. 712) Figure 17-19 Phacoemulsification (p. 713) Figure 17-20 A, Detached retina; B, Scleral buckling procedure (p. 713) Exercises K-M (pp. 730-731) ▸ Discuss the meaning of the 20/20 ratio when referring to the results of the visual acuity test using a Snellen eye chart. *Class Activity Obtain a Snellen eye chart for visual acuity. Have students perform the eye test on each other. For those with corrective lenses, determine the ratio with and without glasses. Have students analyze the findings in various ways, such as finding the average ratio for the class or comparing the ratio among subgroups of the class, etc.*

ELSEVIER

The Language of Medicine, 9th ed.

Chabner

OBJECTIVES	CONTENT	TEACHING RESOURCES
		Class Activity Have students research the current FDA- approved procedures for correction of refractive disorders. Have them report their findings
		Class Activity Have students take turns reading Exercises and giving the answers. Ask them to spell, analyze, and underline the accented syllable in the terms listed.
		Class Activity Divide the students into several teams. Provide each team with unique bingo cards featuring a grid of nine random terms related to the eye. Pick and read aloud definitions for the terms in the section at random, and have students mark the corresponding words on their cards. Keep a record of the terms that have been defined. The game ends when a student is able to correctly mark three terms in a row on his or her card. Have a representative from the team read off the marked terms to verify against the record of terms defined during the game. Correct the student's pronunciation when necessary. Play multiple rounds.

17.2 Homework/Assignments:

17.2 Teacher's Notes:

Chabner

LESSON 17.3

CRITICAL THINKING QUESTION

Abnormalities of sensation can result from disease or dysfunction in the receptors for sensation or along the pathway that sends the signals from the receptors to specific areas of the brain. The abnormality can also be the result of brain abnormalities with no reported problems in the areas of reception or transmission. What is the correct terminology to use to describe these different types of abnormalities as they pertain to the sense of hearing? Give an example of each.

Guidelines: Nerve deafness, also called sensorineural hearing loss, results from impairment of the cochlea or auditory (acoustic) nerve. Acoustic neuroma is a benign tumor arising from the acoustic vestibulocochlear nerve that results in tinnitus (ringing in the ears), vertigo, and decreased hearing. This is a deficit produced at the level of transmission. Conductive deafness results from impairment of the middle ear ossicles and membranes transmitting sound waves into the cochlea. Otosclerosis is hardening of the bony tissue of the labyrinth of the ear, fixing or stiffening the stapes and causing conduction deafness, as the ossicles cannot pass on vibrations when sound enters the ear.

OBJECTIVES	CONTENT	TEACHING RESOURCES
Identify locations and functions of the major parts of the eye and ear.	■ The ear (p. 714) ☐ Anatomy and physiology (p. 714)	PPT 29-33 IRM Exercise Quizzes A-B IRM Diagram Quiz MTO Module 17, Section VI, Lessons 1-2 Figure 17-21 Anatomy of the ear (p. 715) Exercises N, O (pp. 731-732) Companion CD Exercise 17-2 ▶ Discuss the key parts of the ear and their functions. Note the pathway that sound follows through the parts of ear to the brain. *Class Activity Play a telephone game. Assign several students to represent the parts of the ear and brain portrayed in Figure 17-22. Write down a brief message and then verbally tell it only to the student representing the pinna. Ask this student to tell the message only to the student representing the next part in the sound pathway. Continue until the message reaches the cerebral cortex. If students make mistakes choosing the right pathway, then redirect them. The goal is to get the message to the student representing the cerebral cortex.* *Class Activity Pass out copies of the diagram for the ear and ask students to label them with the correct terms. Use them in the next segment to include the combining forms.*

The Language of Medicine, 9th ed.

Chabner

OBJECTIVES	CONTENT	TEACHING RESOURCES
Name the combining forms, prefixes, and suffixes most commonly used to describe these organs and their parts.	☐ Vocabulary (p. 717) ☐ Terminology – The Ear (p. 718) – Combining forms (p. 718) – Suffixes (p. 719)	PPT 34 IRM Terminology –Ear Quiz Figure 17-23 A, Stapedectomy; B, A prosthetic device (p. 719) Exercises O, P (pp. 732-733) *Class Activity Have students choose partners and create flash cards for the key terminology in this section. Have the students quiz each other on the terms.* *Class Activity Using the combining forms, divide the students into groups, and ask them to build as many medical terms as possible. Have one person in each group be the "fact checker" to verify the terms.*
Describe the pathological conditions that may affect the eye and ear.	☐ Pathology (p. 720)	PPT 35-37 IRM Pathology - Ear Quiz IRM Exercise Quiz D MTO Module 17, Section VII, Lesson 1 Figure 17-24 A-D Tympanic membranes with various symptoms (p. 720) Exercise P (p. 733) Companion CD Exercises 17-5, 17-6 ▸ Discuss the pathological conditions that may affect the ear, and describe their treatments.
Identify clinical procedures that pertain to ophthalmology and otology.	☐ Clinical procedures (p. 722)	PPT 38-39 IRM Clinical Procedures - Ear Quiz IRM Exercise Quiz C IRM Dictation and Comprehension Quiz: Ear MTO Module 17, Section VIII, Lesson 1 Figure 17-25 Pure-tone audiometer (p. 722) Figure 17-26 A, Cochlear implant; B, Otoscopic examination (p. 723) ▸ Discuss clinical procedures related to the ears and their purposes.

Chabner

OBJECTIVES	CONTENT	TEACHING RESOURCES
		Class Activity Ask students to find examples of audiograms for various types of hearing disorders. Have them share their findings with the class.
		Class Activity Divide the class into groups, and ask the groups to research the varieties of treatments for hearing disorders. Have them present their findings to the class.
Apply your new knowledge to understanding medical terms in their proper contexts, such as medical reports and records.	■ Practical applications (p. 724)	IRM Exercise Quiz E IRM Abbreviations Quiz MTO Module 17, Sections V and X Review Sheet (pp. 742-743) Companion CD Exercise 17-7 *Class Activity Have students work together to complete IRM Practical Applications A and B. Ask them to analyze each of the terms used and underline the accented syllable.*
Performance Evaluation		IRM Multiple Choice Quiz IRM Terminology Quiz IRM Pathology Quiz IRM Clinical Procedures Quiz IRM Exercise Quizzes IRM Dictation and Comprehension Quizzes IRM Spelling Quiz IRM Pronunciation Quiz IRM Abbreviations Quiz IRM Diagram Quiz IRM Review Sheet Quiz IRM Medical Scramble IRM Crossword Puzzle IRM Practical Applications

ELSEVIER

Chabner

OBJECTIVES	CONTENT	TEACHING RESOURCES
		ESLR Body Spectrum Electronic Anatomy Coloring Book: Senses
		ESLR Student Quiz Chapter 17
		MTO Module 17, Sections I-III and VI-VIII quizzes
		MTO Module 17 Exam
		Companion CD Exercise 17-8, 17-9, 17-10
		iTerms Chapter 17

17.3 Homework/Assignments:

17.3 Teacher's Notes:

The Language of Medicine, 9th ed.

Chabner

Slide 1

Slide 2

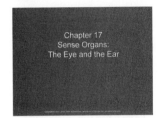

Slide 3

Slide 4

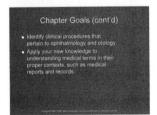

Slide 5

Chabner

Slide 6

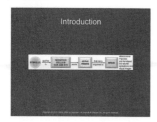

- Light and sound applied to the sense organs of the eye and ear activate receptors that send signals to the appropriate brain regions in the cortex where they are translated into images and sounds.

- What types of receptors exist to process information about our environment?

Slide 7

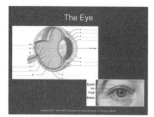

- What are the parts of the eye labeled in the diagram?

- What are the functions of the different parts of the eye?

- See Vocabulary (pp. 674-676) for definitions of the parts of the eye and their functions.

Slide 8

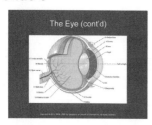

- What are the parts of the eye labeled in the diagram?

- What are the functions of the different parts of the eye?

- See Vocabulary (pp. 674-676) for definitions of the parts of the eye and their functions.

Slide 9

- Why are corneal transplants often successful?

- How many cones and rods are in the retina? (*There are approximately 6.5 million cones and 120 million rods in the retina.*)

- There are three types of cones, each stimulated by one of the primary colors of light (*red, blue, and green*).

- Which cones are most affected by color blindness? (*either the red or green cones*)

Slide 10

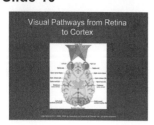

- Describe how light travels through the eye by following the pathways of the color coordinated tracts and visual fields.

- What might happen if there are lesions in areas along the pathway leading to the right and left cerebral cortices?

- Lesions of the cortical areas of the occipital lobe will likewise cause visual disturbance in the areas of the visual field where the information is normally interpreted by the brain.

- See Fig. 17-5 (p. 674) for pathway of light rays from cornea to cerebral cortex.

Slide 11

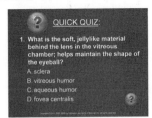

- Correct answer is B: vitreous humor

Slide 12

Slide 13

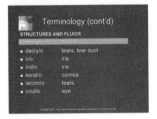

Slide 14

Slide 15

Slide 16

Slide 17

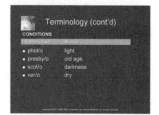

Slide 18

Slide 19

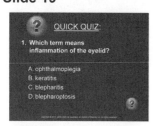

- Correct Answer is C: blepharitis

Slide 20

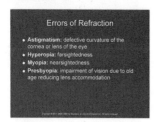

- Do any of the students have any of these conditions? What are the causes?

- How are these conditions corrected? (*The following slide provides images of the errors and the correction.*)

- What is lens accommodation? (*the refractory adjustment resulting when the muscles of the ciliary body produce flattening of the lens [for distant vision] and thickening and rounding [for close vision]*)

The Language of Medicine, 9th ed.

Chabner

Slide 21

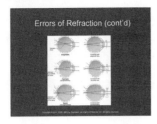

- The dashed lines in B and C indicate the contour and size of the normal eye.

- What error of refraction is associated with presbyopia? (*an inability to adjust the lens for accommodation to near vision*)

Slide 22

- What is the surgical treatment for cataracts? How can vision be corrected in this process?

- Surgical removal of the lens and implantation of an artificial lens behind the iris are treatments for cataracts.

- If surgery isn't possible, are there other treatments?

- If an intraocular lens cannot be inserted, the patient may wear eyeglasses or contact lenses to help refraction.

Slide 23

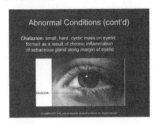

- What is the treatment for this condition?

- Chalazions often require incision and drainage.

- Besides chalazion, what are some of the other eyelid abnormalities? See Table 17-1 Eyelid Abnormalities (p. 683)

Slide 24

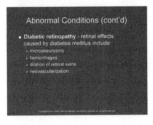

- What is a treatment for diabetic retinopathy?

- For severe hemorrhaging, laser photocoagulation and vitrectomy are helpful.

- What is neovascularization?

- An Internet search will lead to multiple sites focused on diabetes and vision.

Slide 25

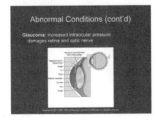

- Discuss the many forms of glaucoma.

- Do most people have glaucoma in one eye or both eyes? Why?

- If a patient has glaucoma in one eye, what is the likely cause? What is the likely treatment?

- What is tonometry?

- Tonometry measures intraocular pressure to detect glaucoma.

ELSEVIER

The Language of Medicine, 9th ed.

Chabner

Slide 26

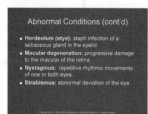

- Discuss the location of the retina and macula.
- Which form of macular degeneration (dry or wet) has a better prognosis and possible treatment?
- Why is it important to treat strabismus in early childhood?

Slide 27

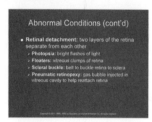

- What are the symptoms, causes, and treatments for retinal detachments?

Slide 28

Slide 29

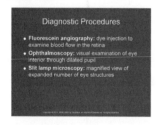

- Ask students to name conditions that are diagnosed by the tests listed.
- What type of eyedrop dilates the pupil? (*mydriatic*)

Slide 30

- How is the Snellen chart used?
- How is the ratio that describes visual acuity interpreted?
- Have students perform the visual acuity test on each other.

ELSEVIER

The Language of Medicine, 9th ed.

Chabner

Slide 31

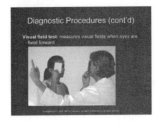

- Have students take the visual field test in class (noted in lesson plan).
- Are students surprised by the results of the test? Why or why not?

Slide 32

- LASIK is an acronym for *laser in situ keratomileusis* (shaping of cornea).
- Why can't LASIK correct presbyopia?

Slide 33

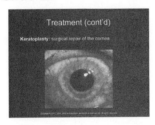

- Keratoplasty: Also known as corneal transplant, the patient's scarred or opaque cornea is replaced with a donor cornea.
- Why does this procedure have such a high success rate compared to other transplants?

Slide 34

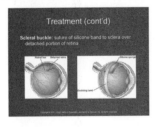

- In this procedure, the band pushes the two parts of the retina against each other to bring together the two layers of the detached retina.

Slide 35

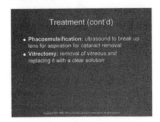

- What sorts of conditions utilize these treatments?
- Are they successful in curing both the symptoms and the cause?

ELSEVIER

The Language of Medicine, 9th ed.

Chabner

Slide 36

Slide 37

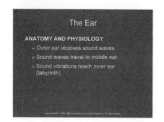

- See Figs. 17-20 (p. 689) and 17-21 (p. 690).

- Name the three bones in the middle ear that move in response to vibrations of the tympanic membrane? (*malleus, incus, stapes*)

- What is another name for the inner ear, and why is it referred to by this name? (*It is called the labyrinth due to its circular, mazelike structure.*)

- What is the name of the bony, snail-shaped structure of the inner ear? (*cochlea*)

- In addition to being the organ for hearing, what other important function is performed by the ear? (*equilibrium*)

Slide 38

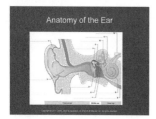

Slide 39

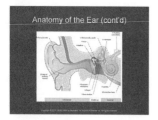

Slide 40

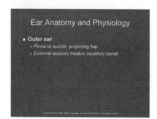

- The external auditory meatus is lined with numerous cerumen glands which produce a waxy substance that lubricates and protects the ear.

- Which part of the ear is most often pierced?

The Language of Medicine, 9th ed.

Chabner

Slide 41

- How do these structures contribute to vibration?
- Why are they susceptible to infection?
- Why do conditions that affect the respiratory system also affect these structures?
- The malleus, incus, and stapes make up the ossicles.

Slide 42

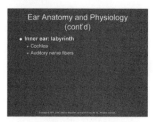

- The oval window separates the middle and inner ear.
- The cochlea contains perilymph and endolymph through which vibrations travel.
- The cochlea also contains the organ of Corti in which tiny hair cells receive vibrations from the auditory liquids and relay the sound waves to the auditory nerve fibers.

Slide 43

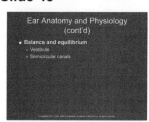

- The semicircular canals contain the saccule and utricle.
- The canals contain endolymph and hair cells.
- Fluid and hair cells fluctuate in response to movement of the head. This information is transmitted through nerve fibers to the brain.
- The brain sends information to the body's muscles to maintain equilibrium.

Slide 44

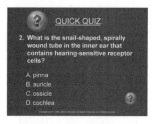

- Correct answer is D: cochlea

Slide 45

Chabner

Slide 46

Slide 47

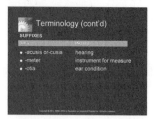

Slide 48

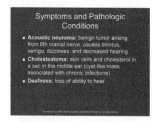

- Why can surgery for acoustic neuroma lead to deafness and facial paralysis?

- Nerve deafness (sensorineural hearing loss) results from impairment of the cochlea or auditory nerve.

- What constitutes conductive deafness? (*It results from impairment of the middle ear ossicles and membranes transmitting sound waves into the cochlea.*)

Slide 49

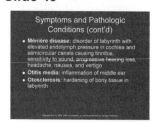

- Why does fixation of the stapes bone cause deafness? What is the current therapy for this condition?

- What is the current therapy for Ménière disease? How effective is the therapy?

- Why do doctors put tubes in the ears?

- What is the proper term for a surgical incision in the tympanic membrane and the insertion of a draining tube device?

- Why does the anatomical structure of the Eustachian tube in children make them more susceptible to otitis media?

Slide 50

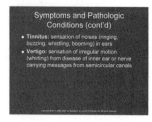

- Ask students to make some quick head movements and ask if any students are experiencing vertigo.

- What sorts of situations induce vertigo (for example, rides at amusement parks, ear infections, elevator rides, and so on)? Does the vertigo described in these situations stem from the wrong message being carried by the vestibular nerve or from movement of the fluids in the semicircular canals?

Slide 51

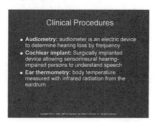

- How is audiometry performed?
- See Fig. 17-24 for an example of an audiometer.
- With a cochlear implant, a small computer converts sound waves to electronic impulses that stimulate nerve fibers in ears.
- What types of pathologies might require a cochlear implant for treatment?

Slide 52

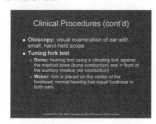

- Obtain tuning forks and ask students to perform the Rinne and Weber tests on each other.
- Obtain ear and oral thermometers. Ask students to compare their temperatures using both methods.
- Is there a difference between the methods? If so, why?

Slide 53

Slide 54

Slide 55

Chabner

Slide 56

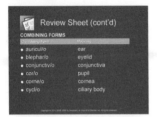

Review Sheet (cont'd)

COMBINING FORMS

Combining Form	Meaning
• auricul/o	ear
• blephar/o	eyelid
• conjunctiv/o	conjunctiva
• cor/o	pupil
• corne/o	cornea
• cycl/o	ciliary body

Slide 57

Review Sheet (cont'd)

COMBINING FORMS

Combining Form	Meaning
• dacry/o	
• dipl/o	
• glauc/o	
• ir/o	
• irid/o	
• kerat/o	
• lacrim/o	

Slide 58

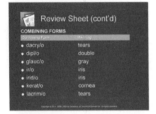

Review Sheet (cont'd)

COMBINING FORMS

Combining Form	Meaning
• dacry/o	tears
• dipl/o	double
• glauc/o	gray
• ir/o	iris
• irid/o	iris
• kerat/o	cornea
• lacrim/o	tears

Slide 59

Review Sheet (cont'd)

COMBINING FORMS

Combining Form	Meaning
• mastoid/o	
• mi/o	
• mydr/o	
• myring/o	
• nyct/o	
• ocul/o	

Slide 60

Review Sheet (cont'd)

COMBINING FORMS

Combining Form	Meaning
• mastoid/o	mastoid process
• mi/o	smaller, less
• mydr/o	widen, enlarge
• myring/o	eardrum
• nyct/o	night
• ocul/o	eye

ELSEVIER

Chabner

Slide 61

Slide 62

Slide 63

Slide 64

Slide 65

Slide 66

Review Sheet (cont'd)

COMBINING FORMS

Combining Form	Meaning
• scot/o	darkness
• staped/o	stapes
• tympan/o	eardrum
• uve/o	uvea
• vestibul/o	vestibule
• vitre/o	glassy
• xer/o	dry

Slide 67

Review Sheet (cont'd)

SUFFIXES

Suffix	Meaning
• -acusis	_____
• -cusis	_____
• -meter	_____
• -metry	_____
• -opia	_____

Slide 68

Review Sheet (cont'd)

SUFFIXES

Suffix	Meaning
• -acusis	hearing
• -cusis	hearing
• -meter	instrument for measure
• -metry	process of measurement
• -opia	vision

Slide 69

Review Sheet (cont'd)

SUFFIXES

Suffix	Meaning
• -opsia	_____
• -otia	_____
• -phobia	_____
• -plegic	_____
• -tropia	_____

Slide 70

Review Sheet (cont'd)

SUFFIXES

Suffix	Meaning
• -opsia	vision
• -otia	ear condition
• -phobia	fear
• -plegic	paralysis; palsy
• -tropia	to turn

18 Endocrine System

TEACHING FOCUS

Students will have the opportunity to learn how the endocrine system regulates many body functions by releasing hormones into the bloodstream. The student will have the opportunity to learn the location of the major endocrine glands and tissues, their primary secretions, sites of action and mechanisms of action, and important bodily functions. Abnormal conditions arising from deregulation of the system and diagnostic tests and procedures related to endocrine abnormalities will be presented for the student to better understand medical terms used by endocrine specialists.

MATERIALS AND RESOURCES

- ☐ Flash cards (Lesson 18.4)
- ☐ Glucose meter (Lesson 18.4)
- ☐ Index cards (Lesson 18.4)
- ☐ Insulin pump (Lesson 18.4)
- ☐ Medical journals about endocrine abnormalities (Lesson 18.2)

- ☐ Medical pathology textbook (Lesson 18.2)
- ☐ Transparency or PowerPoint slide of illustration of endocrine glands (Lesson 18.1)
- ☐ VCR and television (Lesson 18.2)
- ☐ Video about the male and female reproductive systems (Lesson 18.2)

LESSON CHECKLIST

Preparations for this lesson include:

- Demonstration: insulin pump, glucose meter
- Guest speaker: diabetic person who uses glucose meter and insulin pump
- Student performance evaluation of all entry-level skills required for student comprehension and application of endocrine system terminology, including:
  - o location, secretion, and action of endocrine tissue
  - o the major endocrine glands, the hormones they produce, and their actions
  - o abnormal conditions of the endocrine glands

KEY TERMS

Vocabulary (pp. 757-759)

adrenal cortex
adrenal medulla
ovaries
pancreas
parathyroid glands
pituitary gland (hypophysis)
testes
thyroid gland
adrenaline
adrenocorticotropic hormone (ACTH)
aldosterone
androgen
antidiuretic hormone (ADH)
calcitonin
cortisol
epinephrine
estradiol
estrogen
follicle-stimulating hormone (FSH)
glucagon
growth hormone (GH)
insulin
luteinizing hormone (LH)
norepinephrine

oxytocin (OT)
parathormone (PTH)
progesterone
prolactin (PRL)
somatotropin (STH)
testosterone
thryroid-stimulating hormone (TSH)
thyroxine (T_4)
triiodothyronine (T_3)
vasopressin
catecholamines
corticosteroids
electrolyte
glucocorticoid
homeostasis
hormone
hypothalamus
mineralocorticoid
receptor
sella turcica
sex hormones
steroid
sympathomimetic
target tissue

Terminology (pp. 760-763)

aden/o
adren/o
adrenal/o
andr/o
calc/o
cortic/o
crin/o
dips/o
estr/o
gluc/o
glyc/o
gonad/o
home/o
hormon/o
insulin/o
kal/i
lact/o
myx/o
natr/o
pancreat/o
parathyroid/o

phys/o
pituitar/o
somat/o
ster/o
thyr/o
thyroid/o
toc/o
toxic/o
ur/o
-agon
-emia
-in, -ine
-tropin
-uria
eu-
hyper-
hypo-
oxy-
pan-
tetra-
tri-

Pathology (pp. 764-773)

hyperthyroidism
hypothyroidism
thyroid carcinoma
hyperparathyroidism
hypoparathyroidism
adrenal virilism
Cushing's syndrome
Addison's disease
pheochromocytoma

hyperinsulinism
diabetes mellitus
acromegaly
gigantism
dwarfism
panhypopituitarism
syndrome of inappropriate ADH
diabetes insipidus

Laboratory Tests (pp. 773-774)

fasting plasma glucose
serum and urine tests
thyroid function tests
exophthalmometry
computed tomography (CT) scan

magnetic resonance imaging (MRI)
radioactive iodine uptake
thyroid scan
ultrasound examination

REFERENCE LIST

PowerPoint slides (CD, Evolve): 1-78

Legend

CD
Companion
CD

iTerms

IRM
Instructor's
Resource Manual
available on CD
and Evolve

Evolve
Evolve
Resources

PPT
PowerPoint
Slides

MTO
Medical
Terminology
Online

Class Activities are indicated in **bold italic**.

LESSON 18.1

PRETEST
IRM Exercise Quiz A

BACKGROUND ASSESSMENT
Question: What is the function of the endocrine system and how does it work?
Answer: The endocrine system works through the use of certain glands that secrete chemical messengers called hormones. The hormones travel through the bloodstream to receptor sites in the various target tissues and cause a variety of effects.

Question: Janet is taking birth control pills. She knows that they regulate her menstrual periods but is not sure how that keeps her from becoming pregnant. She learns that the pills contain hormones. Where are the female hormones naturally produced and what are their functions?
Answer: The female hormones estrogen and progesterone are produced in the ovaries. Estrogen maintains female secondary sex characteristics and interacts with hormones of the anterior pituitary to promote ovulation and the menstrual cycle. Progesterone also interacts with pituitary hormones, but during pregnancy it maintains and supports the growth of the embryo and surrounding tissues of the uterus. These two hormones ebb and flow during the menstrual cycle; they first cause ovulation (release of an ovum to be fertilized) and then promote an environment for the egg to be nourished and grow. When fertilization does not take place, the uterine environment breaks down in the form of the menses. Birth control pills hormonally mimic pregnancy and inhibit ovulation.

CRITICAL THINKING QUESTION
An enlarged thyroid gland can lead to symptoms that reflect either overproduction or underproduction of thyroid hormones. How are both of these conditions possible from an enlarged thyroid?
Guidelines: An enlarged thyroid (goiter) can result from a lack of iodine in the diet, resulting in the inability of the gland to produce thyroid hormones. This causes the hypothalamus and adenohypophysis (anterior pituitary gland) to secrete releasing factors that tell the thyroid to produce even more of its hormone, leading to an enlarged gland where the prehormones are stored in follicles. On the other hand, tumors of the thyroid (neoplasms) can enlarge the thyroid and produce both hyperthyroidism or, in the case of a malignant tumor, a nonfunctioning gland (hypothyroidism).

OBJECTIVES	CONTENT	TEACHING RESOURCES
Identify the endocrine glands and their hormones and functions.	■ Introduction (p. 746) ■ Thyroid gland (p. 748) ■ Parathyroid glands (p. 749) ■ Adrenal glands (p. 750) ■ Pancreas (p. 752)	▣ PPT 5-28 IRM Exercise Quiz A-C IRM Diagram Quiz MTO Module 18, Section I, Lessons 1-2, 4-6 Figure 18-1 The endocrine system (p. 747) Figure 18-2 The thyroid gland (p. 748) Figure 18-3 The thyroid gland, its hormones and actions (p. 749) Figure 18-4 The parathyroid glands (p. 749) Figure 18-5 The parathyroid glands, their hormone and action (p. 750) Figure 18-6 The adrenal (suprarenal) glands (p. 751)

Chabner

OBJECTIVES	CONTENT	TEACHING RESOURCES
		Figure 18-7 The adrenal cortex and adrenal medulla, their hormones and actions (p. 751)
		Figure 18-8 The pancreas (p. 752)
		Figure 18-9 The pancreas (islets of Langerhans), its hormones and actions (p. 753)
		Table 18-1 Endocrine tissue (p. 747)
		Table 18-2 Major endocrine glands, the hormones they produce, and their actions (p. 756)
		Companion CD Exercise 18-1
		Class Activity Divide the class into two competing teams. Show them a transparency or PowerPoint slide of the illustration of endocrine glands. Call out a number and ask them to identify the gland. The first team to give a correct answer wins a point. Give an additional point for the name of a hormone the gland produces. The team with the most points wins.
		Class Activity Alternately, hand out copies of the blank illustration of the endocrine system. Have the students label the diagram with the organs and their combining forms.
		Class Activity Divide the class into groups, and assign each group one of the major endocrine glands listed in Table 18-2. Assign the anterior and posterior pituitary lobes to two groups. Have each group create a poster listing the gland, its location in the human body, the hormones the gland produces, the hormone's purpose, and the hormone's point of entry into the bloodstream. Then have each group make an oral presentation to the class based on the poster.
		Class Activity Divide the class into two or more competing teams. Play a Jeopardy-style game by giving them "answers" (from the Vocabulary list) such as this: "The male hormone produced by the testes." Award a point for the question, "What is testosterone?"
		Class Activity Prepare a handout with the hormones listed in Table 18-2 in column one, and blank lines in columns two and three. During class, review the list, asking students to name each gland and the hormone each

Chabner

OBJECTIVES	CONTENT	TEACHING RESOURCES
		gland produces. Have all students fill in column two with the correct answer. When the correct answer is provided, ask a student to provide a fact about the hormone or gland to serve as a memory aid. Have students fill in column three with an appropriate memory aid.

18.1 Homework/Assignments:

18.1 Teacher's Notes:

LESSON 18.2

CRITICAL THINKING QUESTION

The abnormal conditions of gigantism, acromegaly, and dwarfism have symptoms that are very different from each other, yet they each result from secretory problems in the same gland—the pituitary. How is this possible?

Guidelines: The timing of the abnormal secretion of the pituitary hormones in relation to the developmental stage of the individual has a strong influence on the resulting symptoms and conditions that arise. Acromegaly results from an excess of growth hormone due to neoplasms of the pituitary gland that occur during adulthood. Overgrowth of the feet, hands, face, and jaw results. In gigantism, the hyperfunctioning of the pituitary occurs before puberty. Benign tumors result in an excess of growth hormone, leading to overgrowth during a period of naturally rapid growth. Dwarfism is the result of hyposecretion of growth hormones; children are normal mentally, but their bones remain small. Some of these conditions can be corrected if the cause of the symptom is discovered early.

OBJECTIVES	CONTENT	TEACHING RESOURCES
Identify the endocrine glands and their hormones and functions.	■ Pituitary gland (p. 753) ■ Ovaries (p. 755) ■ Testes (p. 756)	PPT 30-40 IRM Multiple Choice Quiz IRM Dictation and Comprehension Quiz, IRM Pronunciation Quiz A-B ↖ MTO Module 18, Section I, Lessons 3 and 6 Figure 18-10 The pituitary gland (p. 753) Figure 18-11 The relationship of the hypothalamus to the anterior pituitary gland and the posterior pituitary gland (p. 754) Figure 18-12 The pituitary gland, its hormones and actions (p. 755) Figure 18-13 The ovaries and testes, their hormones and actions (p. 757) Table 18-2 Major endocrine glands, the hormones they produce, and their actions (p. 756) Exercises G-H (pp. 781) ▸ Discuss why a pituitary tumor might cause tunnel vision. *Class Activity Obtain a video about the function of the male and female reproductive systems. Divide the class into four groups. Have two groups per male/female category. Each group within the same sex must report on two topics. One topic is the formation of the germ cells for that organ and how hormones influence that process. The second group explains how hormones regulate*

OBJECTIVES	CONTENT	TEACHING RESOURCES
		secondary sex characteristics and, in the case of females, pregnancy as well. ***Class Activity** Give several competing teams two sets of index cards each. One set has a card for each major endocrine gland; the other set lists the names of corresponding hormones. Have the teams match the hormone with the gland. The first team to complete the task correctly wins. Have the winning team present its answers to the class.*
Analyze medical terms related to the endocrine glands and their hormones.	■ Terminology (p. 760)	PPT 41-49 IRM Multiple Choice Quiz Figure 18-14 Hypophysectomy (p. 762) Exercises A-C (pp. 778-780) Review Sheet (pp. 790-791) Companion CD Exercises 18-2, 18-3, 18-4, 18-5 ***Class Activity** Have each student obtain one article from a leading clinical journal and underline all terms related to the endocrine organs, hormones, and malfunctions of the system. Use only 25 terms from each article. Have students exchange articles and define the terms in the article.* ***Class Activity** Read the Practical Application to the students. Ask them to answer the questions following the report. Have them spell, analyze, and underline the accented syllable in each term.*

18.2 Homework/Assignments:

18.2 Teacher's Notes:

ELSEVIER

Chabner

LESSON 18.3

CRITICAL THINKING QUESTION

Diabetes is a disease of improper metabolism of sugar, starch, and fat. However, there are two types of diabetes, which occur at very different points in life and have a different inheritance pattern. In addition, one type presents with a very thin person, and one type usually presents with an obese person. What are the differences between these two types of diabetes?

Guidelines: Type 1 diabetes has an early onset, usually in childhood, and presents in a very thin person. It involves destruction of the cells in the pancreas (beta cells) that are responsible for producing insulin. It has a rapid onset and often results in ketoacidosis (improper burning of fats leading to ketones and acids in the body). Type 2 diabetes has a different inheritance pattern and presents in older and obese patients. The onset is very gradual. The cells that produce insulin are generally not destroyed, but the ability of insulin to act on its target cells is reduced and ketoacidosis seldom occurs. Both diseases use different approaches to treatment. Type 1 patients can use insulin pumps to maintain glucose levels. Type 2 patients can often change their diets, lose weight, exercise, and, if necessary, use insulin or oral hypoglycemic agents.

OBJECTIVES	CONTENT	TEACHING RESOURCES
Describe the abnormal conditions resulting from excessive and deficient secretions of the endocrine glands.	■ Pathology (p. 764) □ Thyroid gland (p. 764) □ Parathyroid glands (p. 765) □ Adrenal cortex (p. 766) □ Adrenal medulla (p. 767) □ Pancreas (p. 768) □ Pituitary gland (anterior lobe) (p. 771) □ Pituitary gland (posterior lobe) (p. 772)	PPT 51-59 IRM Pathology Quiz IRM Exercise Quiz D-G IRM Practical Application A questions 1-4 IRM Practical Application B questions 1, 2 IRM Dictation and Comprehension Quizzes MTO Module 18, Section II, Lessons 1-4 Figure 18-15 A, Goiter; B, Exophthalmos (p. 764) Figure 18-16 (A) Myxedema; (B) Cushing syndrome (p. 766) Figure 18-17 Addison's disease (p. 767) Figure 18-18 Insulin pump (p. 769) Figure 18-19 Secondary complications of diabetes mellitus (p. 770) Figure 18-20 Progression of acromegaly (p. 771) Figure 18-21 Gigantism (p. 772) Table 18-3 Comparison of type 1 and type 2 diabetes mellitus (p. 769) Table 18-4 Abnormal conditions of endocrine glands (p. 773) Exercises D-F, I (pp. 779-780)

The Language of Medicine, 9th ed.

Chabner

OBJECTIVES	CONTENT	TEACHING RESOURCES
		Companion CD Exercises 18-6, 18-7
		▸ Discuss famous people who suffered from abnormal conditions of the endocrine system. If students have difficulty finding references, they can start with the medical histories of the U.S. presidents. How did they learn to cope with their conditions?
		▸ Discuss why some adrenal gland tumors cause virilism. Why do people get cortisone shots when they have musculoskeletal disorders?
		Class Activity Have small groups each pick a card from a set of index cards with the names of abnormal conditions on them. Ask each group to name the gland involved and describe the causes and effects of the condition. Have a representative of each group share the description with the class. Have the class offer improvements.
		Class Activity Use a library or the Internet to locate four to six photographs of patients with visible signs of abnormal endocrine activity. Print out or photocopy relevant photos and number each copy. Pass the numbered copies through the class, asking students to write the underlying cause of each patient's appearance and the gland involved on a separate piece of paper. Discuss the results as a class activity, or break the class into smaller groups and ask each group to reach a consensus for each patient.

18.3 Homework/Assignments:

18.3 Teacher's Notes:

LESSON 18.4

CRITICAL THINKING QUESTION

Why is a radioactive iodine uptake test useful for evaluating an enlarged thyroid?

Guidelines: There are several reasons why a thyroid can be enlarged. A thyroid uptake test will show not only the anatomy of the gland but also the function of the gland, which will aid in the diagnosis of why the gland is enlarged. Radioactive iodine is administered orally, and the uptake into the gland is evidence of thyroid function. Functional tests aid in the evaluation of tumors to help distinguish between benign and malignant conditions.

OBJECTIVES	CONTENT	TEACHING RESOURCES
Identify laboratory tests, clinical procedures, and abbreviations related to endocrinology.	■ Laboratory tests (p. 773) ■ Clinical procedures (p. 774) ■ Abbreviations (p. 775)	PPT 61-62 IRM Laboratory Tests and Clinical Procedures Quiz IRM Abbreviations Quiz MTO Module 18, Section III, Lessons 1-3 Exercise B (p. 778) *Class Activity Have a person who uses a glucose meter and insulin pump come to class and demonstrate their use.* *Class Activity Divide the class into two competing teams. Give each team a set of different flash cards with the names on them of laboratory tests, clinical procedures, or abbreviations related to endocrinology. The teams take turns showing a card to the opponent, who has to define the test or procedure, or give the abbreviated term. The correct answer wins a point. However, the first team loses a point for accepting an incorrect answer or rejecting a correct answer. The team with the most points wins.* *Class Activity Have students research the newest findings in treatment for diabetes mellitus. Ask them to present their findings to the class.*
Apply your new knowledge to understanding medical terms in their proper contexts, such as medical reports and records.	■ Practical applications (p. 776)	PPT 63-77 IRM Practical Applications MTO Module 18, Section V Companion CD Exercise 18-8 *Class Activity Have students take turns reading the sentences in Exercise K. The student reading the question will answer it:*

OBJECTIVES	CONTENT	TEACHING RESOURCES
		the class will spell, analyze, define, and underline the accented syllable in each answer.
Performance Evaluation		IRM Multiple Choice Quiz
		IRM Terminology Quiz
		IRM Pathology Quiz
		IRM Laboratory Tests and Clinical Procedures Quiz
		IRM Exercise Quiz
		IRM Dictation and Comprehension Quiz
		IRM Spelling Quiz
		IRM Pronunciation Quiz
		IRM Abbreviations Quiz
		IRM Diagram Quiz
		IRM Vocabulary Quiz
		IRM Review Sheet Quiz
		IRM Medical Scramble
		IRM Crossword puzzle
		IRM Practical Applications
		ESLR Student Quiz Chapter 18
		MTO Module 18, Sections I-III quizzes
		MTO Module 18 Exam
		Companion CD Exercises 18-9, 18-10
		iTerms Chapter 18

18.4 Homework/Assignments:

18.4 Teacher's Notes:

Chabner

Slide 1

The Language Of Medicine

9th edition

Davi-Ellen Chabner

Slide 2

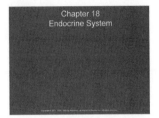

Chapter 18
Endocrine System

Slide 3

Chapter Goals

- Identify the endocrine glands and their hormones
- Gain an understanding of the functions of these hormones in the body.
- Analyze medical terms related to the endocrine glands and their hormones.

Slide 4

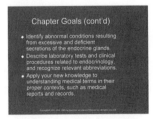

Chapter Goals (cont'd)

- Identify abnormal conditions resulting from excessive and deficient secretions of the endocrine glands.
- Describe laboratory tests and clinical procedures related to endocrinology, and recognize relevant abbreviations.
- Apply your new knowledge to understanding medical terms in their proper contexts, such as medical reports and records.

Slide 5

Chapter 18
Lesson 18.1

ELSEVIER

Slide 6

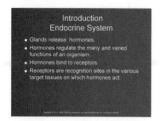

Slide 7

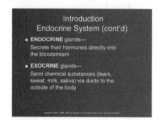

Slide 8

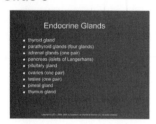

- How are endocrine glands different from exocrine glands?

- Endocrine glands secrete hormones directly into the bloodstream; exocrine glands send their chemical substances into ducts and out of the body.

Slide 9

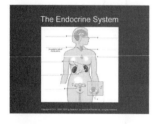

- Ask students to label the figure. Next image has labels completed.

Slide 10

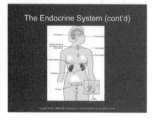

- See p. 722-723 in text for more information.

Chabner

Slide 11

- Identify other locations (tissues) in the body that secrete hormones apart from the major glands.

- Hormones are secreted from endocrine tissue throughout the body. These hormones play an important role in body functions and they should not be understated or ignored just because they are produced by cells in organs that are not endocrine.

- Many of these organs have both endocrine and exocrine functions, and should be examined by students who later report their findings to the class.

Slide 12

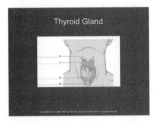

- Right and left lobe on either side of the trachea

- Thyroid cartilage produces the "Adam's apple"

- Isthmus connects two lobes

Slide 13

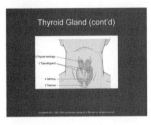

- Right and left lobe on either side of the trachea

- Thyroid cartilage produces the "Adam's apple"

- Isthmus connects two lobes

Slide 14

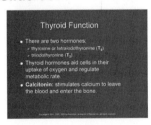

- What are some of the hormones secreted by the thyroid gland?

Slide 15

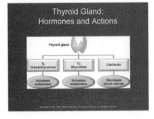

- What are some of the hormones secreted by the thyroid gland?

Slide 16

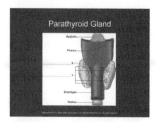

- What are some of the hormones secreted by the thyroid gland?

Slide 17

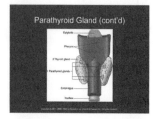

- What are some of the hormones secreted by the thyroid gland?

Slide 18

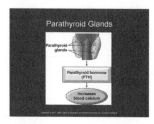

- Four glands located in the dorsal aspect of the thyroid gland.
- What hormone is secreted by the parathyroid glands, and what role does it play in regulating the level of calcium in the blood?

Slide 19

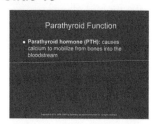

- How is the adjustment of the level of calcium in the blood a good example of the way hormones control the homeostasis of the body?

Slide 20

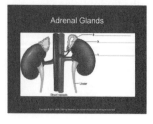

- Two small glands: one on top of each kidney

Slide 21

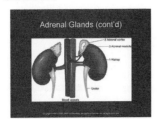

- Two small glands: one on top of each kidney

Slide 22

Slide 23

- What are the three types of corticosteroids secreted by the adrenal cortex?
- Glucocorticoids: influence metabolism of sugars, fats, and proteins. Antiinflammatory efffect.
- Mineralocorticoids: regulate level of mineral salts (electrolytes) in the body.
- Gonadocorticoids: sex hormones that influence secondary sex characteristics.

Slide 24

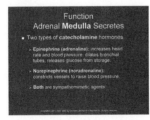

- What are two types of catecholamine secreted by the adrenal medulla?
- Epinephrine: increases cardiac rate, dilates bronchial tubes, stimulates glucose production.
- Norepinephrine: constricts vessels, raises blood pressure.

Slide 25

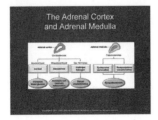

Slide 26

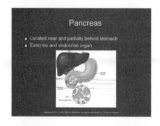

- The endocrine tissue of the pancreas consists of hormone-producing cells: islets of Langerhans.

- Most of the pancreas consists of exocrine cells that secrete digestive enzymes.

- What percent of the pancreas consists of exocrine cells? (*98%.*)

Slide 27

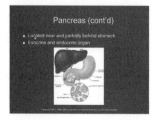

- The endocrine tissue of the pancreas consists of hormone-producing cells: islets of Langerhans.

- Most of the pancreas consists of exocrine cells that secrete digestive enzymes.

- What percent of the pancreas consists of exocrine cells? (*98%.*)

Slide 28

- How is the movement of glucose out of the blood and into cells promoted by insulin?

- How is the movement of glucose into the blood promoted by glucagon?

Slide 29

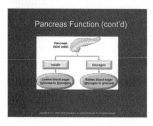

- How is the movement of glucose out of the blood and into cells promoted by insulin?

- How is the movement of glucose into the blood promoted by glucagon?

Slide 30

Chabner

Slide 31

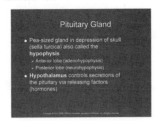

- Describe the interactions between the hypothalamus and the pituitary gland that control the secretions by the pituitary gland.

Slide 32

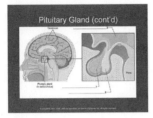

Slide 33

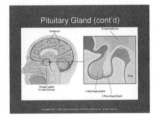

Slide 34

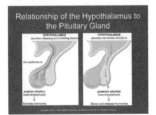

Slide 35

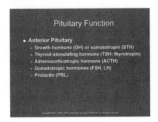

- Go over the basic function of each of these hormones/factors.
- Use Fig. 18-12.
- Show where there is feedback inhibition.
- Discuss how feedback from the targets regulates further release and the general concept of regulation.

Slide 36

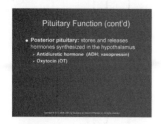

- What are two important hormones released by the posterior pituitary gland?

- Antidiuretic hormone (ADH) and oxytocin (OT)

Slide 37

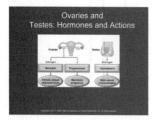

- Review this chart; then go over Table 18-2 from p. 733 of the text.

Slide 38

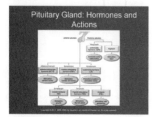

Slide 39

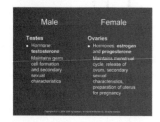

- Review the menstrual cycle and a graph of changes of levels of estrogen and progesterone during the cycle.

- Describe how these hormones promote the ovulation and development of the uterus for potential pregnancy.

Slide 40

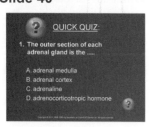

- Correct answer is B: adrenal cortex

Slide 41

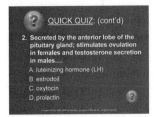

- Correct answer is A: luteinizing hormone (LH).

Slide 42

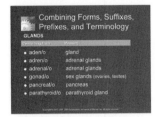

Slide 43

Slide 44

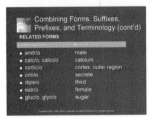

Slide 45

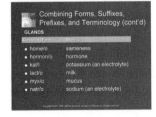

Slide 46

Slide 47

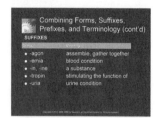

Slide 48

Slide 49

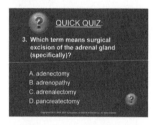

- Correct answer is C: adrenalectomy specifically means excision of the adrenal gland.

Slide 50

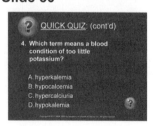

- Correct answer is D: hypokalemia

Chabner

Slide 51

Slide 52

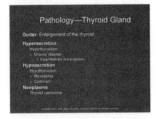

- What are some treatment options for goiter?

- Increased supply of iodine, thyroid-blocking drugs, radioactive iodine.

- What are some conditions that can produce hypothyroidism?

- What symptoms are associated with hypothyroidism? (*fatigue, muscular and mental sluggishness, weight gain, fluid retention, slow heart rate, low body temperature, constipation*)

Slide 53

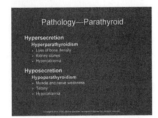

- What is hypercalcemia and what are its effects?

- What is hypocalcemia and what are its effects?

Slide 54

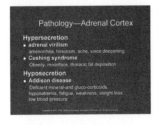

- Have students state the potential causes of these abnormalities and whether or not they can be treated.

- If so, how are they treated and what is the prognosis?

Slide 55

Chabner

Slide 56

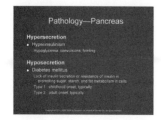

Slide 57

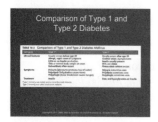

- After reviewing the table, discuss the secondary complications of diabetes.

Slide 58

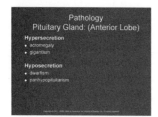

Slide 59

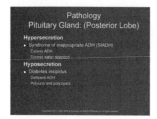

Slide 60

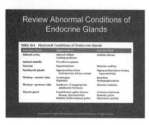

- Review all the abnormalities.
- Ask students to create the table first and then show this slide to review.

Chabner

Slide 61

Slide 62

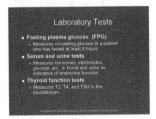

- What symptoms would prompt these tests to be ordered?

Slide 63

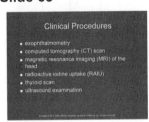

- When would these procedures be ordered?
- For what symptoms?
- Review previous lessons.

Slide 64

Slide 65

Slide 66

Slide 67

Slide 68

Slide 69

Slide 70

ELSEVIER

The Language of Medicine, 9th ed.
Chabner

Slide 71

Slide 72

Slide 73

Slide 74

Slide 75

Slide 76

Slide 77

Slide 78

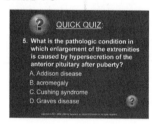

- Correct answeris B: Acromegaly. See p. 746 in 8e for more information.

TEACHING FOCUS

Students will have the opportunity to gain familiarity with terms that describe the classifications of tumors and those terms related to the causes, diagnoses, and treatment of cancer. The laboratory tests that are used to determine not only the presence of a tumor but the degree to which it has spread also will be described in this chapter. Finally, abbreviations and terms associated with the care of cancer patients will also be presented in this chapter.

MATERIALS AND RESOURCES

- ☐ Flash cards (Lesson 19.1, 19.3, 19.4)
- ☐ Index cards (Lesson 19.2)
- ☐ Leading cancer journals (all Lessons)
- ☐ Medical atlas of histology (Lesson 19.2)
- ☐ Medical pathology textbooks (all Lessons)
- ☐ Microscopic pathology atlas (Lesson 19.2)
- ☐ Paper (Lesson 19.1)
- ☐ Pathology reports (Lesson 19.2)
- ☐ Transparencies or PowerPoint slides (Lessons 19.3, 19.4)

LESSON CHECKLIST

Preparations for this lesson include:

- Lecture
- Field trip: visit to cancer treatment facility
- Cancer registrar
- Student performance evaluation of all entry-level skills required for student comprehension and application of oncology principles, including:
  - o understanding cancer treatment
  - o listing grading and staging systems
  - o providing pathological descriptions
  - o understanding characteristics and classification of tumors
  - o understanding medical terms related to oncology

KEY TERMS

Vocabulary (pp. 815-818)

adjuvant therapy
alkylating agents
anaplasia
antibiotics
antimetabolites
antimitotics
apoptosis
benign
biological response modifiers
biological therapy
carcinogens
carcinoma
cellular oncogenes
chemotherapy
combination chemotherapy
dedifferentiation
deoxyribonucleic acid (DNA)
differentiated
differentiating agents
differentiation
electron beams
encapsulated

external beam radiation
fractionation
genetic screening
grading of tumors
gray (Gy)
gross description of tumors
infiltrative
invasive
linear accelerator
malignant tumor
mesenchymal
metastasis
microscopic description (of tumors)
mitosis
mixed-tissue tumors
modality
molecularly targeted drugs
morbidity
mucinous
mutation
neoplasm
nucleotide

oncogene
palliative
pedunculated
pharmacokinetics
protocol
rad
radiation
radiocurable tumor
radioresistant tumor
radiosensitive tumor
radiosensitizers
radiotherapy
relapse

remission
ribonucleic acid (RNA)
sarcoma
serous
sessile
solid tumor
staging of tumors
steroids
surgical procedures to treat cancer
tumors
ultraviolet radiation
viral oncogenes
virus

Terminology (pp. 818-820)

alveol/o
cac/o
carcin/o
cauter/o
chem/o
cry/o
cyst/o
fibr/o
follicul/o
fung/i
medull/o
mucos/o
mut/a
mutagen/o
necr/o
onc/o
papill/o
pharmac/o
plas/o
ple/o

polyp/o
prot/o
radi/o
sarc/o
scirrh/p
xer/o
-blastoma
-genesis
-oma
-plasia
-plasm
-suppression
-therapy
ana-
apo-
brachy-
epi-
meta-
tele-

REFERENCE LIST

PowerPoint slides (CD, Evolve): 1-40

Legend

 CD
Companion
CD

 iTerms

 IRM
Instructor's
Resource Manual
available on CD
and Evolve

 Evolve
Evolve
Resources

 PPT
PowerPoint
Slides

 MTO
Medical
Terminology
Online

Class Activities are indicated in ***bold italic***.

LESSON 19.1

PRETEST
IRM Exercise Quiz B

BACKGROUND ASSESSMENT
Question: The term *neoplasm* refers to tumors that are masses or growths that arise from normal tissue. A growth can occur at any time in life. Are all neoplasms life threatening?
Answer: The term neoplasm refers to the growth. Neoplasms may be either malignant or benign. Benign growths are noninvasive and do not spread to other sites. They can be life threatening if their removal would be difficult and destroy other important organs (as with some benign brain tumors). Malignant tumors compress, invade, and ultimately destroy surrounding tissues. They spread to other sites and are life threatening.

Question: There are agents in the environment that, upon exposure, are known to increase an individual's risk of developing cancer. What are some of those environmental agents, and how do they contribute to increasing cancer risk?
Answer: Environmental agents that contribute to cancer risk do so by damaging the genetic material in cells that regulate growth, division, and protein synthesis. They cause chemical changes in the nucleotide components of the cell's DNA and get passed on to daughter cells. They affect not only cell growth, but also cell repair and the ability of a cell to know when to die or disintegrate (apoptosis). Some of these environmental agents include chemicals in cigarettes, automobile exhaust, insecticides, dyes, industrial chemicals, insulation, and hormones. Radiation also contributes to cancer risk in the form of sunlight, x-rays, radioactive substances, and nuclear fission. Viruses in the environment may also be carcinogenic because of their ability to transform cells and alter their genetic material.

CRITICAL THINKING QUESTION
Radiation therapy is a way of treating cancer by irradiating the tumor with a maximal dose of ionizing radiation in order to destroy the cells. Exposure to radiation, however, poses a risk in itself for increasing the development of cancers. How does cancer therapy reconcile this risk?
Guidelines: The goal of radiation therapy is to deliver the maximal dose to the tumor with minimal damage to surrounding healthy tissues. There is no doubt that high-dose radiation damages DNA. Radiation also causes many undesirable side effects, some that reverse after radiotherapy is completed, and some that do not. Newer radiation techniques use high-energy protons to increase the focus of the electron beams being used to destroy the tumor. This decreases tissue damage to surrounding healthy tissues. Fractionation—small, repeated doses of radiation, rather than fewer, large doses—is also used, allowing larger total doses to be given while causing less damage to normal tissue.

OBJECTIVES	CONTENT	TEACHING RESOURCES
Learn medical terms that describe the growth and spread of tumors.	■ Introduction (p. 794) ■ Characteristics of tumors (p. 794)	▨ PPT 5-10 ⊕ IRM Multiple Choice Quiz question 1 ⊕ IRM Exercise Quiz A ↖ MTO Module 19, Section I, Lesson 1 Figure 19-1 A, Photomicrograph of normal skeletal muscle cells; B, Anaplastic tumor cells of the skeletal muscle (p. 794) Figure 19-2 A liver studded with metastatic cancer (p. 795)

ELSEVIER

Chabner

OBJECTIVES	CONTENT	TEACHING RESOURCES
		Figure 19-3 Differences between benign and malignant tumors (p. 795)
		Exercise A (p. 827)
		Companion CD Exercise 19-1
		Class Activity Have groups of three develop a list of characteristics of tumors, both benign and malignant. Pick a group to present the description. Have the class offer improvements.
		Class Activity Have students interview family members and other students about their daily exposure to carcinogens. Students should ask what they have done to prevent cancer (e.g., wear SPF sunscreen). Have students report their findings in class. See whether males and females engage in different preventative behaviors and whether they think males or females are exposed to more carcinogens.
Become familiar with terms related to the causes, diagnosis, and treatment of cancer.	■ Carcinogenesis (p. 796) □ What causes cancer? (p. 796) □ Environmental agents (p. 797) □ Heredity (p. 798)	PPT 11-13
		IRM Multiple Choice Quiz
		MTO Module 19, Section I, Lesson 2
		Figure 19-4 Two functions of DNA (p. 796)
		Figure 19-5 Chromosomal (oncogene) translocation (p. 798)
		Table 19-1 Genes implicated in hereditary cancers (p. 799)
		Figure 19-6 Role of environmental agents and heredity in carcinogenesis (p. 799)
		Exercise B (p. 827)
		▶ Discuss Table 19-1 regarding how risk of cancer can be inherited through suppressor genes and how genes can be analyzed for risk.
		Class Activity Divide the class into two competing teams. Give each team a set of different flash cards with the names of cancer treatments on them. The teams take turns showing a card to the opponent, who has to define or describe the treatment. The correct answer wins a point. However, the first team loses a point for accepting an incorrect answer or rejecting a correct answer. The team with the most points wins.

The Language of Medicine, 9th ed.

Chabner

OBJECTIVES	CONTENT	TEACHING RESOURCES
		Class Activity Divide students into groups. Assign a known carcinogen to each group. Groups should report back to the class on the topic and explain the cancer the toxin is associated with, as well as how it may produce cancer (e.g., asbestos, cigarettes, radioactive fallout from bomb explosions, and power plants, UV light).
Recognize how tumors are classified and described by pathologists.	■ Classification of cancerous tumors (p. 799) □ Carcinomas (p. 800) □ Sarcomas (p. 800) □ Mixed-tissue tumors (p. 802)	PPT 14-20 IRM Multiple Choice Quiz IRM Exercise Quiz C Table 19-2 Carcinomas and the epithelial tissues from which they derive (p. 800) Table 19-3 Sarcomas and the connective tissues from which they derive (p. 801) Table 19-4 Mixed-tissue tumors (p. 802) Exercise C (p. 828) Companion CD Exercise 19-2 ▸ Discuss Tables 19-2 and 19-3 with respect to the tissues from which carcinomas and sarcomas derive. *Class Activity Have students cut out paper images of chromosomes and go over how replication and cell division create daughter cells (mitosis) and how germ cells are created (meiosis). Then have two groups explain at what point carcinogens can thwart the process of cell division. Have another group explain how mutations lead to damaged DNA and malignancy. This group should focus on other cell processes besides division (e.g., protein synthesis, programmed cell death).* *Class Activity Ask students to find videos illustrating the process of oncogenesis that can be shared with the class.*

ELSEVIER

19.1 Homework/Assignments:

Have students research cancer survival rates and treatments for men vs. women.

19.1 Teacher's Notes:

LESSON 19.2

CRITICAL THINKING QUESTION

Dr. Duke is an oncologist. He recently biopsied tissue from a tumor on Sara's face. He told her that her tumor is malignant but that it still looks very much like its parent tissue. He also told her that T is less than one, N is zero, and M is zero. What can she tell about her prognosis from this information? **Guidelines:** Her prognosis is very good. Her cancer is treatable and caught in its early stages, so her chances of long-term survival are very high. The tissue looks much like its original form; thus, it is still well differentiated and in its early stages of transformation. T refers to the size of the tumor, N refers to the number of lymph nodes that are invaded, and M refers to metastases to other organs. Her biopsy report indicates that her tumor is small, differentiated, and has not spread. This is good for treatment and prognosis.

OBJECTIVES	CONTENT	TEACHING RESOURCES
Recognize how tumors are classified and described by pathologists.	■ Pathologic descriptions (p. 802) □ Gross descriptions (p. 802) □ Microscopic descriptions (p. 803)	PPT 22-26 IRM Multiple Choice Quiz IRM Exercise Quiz D, E IRM Dictation and Comprehension Quiz MTO Module 19, Section II, Lessons 1-2 Figure 19-7 A, Cystic ovarian adenocarcinoma; B, medullary carcinoma (p. 802) Figure 19-8 A, Adenomatous polyposis; B, Gastric carcinoma (p. 803) Figure 19-9 A, Follicular non-Hodgkin lymphoma; B, Papillary carcinoma (p. 804) Exercises D, E (p. 828-829) Companion CD Exercises 19-3, 19-4 *Class Activity Give small groups copies of actual pathology reports. Have them find terms for gross and microscopic pathological descriptions and define them. Have them share their findings with the class.* *Class Activity Divide the class into two or more competing teams. Play a Jeopardy-style game by giving them "answers" from pathological descriptions such as, "It forms large open spaces filled with fluid." Award a point for the question, "What is a cystic tumor?" The team with the most points wins.* *Class Activity Using the medical pathology textbooks, have students find pictures of the gross descriptions in the textbook. Have them report back to the class with the pictures, describing the characteristics of each tumor.*

OBJECTIVES	CONTENT	TEACHING RESOURCES
		Class Activity Using an atlas of microscopic pathology, divide the class into groups. Assign each group a cancer of a particular organ system. Have students pick out micrographs of their disease category, and then find micrographs of healthy organ systems using a medical atlas of histology. Have the students point out the most obvious differences in the structure of the diseased versus healthy organ. See an example of a similar comparison in the text, Figure 19-1.
Understand the x-rays, laboratory tests, and procedures used by physicians for determining the presence and extent of spread (staging) of tumors.	■ Grading and staging systems (p. 804)	⊠ PPT 28-30 IRM Multiple choice Quiz Table 19-5 International TNM staging system for lung cancer (p. 805) Exercise F (p. 829) *Class Activity Have students look up at least two different types of staging systems for two different cancers (e.g., lung and cervical). What is the importance of grading systems, and why do they exist?* *Class Activity Ask a local cancer registrar to come in and explain his/her job responsibilities, including examples of how various cancers are staged. Have a discussion of why accurate data are important in cancer research.* *Class Activity Divide the class into groups of three. Give each a set of index cards with three different lung cancer diagnoses with staging abbreviations from the TNM system (Table 19-5). Have students take turns role-playing an allied health professional explaining the diagnosis and prognosis to the patient. Have groups share highlights of their exchanges with the class.* *Class Activity Divide the class into small groups. Have each group debate whether or not a standardized system of grading cancerous tumors would be beneficial to the medical community. Have each group vote on a final decision and appoint a spokesperson to explain the group's decision to the class.*

19.2 Homework/Assignments:

Have students investigate cancer registries: Which hospitals in the area have them? What is their purpose? Cancer is a reportable disease. If there is no registry, who receives and compiles reports?

Ask students to explore the National Cancer Registrars Web site (http://www.ncra-usa.org) to find out more about the career of cancer registry/oncology data registrars.

19.2 Teacher's Notes:

LESSON 19.3

CRITICAL THINKING QUESTION

Lois has been notified that she must undergo surgery to remove a malignant growth from her uterus. She asks her doctor whether she will need adjuvant therapy after her surgery. Her doctor tells her she will know that only after the surgery. What sorts of information might her doctor obtain from the surgery to determine whether she needs additional treatment?

Guidelines: Lois's doctor will try to determine whether her tumor has spread beyond the tissue she plans to remove. If it is early, the doctor may find that she can remove the entire tumor, and surgery alone might cure Lois's cancer. A debulking procedure may be used if the tumor is attached to a vital organ and cannot be completely removed. In that case, her doctor will remove as much tissue as possible with additional radiation or chemotherapy needed later. Her doctor will do what is called an excisional biopsy that will be used for diagnosis but might also be curative.

OBJECTIVES	CONTENT	TEACHING RESOURCES
Recognize procedures, tests, and abbreviations that pertain to the care of cancer patients.	■ Cancer treatment (p. 806) ☐ Surgery (p. 806) ☐ Radiation therapy (radiation oncology) (p. 806) ☐ Chemotherapy, biological therapy, and differentiating agents (p. 810)	PPT 32-36 IRM Multiple Choice Quiz IRM Exercise Quiz F MTO, Module 19, Section II, Lessons 3-4 Figure 19-10 Linear accelerator (p. 807) Figure 19-11 Proton therapy machine (p.808) Figure 19-12 Hodgkin's disease before and after radiation therapy (p. 809) Table 19-6 Selected cancer chemotherapeutic agents and the cancers they treat (p. 811) Figure 19-13 Mechanisms of action of cancer chemotherapeutic agents (p. 813) Table 19-7 Cancers and chemotherapeutic regimens (p. 812) Table 19-8 Biological agents and their modes of action (p. 814) Table 19-9 Newest anticancer drugs and their modes (p. 814) Exercises G-I (pp. 830-831) Companion CD Exercise 19-5 *Class Activity Invite a spokesperson from a local cancer group to speak to the class about his or her organization. A cancer survivor might also discuss the disease and treatment.* *Class Activity Divide students into groups. Assign each group a specific cancer treatment (e.g., surgery, radiation therapy, chemotherapy). Class size permitting, groups*

ELSEVIER

The Language of Medicine, 9th ed.

Chabner

OBJECTIVES	CONTENT	TEACHING RESOURCES
		can be assigned specific forms of surgery or specific chemo- or biological therapies. Have each group research and prepare a report for a patient who has been recommended to undergo the assigned therapy. Each report should include how to prepare for therapy, what to expect immediately after therapy, and any potential side effects. Have each group present its findings to the class.
		Class Activity *Divide the class into three groups and have each choose a contestant for a quiz show. Using transparencies or flash cards, show the contestants a variety of words one at a time. Ask them to pronounce each word correctly and define it. The first contestant to answer correctly wins a point. When a contestant answers incorrectly, the team chooses a new contestant.*
		Class Activity *Use the Internet to find current treatments for cancer, including alternative treatments. The American Cancer Society Web site, WebMD, and the government website for complementary and alternative medicine (http://nccam.nih.gov/health/whatiscam) can be used.*

19.3 Homework/Assignments:

19.3 Teacher's Notes:

LESSON 19.4

CRITICAL THINKING QUESTION

Why do some cancer chemotherapeutic agents, such as antimetabolites, have noxious side effects in certain organ systems? What other classes of cancer chemotherapy might have similar treatment effects?

Guidelines: Drugs that target quickly dividing tumor cells attach to DNA molecules to disrupt DNA synthesis or block replication to kill the cells. Cells in the body that normally divide often also take up these drugs. These include cells that form blood and hair elements and which line the intestine. The drug is meant to disrupt cell duplication; alopecia (hair loss), myelosuppression (bone marrow depression), and gastrointestinal distress (nausea) are common side effects. Alkylating agents, antimitotics, and antimetabolites all have toxic side effects because they work on quickly dividing cells via these similar mechanisms.

OBJECTIVES	CONTENT	TEACHING RESOURCES
Recognize procedures, tests, and abbreviations that pertain to the care of cancer patients.	■ Terminology (p. 818) ☐ Combining forms (p. 818) ☐ Suffixes (p. 820) ☐ Prefixes (p. 820) ■ Laboratory tests (p. 821) ■ Clinical procedures (p. 821) ■ Abbreviations (p. 823)	PPT 37-39 IRM Multiple Choice Quiz IRM Terminology Quiz IRM Laboratory Tests and Clinical Procedures Quiz IRM Exercise Quiz G, H IRM Pronunciation Quiz IRM Abbreviations Quiz IRM Practical Applications, Case Study A questions, 1-5 IRM Practical Applications, Chart Note C MTO Module 19, Section I, Lessons 3-4 Figure 19-14 (A) Normal smear from the cervicovaginal region; (B) Abnormal cervicovaginal smear (p. 822) Exercises J-K (pp. 831-832) *Class Activity Divide the class into two competing teams. Show them a flash card, transparency, or PowerPoint slide of an abbreviation. Ask them to provide the term it stands for. The first team to give a correct answer wins a point. Give an additional point for a definition of the term.* *Class Activity Play a Jeopardy-style game with chemotherapy and biological therapy terms. For example, instructor may give students*

Chabner

OBJECTIVES	CONTENT	TEACHING RESOURCES
		answers, such as, "these are synthetic compounds containing one or more alkyl groups that interfere with DNA synthesis by attaching to DNA molecules." Students will answer with "What are alkylating agents?" Instructor can divide the class into groups and keep score.
Apply your new knowledge to understanding medical terms in their proper contexts, such as medical reports and records.	■ Practical Applications (p. 824)	IRM Practical Applications A-C MTO Module 19, Section IV Practical Applications (pp. 824-826) *Class Activity Have students find an article from a leading cancer journal. Have them underline 25 medical terms used for cancer diagnosis or therapy. Have each student switch articles with a classmate and define the terms.* *Class Activity Have students take turns reading the sentences from exercise L. Ask them to spell, analyze, define, and underline the accented syllable.*
Performance Evaluation		IRM Multiple Choice Quiz IRM Terminology Quiz IRM Laboratory Tests and Clinical Procedures Quiz IRM Exercise Quiz IRM Dictation and Comprehension Quiz IRM Spelling Quiz IRM Pronunciation Quiz IRM Abbreviations Quiz IRM Vocabulary Quiz IRM Review Sheet Quiz IRM Pronunciation Quiz IRM Crossword Puzzle IRM Practical Applications

ELSEVIER

OBJECTIVES	CONTENT	TEACHING RESOURCES
		ESLR Student Quiz Chapter 19
		MTO Module 19, Sections I-II quizzes
		MTO Module 19 Exam.
		Companion CD Exercises 19-6, 19-7, 19-8
		iTerms Chapter 19

19.4 Homework/Assignments:

Have students look up chemotherapeutic agents and report back on the side effects of these agents. Assign groups to different types of cancer (such as gastric sarcoma and melanoma). What are the available drugs to help patients deal with their side effects? Are there many? How do they work?

19.4 Teacher's Notes:

ELSEVIER

The Language of Medicine, 9th ed.

Chabner

Slide 1

Slide 2

Slide 3

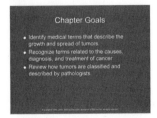

Slide 4

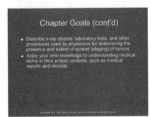

Slide 5

Chabner

Slide 6

- Go over recent morbidity numbers that you can obtain from the NIH Web site.

- How do cancer cells spread throughout the body?

Slide 7

- What are the most common causes of cancer death in the U.S.? In men? In women?

Slide 8

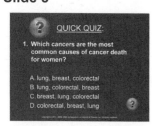

- Correct answer is A: For women, it is lung, breast, then colorectal that are the most common causes of death from cancer

Slide 9

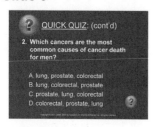

- Correct answer is B: For men it is lung, colorectal, then prostate that are the most common causes of cancer death for men.

Slide 10

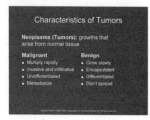

- What is an encapsulated tumor? (*a tumor contained within a fibrous capsule*)

- What is a differentiated tumor? (*a tumor composed of cells that resemble the normal tissue from which they are derived*)

Slide 11

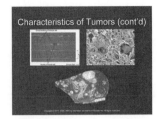

Slide 12

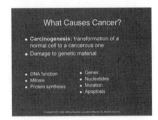

- What is the relationship between DNA and cell function?

- Explain how cell function can be disrupted by DNA damage and how that damage could lead to mutations and apoptosis.

Slide 13

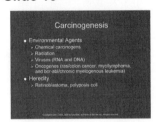

- What are some chemical carcinogens? (*cigarette smoke, exhaust, insecticides, etc.*)

- Name some sources of radiation. (*sunlight, x-rays, etc.*)

- What are oncogenes? (*pieces of normal DNA that cause normal cells to become malignant when activated by mutation*)

Slide 14

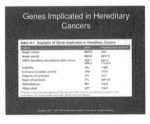

- What is genetic screening? (*testing family members' blood to determine whether the cancer is inherited*)

Slide 15

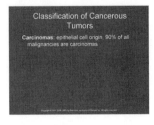

- What does histogenesis mean?

- What type of tissue are carcinomas derived from?

- What is the name for benign tumors? Malignant tumors?

Chabner

Slide 16

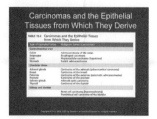

Slide 17

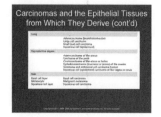

Slide 18

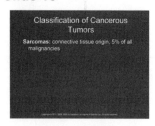

- What type of tissue are sarcomas derived from? Give specific examples.

- What are benign tumors called? Malignant tumors?

Slide 19

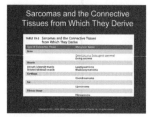

Slide 20

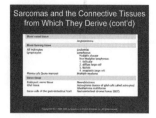

Chabner

Slide 21

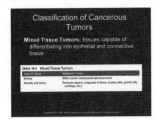

- Where are mixed-tissue tumors commonly found?

Slide 22

Slide 23

- Describe each of the above types of tumors. Where is each likely to be found?
- List and describe the two types of polypoid tumors and cystic tumors.

Slide 24

- What are alveolar tumors?
- What are dysplastic tumors?
- What does *scirrhous* mean when referring to tumors?

Slide 25

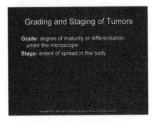

- Describe how a tumor is graded and staged.
- Explain how this relates to therapy and prognosis.

Chabner

Slide 26

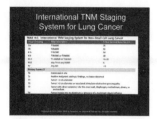

Slide 27

Slide 28

Slide 29

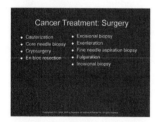

- What is a debulking procedure?
- What is adjuvant therapy?

Slide 30

- What is normal cell damage referred to in radiation? (*morbidity*)

Slide 31

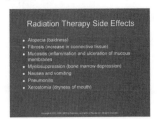

- Discuss the possible causes of these side effects.
- Which side effects reverse after treatment is discontinued?

Slide 32

Slide 33

- What are common side effects of alkylating agents?
- How do antibiotic drugs work in cancer therapy?
- What are antimitotics derived from?
- Name a particular type of cancer on which hormonal agents might be effective.

Slide 34

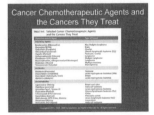

Slide 35

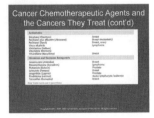

ELSEVIER

The Language of Medicine, 9th ed.
Chabner

Slide 36

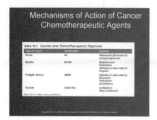

- Discuss how the agents might act as carcinogens to normal tissue.
- How is this true for radiation therapy as well?
- Discuss new gene-targeted research and drug discovery that might make these old treatments look archaic in the future

Slide 37

Slide 38

- Name three terms in cancer medicine that use one of the above forms. (*carcinoma, mutation, radiotherapy*)

Slide 39

- Name three words in cancer medicine that contain of one of the above suffixes or prefixes. (*neoplasm, histogenesis, sarcoma*)

Slide 40

- Describe a bone marrow biopsy and how it can detect cancer.
- What is exfoliative cytology and what types of cancer does it detect?
- What is a needle biopsy and what types of cancer can it detect?

TEACHING FOCUS

Students will have the opportunity to learn about the role of radioactivity in the diagnosis and treatment of disease. They will become acquainted with the health professions and the training necessary to use radioactive substances for these purposes. They will have a chance to become familiar with the unique properties of x-rays and radioisotopes that make these diagnostic tools useful in medicine and the unique advantages of various methods of scanning. Students will also be shown the difference between diagnostic tests that are done in a test tube *(in vitro)* versus the whole body *(in vivo)* and the advantages and disadvantages of these procedures.

MATERIALS AND RESOURCES

- ☐ CT scans (Lesson 20.1)
- ☐ Film badge (Lesson 20.1)
- ☐ Flash cards, transparencies, or PowerPoint slides (Lesson 20.2)
- ☐ Fluoroscopic images (Lesson 20.1)
- ☐ Gross anatomy atlas (Lesson 20.1)
- ☐ Medical forms (Lesson 20.2)
- ☐ Ultrasound images (Lesson 20.1)
- ☐ X-ray photographs (Lesson 20.1)

LESSON CHECKLIST

Preparations for this lesson include:

- Lecture
- Demonstration: ultrasound, PET, MRI, x-ray, CT scan images
- Method of student evaluation for entry-level knowledge to achieve competency in the comprehension and application of terminology relating to radiology and nuclear medicine, including:
  - o physical properties of x-rays
  - o diagnostic techniques used by radiologists and nuclear physicists
  - o x-ray views and patient positions in x-ray examinations
  - o radioactivity's role in diagnosis
  - o medical terms used in radiology and nuclear medicine
  - o medical terms in proper context, such as medical reports and records

KEY TERMS

Diagnostic Techniques (pp. 846-853)

angiography
arthrography
cholangiography
digital subtraction angiography (DSA)
hysterosalpingography
myelography
pyelography

Vocabulary (pp. 858-859)

cineradiography
computed tomography (CT)
contrast studies
fluorescence
gamma camera
gamma rays half-life
interventional radiology
in vitro
in vivo
ionization
labeled compound

magnetic resonance (MR)
nuclear medicine
positron emission tomography (PET)
radioimmunoassay
radioisotope radiology
radiolucent
radionuclide
radiopaque
radiopharmaceutical
roentgenology
scan
scintigraphy
single-photon emission computed tomography (SPECT)
tagging
tracer studies
transducer
ultrasound (US, U/S)
uptake
ventilation/perfusion studies

Terminology (pp. 859-860)

is/o

pharmaceut/o

radi/o

son/o

therapeut/o

vitr/o

viv/o

-gram

-graphy

-lucent

-opaque

echo-

ultra-

REFERENCE LIST

PowerPoint slides (CD, Evolve): 1-31

Legend

 CD
Companion
CD

 iTerms

 IRM
Instructor's
Resource Manual
available on CD
and Evolve

 Evolve
Evolve
Resources

 PPT
PowerPoint
Slides

 MTO
Medical
Terminology
Online

Class Activities are indicated in **bold italic**.

ELSEVIER

LESSON 20.1

PRETEST
IRM Exercise Quiz A

BACKGROUND ASSESSMENT

Question: Henry was climbing a tree when he fell and hurt his arm. His mother took him to the emergency room where she demanded to see a doctor. After an initial examination, she was surprised that she saw little of the doctor and instead saw many other health professionals who were involved in determining whether Henry's arm was indeed broken. What sort of personnel might be involved in diagnosing the condition of Henry's arm?

Answer: Many allied health professionals work with physicians in radiology and nuclear medicine. Depending on the type of injury, Henry might be seen by various radiologic technologists. A radiologist is a physician who specializes in the practice of diagnostic radiology. A nuclear physician specializes in administering diagnostic procedures that require nuclear medicine. Radiographers aid physicians in administering diagnostic x-rays, and nuclear medicine technologists attend to patients undergoing those procedures requiring nuclear medicines (e.g., radiopharmaceuticals) and operate gamma cameras under the direction of a nuclear physician. Sonographers perform ultrasound, which does not require radioisotopes or x-rays, but can be important in diagnosing body cavity disorders that cannot be seen with the naked eye (such as those in blood vessels, heart chambers, unborn fetuses).

Question: Dr. Fuller has a patient she suspects has a malfunctioning thyroid gland. She is not certain about the nature of the problem and would like to obtain information about this patient. What type of diagnostic tool should she use, and what sorts of information might she obtain about the state of the thyroid?

Answer: A thyroid scan can gather multiple types of information about the thyroid gland. The size and shape of the thyroid gland can be visualized following the oral ingestion of iodine-123 (^{123}I) by the patient. In addition, the radioactive iodine will accumulate in "hot spots" where the thyroid gland is hyperfunctioning. Thyroid malignancies appear as "cold spots" because the carcinoma does not concentrate the ^{123}I and thus identifies a nonfunctioning region of the gland.

CRITICAL THINKING QUESTION

How can one patient have a radiologic procedure to diagnose a condition, while another has radiation treatment to destroy a tumor?

Guidelines: As radiation treatment, the ionizing effect of radiation can kill tumor cells. Smaller doses of those same ionizing rays can be used to image tissues.

OBJECTIVES	CONTENT	TEACHING RESOURCES
Learn the physical properties of x-rays.	■ Introduction (p. 844) ■ Radiology (p. 844) □ Characteristics of x-rays (p. 844)	⊠▥ PPT 5-7 🡔 MTO Module 20, Section I, Lessons 1-2 Figure 20-1 X-ray photograph (radiograph) of the hand (p. 845) Exercises A, B (pp. 864) Demonstrate the uses of a film badge in the workplace. *Class Activity Ask pairs of students to imagine that the technology of x-rays has only recently been developed. Have them take turns role-playing a salesperson for an x-ray company trying to convince a skeptical hospital director to purchase the new*

The Language of Medicine, 9th ed.

OBJECTIVES	CONTENT	TEACHING RESOURCES
		equipment. *Have them share highlights of their exchanges with the class.*
		Class Activity Compare a traditional x-ray with a CT scan of a similar region of the body. These pictures can be obtained from books or online sources. Compare and contrast the details obtained about the organ or region of the body. Using a gross anatomy atlas, see how many structures you can identify from both types of images.
Become familiar with diagnostic techniques used by radiologists and nuclear physicians.	☐ Diagnostic techniques (p. 846)	PPT 8-9 MTO Module 20, Section I, Lessons 4-6 Figure 20-2 (A) CT scanner; (B) Patient in a CT scanner (p. 8202 through various regions of the body (p. 846) Figure 20-3 CT scans through various regions of the body (p. 847) Figure 20-4 Coronary angiography (p. 848) Figure 20-5 Coronary angiograms before and after stent placement (p. 849) Figure 20-6 Percutaneous transhepatic cholangiography (p. 849) Figure 20-7 Fetal measurements taken with ultrasound imaging (p. 850) Figure 20-8 A, Doppler ultrasound scan; B, Color-flow imaging in a patient with aortic regurgitation (p. 851) Figure 20-9 Magnetic resonance images (p. 852) Exercise C (p. 865) *Class Activity Have students take a poll of classmates, friends, and family members about the types of medical imaging they have experienced in their lifetimes. Have the students determine whether there is a correlation with age and numbers or types of procedures that individuals have experienced. Determine whether there is a difference between men and women in the number and types of scans they have undergone.* *Class Activity Divide the class into three or six groups. Ask one or two groups to prepare a presentation on the advantages and*

OBJECTIVES	CONTENT	TEACHING RESOURCES
		disadvantages of a diagnostic technique: x-rays, ultrasound, or magnetic imaging. Pick representatives to present to the class. Have the class offer improvements. Ask them to analyze and define any medical terms that are used. *Class Activity Compare the images of the female reproductive organs obtained from a fluoroscope with those obtained via ultrasound. What are the advantages and disadvantages of each of these procedures? Have each student write a case study that utilizes each of these procedures.*
Identify the x-ray views and patient positions used in x-ray examinations.	☐ X-ray positioning (p. 853)	⊠▤ PPT 10-16 🔧 IRM Multiple Choice Quiz ↖ MTO Module 20, Section I, Lesson 3 Figure 20-10 Summary of radiological diagnostic techniques (p. 853) Figure 20-11 Positions for x-ray views (p. 853) Exercise D (p. 865) ◉ Companion CD Exercise 20-1 *Class Activity Divide the class into two teams. Call out an x-ray position. Ask them to demonstrate the position and to state the direction of the x-ray beam and the position of the x-ray film. The first team to do so correctly gets a point.*

20.1 Homework/Assignments:

20.1 Teacher's Notes:

ELSEVIER

Chabner

LESSON 20.2

CRITICAL THINKING QUESTION

Sonja is 42 years old and pregnant with her first child. Her doctor thinks she ought to have a procedure called amniocentesis to harvest fetal cells for genetic analysis. He tells Sonja that he will use a large needle inserted through her abdomen to obtain these cells from the amniotic fluid around the baby. He tells her that he will be able to visualize the needle so she needn't worry about sticking her baby. She decides that she still thinks it is dangerous because of the radioactivity her baby will be exposed to. Need she be concerned?

Guidelines: Her doctor will be using ultrasound, not x-rays, to detect the needle. The technique uses high-frequency sound waves that bounce off body tissues to detect interfaces between tissues of different densities. Ultrasonic echoes are recorded as a composite picture of the area producing a sonogram. The sound waves are nonionizing and noninjurious to tissues at the energy ranges used for this procedure, so the fetus will be safe and the needle can be visualized.

OBJECTIVES	CONTENT	TEACHING RESOURCES
Learn about the role of radioactivity in the diagnosis of disease.	■ Nuclear medicine (p. 854) ☐ Radioactivity and radionuclides (p. 854) ☐ Nuclear medicine tests: in vitro and in vivo procedures (p. 854)	PPT 18-24 IRM Multiple Choice Quiz MTO Module 20, Section II, Lessons 1-2 Figure 20-12 A, Patient receiving intravenous injection of radionuclide; B, Gamma camera (p. 855) Figure 20-13 Whole-body PET images (p. 856) Figure 20-14 Thyroid scans (p. 857) Figure 20-15 In vitro and in vivo nuclear medicine diagnostic tests (p. 857) Exercises E, F (pp. 866) Companion CD Exercise 20-2 *Class Activity Have students visit a medical library (or the Internet) to obtain photos of ultrasounds used to diagnose heart, gastrointestinal, reproductive, or obstetric disease. Have students display their findings and ask them to determine whether these scans provide the level of contrast obtained via scan using radiopharmaceuticals. Determine the advantages and disadvantages of ultrasound, other than nonionizing energy requirements.* *Class Activity Have groups of three develop an explanation of how radioactivity is used in the diagnosis of disease. Pick a group to present its explanation to the class. Have the class offer improvements.*

The Language of Medicine, 9th ed.

Chabner

OBJECTIVES	CONTENT	TEACHING RESOURCES
		Class Activity Have each student pick a particular type of scan that is of interest to him or her. Have the student contact a medical professional who conducts this sort of scanning to inquire whether examples of each type may be acquired for educational purposes. Have a show-and-tell atmosphere for viewing the scans. Then, have the class vote on which type of scan offers the most information about the status of the anatomy or function of the organ. *Class Activity Obtain a newspaper or magazine article about a topic related to nuclear medicine, Underline all the combining forms, suffixes, and prefixes in the terminology related to nuclear medicine. You may want to send students to the offices of radiologists to obtain a trade journal or magazine on the topic.*
Become familiar with medical terms used in the specialties of radiology and nuclear medicine.	■ Vocabulary (p. 858) ■ Terminology (p. 859) ■ Abbreviations (p. 861)	PPT 25-28 IRM Terminology Quiz IRM Abbreviations Quiz IRM Dictation and Comprehension Quizzes IRM Spelling Quiz A, B Exercises G-H (pp. 866-867) Companion CD Exercise 20-3 *Class Activity Divide the class into three groups and have each choose a contestant for a quiz show. Using transparencies or flash cards, show the contestants a variety of words one at a time. Ask them to pronounce each word correctly and define it. The first contestant to answer correctly wins a point. When a contestant answers incorrectly, the team chooses a new contestant. The team with the most correct answers wins.* *Class Activity Obtain online medical forms related to scans and x-rays. Have a competition to obtain the most abbreviations related to this topic. Divide the class into three groups before they obtain the abbreviations. Be certain to identify the correct words associated with the abbreviation.*

OBJECTIVES	CONTENT	TEACHING RESOURCES
Apply your new knowledge to understanding medical terms in their proper contexts, such as medical reports and records.	■ Practical Applications (p. 862)	PPT 29-30 IRM Multiple Choice Quiz IRM Crossword Puzzle IRM Practical Applications MTO Module 20, Section IV Companion CD Exercise 20-4 *Class Activity **Divide the class into two competing teams. Show them a flashcard, transparency, or PowerPoint slide of an abbreviation. Ask them to provide the term it stands for. The first team to give a correct answer wins a point. Give an additional point for a definition of the term. The team with the most points wins.*** *Class Activity **Read the first Case Report to the students. Ask them to answer the questions and spell, analyze, define, and underline the accented syllable in the terms used.***
Performance Evaluation		IRM Multiple Choice Quiz IRM Terminology Quiz IRM Exercise Quiz IRM Dictation and Comprehension Quiz IRM Spelling Quiz IRM Pronunciation Quiz IRM Abbreviations Quiz IRM Vocabulary Quiz IRM Review Sheet Quiz IRM Medical Scramble IRM Crossword Puzzle IRM Practical Applications ESLR Student Quiz Chapter 20 MTO Module 20, Sections I-II quizzes

Chabner

OBJECTIVES	CONTENT	TEACHING RESOURCES
		⬧ MTO Module 20 Exam
		💿 Companion CD Exercise 20-5, 20-6, 20-7
		📟 iTerms Chapter 20

20.2 Homework/Assignments:

20.2 Teacher's Notes:

Slide 1

The Language Of
Medicine
9th edition
Davi-Ellen Chabner

Slide 2

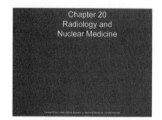

Chapter 20
Radiology and
Nuclear Medicine

Slide 3

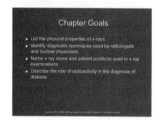

Chapter Goals

- List the physical properties of x-rays.
- Identify diagnostic techniques used by radiologists and nuclear physicians.
- Name x-ray views and patient positions used in x-ray examinations.
- Describe the role of radioactivity in the diagnosis of disease.

Slide 4

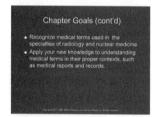

Chapter Goals (cont'd)

- Recognize medical terms used in the specialties of radiology and nuclear medicine.
- Apply your new knowledge to understanding medical terms in their proper contexts, such as medical reports and records.

Slide 5

Chapter 20
Lesson 20.1

The Language of Medicine, 9th ed.

Chabner

Slide 6

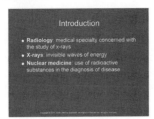

- What is another name for radiology? (*roentgenology*)
- What is the name for a physician who practices radiology? (*radiologist*)
- Name the three types of radioactivity. (*alpha parcticles, beta particles, and gamma rays*)

Slide 7

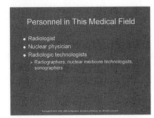

- What functions does a radiologist perform? (*the practice of diagnostic radiology*)
- What are the functions of each type of radiologic technician?

Slide 8

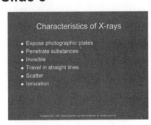

- What is the characteristic of a substance if it permits passage of most x-rays? (*radiolucent*)
- Substances that absorb most x-rays are _____? (*radiopague*)
- What is ionization?
- Scatter and ionization causes tissue damage.

Slide 9

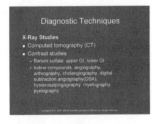

- Make sure all these terms are defined as in text.
- Why are contrast media used?
- What is a "double-contrast study"?
- Which test is also known as "urography"?

Slide 10

- Note which techniques require the use of radioactive substances.
- Which of the techniques listed can be used with a patient in motion?
- What are the specialized ultrasound techniques used to record blood velocity or flow?

The Language of Medicine, 9th ed.

Chabner

Slide 11

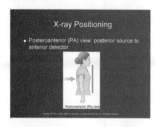

- The posteroanterior view of the chest is the most commonly requested chest x-ray.

- What is the likely reason for this?

- What structures are best viewed with the anteroposterior view?

Slide 12

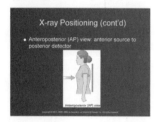

- The posteroanterior view of the chest is the most commonly requested chest x-ray.

- What is the likely reason for this?

- What structures are best viewed with the anteroposterior view?

Slide 13

- Why are oblique views necessary?

Slide 14

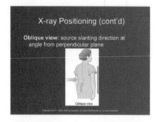

- Why are oblique views necessary?

Slide 15

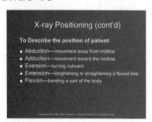

Chabner

Slide 16

Slide 17

- Correct answer is A: radiopaque

Slide 18

Slide 19

- Half-life of a particle is the time required to lose half of its radioactivity (disintegration).

- Important to know this because the length of time the diagnostic tool will stay in the body is critical to the test and critical in keeping the patient safe from radiation effects.

Slide 20

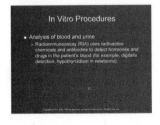

- What is the meaning of in vitro? (*Latin for "in the test tube"*)

- Describe in vivo tests.

The Language of Medicine, 9th ed.

Chabner

Slide 21

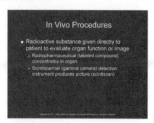

- Amounts of radiopharmaceuticals detected at a given location or organ are proportional to the rate at which the gamma rays are emitted.
- What is the meaning of in vivo? (*Latin for "in the body"*)

Slide 22

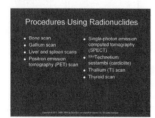

- What name can be applied to this group of tests? (*tracer studies*)
- What is another name for radionuclide scanning? (*scintigraphy*)

Slide 23

- PET is an acronym for Positron Emission Tomography.
- How are the radionuclides incorporated into the tissue?

Slide 24

- SPECT is an acronym for Single-Photon Emission Computed Tomography.
- What is an example of a radioactive tracer?

Slide 25

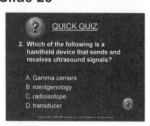

- Correct answer is D: transducer

Chabner

Slide 26

Slide 27

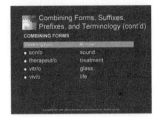

Slide 28

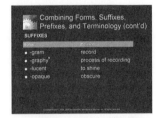

Slide 29

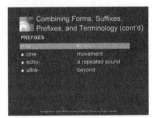

Slide 30

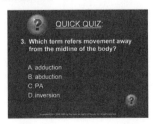

- Correct answer is B: abduction.

Chabner

Slide 31

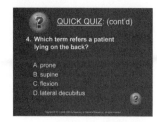

- Correct answer is B: supine

TEACHING FOCUS

Students will have the opportunity to learn about the classification of drugs and the terminology associated with their derivation, administration, mechanisms of actions on the body, and potential toxicity. Students will discover professions associated with pharmacology, including medicinal chemistry, molecular pharmacology, chemotherapy, and toxicology.

MATERIALS AND RESOURCES

- ☐ Hospital Formulary (Lesson 21.1)
- ☐ *Physicians' Desk Reference® (PDR®)* (Lesson 21.1)
- ☐ Slips of paper with vocabulary words, combining forms, and suffixes (Lesson 21.2)

LESSON CHECKLIST

Preparations for this lesson include:
- Lecture
- Demonstration
- Field trip: pharmacy
- Student performance evaluation of all entry-level skills required for student comprehension and application of pharmacology principles, including:
  - administering drugs
  - applying medical terminology
  - combining word elements to form medical words
  - knowing the basic structure of medical words and medical abbreviations
  - recognizing classes of drugs
  - understanding drug names, standards, and references

KEY TERMS

Vocabulary (pp. 890-894)

addiction
additive action
aerosol
anaphylaxis
antagonistic action
antidote
brand name
chemical name
contraindications
controlled substances
dependence
dose
Food and Drug Administration (FDA)
generic name
iatrogenic
idiosyncrasy
inhalation
medicinal chemistry
molecular pharmacology
oral administration
parenteral administration
pharmacist
pharmacy
pharmacodynamics

pharmacokinetics
pharmacologist
pharmacology
Physicians' Desk Reference® (PDR®)
receptor
rectal administration
side effect
sublingual administration
synergism
syringe
tolerance
topical application
toxicity
toxicology
transport
United States Pharmacopeia (USP.)
vitamin
ACE inhibitor
amphetamine
analgesic
androgen
anesthetic
angiotensin II receptor blocker
antacid

ELSEVIER

The Language of Medicine, 9th ed.
Chabner

antiandrogen
antiarrhythmic
antibiotic
anticoagulant
anticonvulsant
antidepressant
antidiabetic
antidiarrheal
antiemetic
antihistamine
antinauseant
antiplatelet
antiulcer
antiviral
aromatase inhibitor
bactericidal
bacteriostatic
beta-blocker
bisphosphonate
caffeine

calcium blocker
cardiac glycoside
cardiovascular drug
cathartic
diuretic
emetic
endocrine
estrogen
gastrointestinal drug
glucocorticoid
hypnotic
laxative
narcotic
progestin
purgative
respiratory drug
sedative
stimulant
thyroid hormone
tranquilizer

Terminology (pp. 894-896)

aer/o
alges/o
bronch/o
chem/o
cras/o
cutane/o
derm/o
erg/o
esthes/o
hist/o
hypn/o
iatr/o
lingu/o
myc/o
narc/o

or/o
pharmac/o
prurit/o
pyret/o
thec/o
tox/o
toxic/o
vas/o
ven/o
vit/o
ana-
anti-
contra-
par-
syn-

REFERENCE LIST

PowerPoint slides (CD, Evolve): 1-25

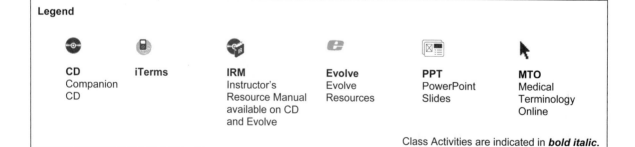

Legend

CD Companion CD

iTerms

IRM Instructor's Resource Manual available on CD and Evolve

Evolve Evolve Resources

PPT PowerPoint Slides

MTO Medical Terminology Online

Class Activities are indicated in **bold italic**.

LESSON 21.1

PRETEST
IRM Exercise Quiz B

BACKGROUND ASSESSMENT

Question: Jon goes to the doctor for an infection. His doctor writes two prescriptions and tells him that he must take both drugs if he wants to get better and that if he takes only one drug, he might not get better. He notices that they are both antibiotics and wonders why he must take two instead of one. Is the doctor just trying to make Jon buy more drugs?

Answer: Jon's doctor is operating under the assumption that each antibiotic alone will work less effectively than the two given together. Sometimes two drugs together produce an effect that is greater than the sum of the individual drugs or each drug alone. This is called synergism. This is especially true if each drug has a slightly different mechanism of action. The mechanism of one drug might actually make the mechanism of the other drug more effective. An example would be one antibiotic that is bacteriostatic and inhibits the growth of the bacteria and another antibiotic that is bactericidal and actually kills the bacteria.

Question: Maria has a school-age child who has been told that she is hyperkinetic in school and must be prescribed stimulants. Maria is very confused because she knows that caffeine is a stimulant and she uses it everyday to be more alert and increase her energy level in the morning. Has her school psychologist made a mistake?

Answer: Stimulants increase alertness and inhibit hyperactive behavior in some children. High doses can have the opposite effect. Children with hyperactive disorders often cannot sit still in school and concentrate. They are prescribed stimulants such as amphetamines or Ritalin.

CRITICAL THINKING QUESTION

Tina is caring for an infant who is running a very high fever and vomiting whenever Tina tries to feed him some water to keep him hydrated. If she continues to give him water to try to lower his body temperature and increase hydration and, as a result, he vomits more fluid than he is drinking, then he will only get more dehydrated, and his body temperature will rise. What do you think Tina should do to reduce the child's fever, make him more comfortable, and enhance his ability to drink liquids?

Guidelines: Since drinking water is causing the child to vomit, it is likely that the oral route of administration for antifever medications will only make matters worse. The child will probably vomit the medication. Therefore the physician may direct Tina to purchase acetaminophen (Tylenol) as a suppository and tell the medical assistant to instruct Tina how to administer the Tylenol via the rectal route. When his fever comes down, the child will likely be less nauseated and able to tolerate liquids. Tina can then try forcing fluids to rehydrate him.

OBJECTIVES	CONTENT	TEACHING RESOURCES
Learn the various subspecialty areas of pharmacology.	■ Introduction (p. 876) ■ Drug names, standards, and references (p. 877) □ Names (p. 877) □ Standards (p. 877) □ References (p. 877)	PPT 1-7 IRM Multiple Choice Quiz questions 1-4 IRM Exercise Quiz A MTO Module 21, Section I, Lessons 1-2 Figure 21-1 Subspecialty areas of pharmacology (p. 876) Exercises A, B (p. 900) ***Class Activity Divide the class into four groups. Each group represents a particular class of drug. Pick one drug from that class***

ELSEVIER

Chabner

OBJECTIVES	CONTENT	TEACHING RESOURCES
		and look it up in three different references. Then describe how those references provide different types of information. What are their respective strengths/weaknesses for providing information?
		Class Activity Using the Internet, find a Web site that lists the 100 most commonly prescribed drugs. Calculate the percentages of the various categories listed. Which ones are most frequently prescribed?
Identify the various routes of drug administration.	■ Administration of drugs (p. 878) ■ Drug actions and Interactions (p. 880) ■ Drug toxicity (p. 880)	PPT 8-12 IRM Multiple Choice Quiz questions 5-11 IRM Exercise Quizzes B-D MTO Module 21, Section I, Lessons 3-4 Table 21-1 Examples of vehicles for drug administration (p. 879) Figure 21-2 Drug administration (p. 879) Exercises C-F (pp. 901-902) Companion CD Exercises 21-1, 21-2 *Class Activity Have a pharmaceutical company representative give a talk to the class about the types of professionals that exist at the company and what sort of training is required for pharmaceutical jobs.* *Class Activity Ask students to spell, analyze, define, and underline the accented syllable in the terms for the various routes of administration.* *Class Activity In groups, have students create brochures for a drug company explaining all the different routes of drug administration. Students should explain when each route is used, how the drug is administered, and what types of drugs each route requires. Have groups present their brochures to the class.*

21.1 Homework/Assignments:

21.1 Teacher's Notes:

The Language of Medicine, 9th ed.

Chabner

CRITICAL THINKING QUESTION

Theo is in a car accident and is taken to the emergency room (ER). He tells the ER doctor that he has coronary heart disease and is taking medications to control his condition. The ER doctor notices that Theo has a large contusion on his leg and is bleeding profusely from his right arm. What does the doctor have to consider now that he has a better understanding of Theo's medical history?

Guidelines: Theo is likely taking medications that are anticoagulants. People with coronary heart disease often take warfarin (Coumadin) or are advised to take a daily aspirin to prevent the formation of clots or to break up clots in blood vessels. Aspirin is a natural antiplatelet drug. The ER doctor has to be concerned that these drugs will diminish Theo's ability to form a clot, so his bleeding from the accident might be difficult to control.

OBJECTIVES	CONTENT	TEACHING RESOURCES
Differentiate among the various classes of drugs and learn their actions and side effects.	■ Classes of drugs (p. 881) ☐ Analgesics (p. 881) ☐ Anesthetics (p. 882) ☐ Antibiotics and antivirals (p. 882) ☐ Anticoagulants and antiplatelet drugs (p. 883) ☐ Anticonvulsants (p. 884) ☐ Antidepressants (p. 884) ☐ Antidiabetics (p. 884) ☐ Antihistamines (p. 884) ☐ Antiosteoporosis drugs (p. 885) ☐ Cardiovascular drugs (p. 885) ☐ Endocrine drugs (p. 886) ☐ Gastrointestinal drugs (p.887) ☐ Respiratory drugs (p. 888) ☐ Sedatives-hypnotics (p. 889) ☐ Stimulants (p. 890) ☐ Tranquilizers (p. 890)	PPT 13-19 IRM Multiple Choice Quiz questions 12-25 IRM Exercise Quizzes E-G MTO, Module 21, Section II, Lessons 1-4 Table 21-2 Analgesics and anesthetics (p. 881) Table 21-3 Antibiotics and antivirals (p. 882) Table 21-4 Anticoagulants, anticonvulsants, antidepressants, and antidiabetics (p. 883) Table 21-5 Antihistamines and antiosteoporosis (p. 885) Table 21-6 Cardiovascular drugs (p. 886) Table 21-7 Endocrine drugs (p. 887) Table 21-8 Gastrointestinal drugs (p. 888) Table 21-9 Respiratory drugs (p. 889) Table 21-10 Sedatives/hypnotics, stimulants, tranquilizers (p. 889) Table 21-11 Vitamins (p. 895) Exercises G-L (pp. 902-904) Companion CD Exercises 21-3, 21-5 *Class Activity Make a chart like the one in Table 21-6. Divide the class into four groups. Each group takes a category from the chart and reports on the detailed mechanisms of action of that class of drugs. Each group gives the brand name and generic name of examples of that class of cardiovascular drug and explains whether the drug follows all the*

OBJECTIVES	CONTENT	TEACHING RESOURCES
		principles of the category in which it was included. Discuss whether the drug treats symptoms or the cause of cardiovascular disease.
		Class Activity Differentiate among classes of drugs that require a prescription and those that do not. Use the PDR® to determine availability.
		Class Activity Use the FDA Web site for approved, tentatively approved, over-the-counter and discontinued drugs. Divide the class into four groups and have each group report on a drug in each of those four categories. http://www.accessdata.fda.gov/scripts/cder/drugsatfda/
		Class Activity Have each student find two articles from newspapers or magazines about drug-related issues. Have them bring them to class and exchange articles between students. Then have each student underline drug-related terms in each article. Have each student exchange articles again and have them define underlined terms.
Define medical terms using combining forms, prefixes, and suffixes that relate to pharmacology.	■ Terminology (p. 894) ■ Abbreviations (p. 896)	▦ PPT 18-19 🔖 IRM Terminology Quiz Exercise K (p. 903) Exercise M (p. 905) 💿 Companion CD Exercise 21-4 *Class Activity Have students practice spelling, analyzing, defining and underlining the accented syllable in the terms in the combining form terminology list.*
Apply your new knowledge to understanding medical terms in their proper contexts, such as medical reports and records.	■ Practical applications (p. 897)	🔖 IRM Practical Applications 🔻 MTO Module 21, Section IV Exercise N (p. 905) *Class Activity Write vocabulary words, combining forms, and prefixes on small slips of paper and place them in a hat. Go around the room and have students draw a slip of paper and define the term (or use it to create a term) and create a context for the term by*

The Language of Medicine, 9th ed.

Chabner

OBJECTIVES	CONTENT	TEACHING RESOURCES
		using it in a sentence or scenario. Continue until all terms have been defined.
		Class Activity Using Exercise N, have the students take turns reading the sentences. Have the remainder of the class spell, analyze, define, and underline the accented syllable in the terms that are used.
Performance Evaluation		IRM Multiple Choice Quiz
		IRM Terminology Quiz
		IRM Exercise Quiz
		IRM Dictation and Comprehension Quiz
		IRM Spelling Quiz
		IRM Pronunciation Quiz
		IRM Vocabulary Quiz
		IRM Review Sheet Quiz
		IRM Medical Scramble
		IRM Crossword Puzzle
		IRM Practical Applications
		ESLR Student Quiz Chapter 21
		MTO Module 21 Sections I-II quizzes
		MTO Module 21 Exam
		Companion CD Exercises 21-6, 21-7, 21-8
		iTerms Chapter 21

21.2 Homework/Assignments:

How are prescription drugs regulated? Have students determine and report on the various government agencies that regulate the production, distribution, and prescription of drugs. What sort of statistical and epidemiological information can be obtained from these agencies? Give examples of agencies that are found on the Internet as well as in library-bound resources.

Assign the class a field trip to a local pharmacy as a homework assignment. Ask each student to write down all the categories of pharmaceuticals that are available over the counter.

21.2 Teacher's Notes:

Chabner

Slide 1

Slide 2

Slide 3

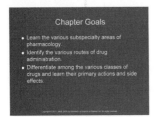

Slide 4

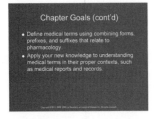

Slide 5

Chabner

Slide 6

- Ask the class to give examples of what they might consider to be a "drug." Is a drug something that can be abused?

- Can caffeine be considered a drug?

- Does a drug have to treat a disease in order to be classified as such?

- Name drugs with which the class is most familiar. Which are generic names and which are brand names?

Slide 7

- Only M.D.s can prescribe drugs in this country. Is this the same in other countries?

- Are there prescribed drugs in this country that are available as over-the-counter drugs in other countries?

Slide 8

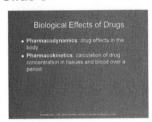

- How does the body alter drugs when they are ingested?

- What does "first pass" effect mean? Have students look up the definition of this term.

- What sorts of things might professionals who develop medicines have to consider about pharmacokinetics when they develop a drug?

Slide 9

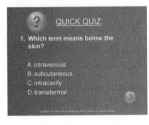

- Correct answer is B: subcutaneous

Slide 10

- Look up examples in the PDR or a drug manufacturer's manual and show students the many ways that drugs are listed and referenced. Also look up pictures of pills, tablets, etc. in the PDR.

- Is there an advantage to this system?

Chabner

Slide 11

Slide 12

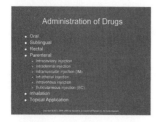

- Ask students for one example of the benefits of each of these routes of drug administration.

- Give examples of specific drugs that are more effective via a certain route.

- Discuss how changing the route can make a therapeutic drug toxic, or easily abused. (*Ritalin is an example. When taken orally, it has therapeutic effects on attention. When taken intranasally or inhaled, a person gets high and might start to abuse it like cocaine.*)

Slide 13

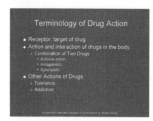

- What is the difference between tolerance and addiction?

- Ask students why a person can become sensitized to a drug (reverse tolerance) and be addicted even though it takes less of the drug to have the same effect. How does this phenomenon cause drug overdoses?

Slide 14

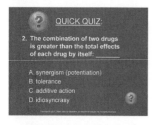

- Correct answer is A: synergism

Slide 15

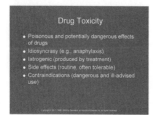

- Give examples of each of these toxic effects of drugs and make certain the student knows which effects are common and which are dangerous.

- What are some of the things that must be considered when prescribing drugs?

- Give examples of drugs that use the kidneys for elimination and what must be considered by the physician in this scenario.

- Give examples of specific drugs and ask students to look up and report contraindications for each drug.

- Pregnancy is an example of a contraindication for most drugs.

The Language of Medicine, 9th ed.

Chabner

Slide 16

Slide 17

- Students can look up all the examples of these drugs and be given assignments to report back to class.
- What are the different types of analgesics, and how do they compare in potency, action, etc.?

Slide 18

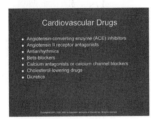

- These are the classes of cardiovascular drugs. There are complex mechanisms for making the heart work better. These mechanisms are based on principles regulating blood pressure, and the biophysics of the electrical properties of the heart muscle, which is innervated by the sympathetic and parasympathetic nervous systems.
- Know some examples of each class of cardiac drugs and their actions on the heart.
- Ask students how cardiovascular drugs differ in their action on the heart.

Slide 19

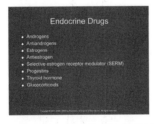

- Here is an expanded list of the endocrine class of drug therapy. This class is important because of our aging population and many of these drugs (e.g., tamoxifen) are used to treat not only symptoms of aging (menopause), but also degenerative diseases such as cancers that arise from the reproductive organs.
- Students can be asked to give examples of endocrine drugs.

Slide 20

- There are many mechanisms of action in this classification. Know some examples and the mechanisms.
- It is also important to know whether the drug relieves the symptom or the cause. For example, where in a series of events leading to increased stomach acid does the drug work?
- Ask students to provide examples of drugs that relieve symptoms and drugs that affect the cause of a disease.

Slide 21

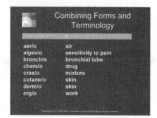

Slide 22

Slide 23

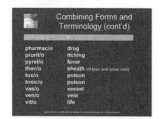

Slide 24

Slide 25

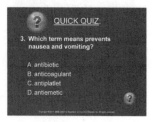

- Correct answer is D: antiemetic.

22 Lesson Plan
Psychiatry

TEACHING FOCUS

Students will have the opportunity to learn about the training required for classified professionals who provide diagnosis and therapy for individuals with mental disorders. Students will be exposed to the proper definition, pronunciation, and abbreviations for medical terms associated with the diagnosis and treatment of psychiatric disorders. Students will be shown some examples of tests used by clinical psychologists to evaluate patients' mental health, intelligence, personality, memory, mental processing, and potential brain damage.

MATERIALS AND RESOURCES

☐ Current newspaper (Lesson 22.1)
☐ Diagnostic and Statistical Manual of Mental Health Disorders (DSM-IV), 4th ed. (Lesson 22.1)

☐ Flash cards (Lesson 22.2)
☐ Paper (Lesson 22.1 and 22.3)
☐ *Physicians' Desk Reference®* (Lesson 22.3)

LESSON CHECKLIST

Preparations for this lesson include:

- Lecture
- Demonstration: tests used by clinical psychologists
- Method of student evaluation for entry-level knowledge to achieve competency in the appropriate application of terminology relating to psychiatry, including:
  - means by which intelligence and mental health status is assessed
  - names of commonly prescribed psychiatric drugs
  - terms for psychiatric disorders and therapies
  - differences between psychological and psychiatric specialties

KEY TERMS

Psychiatric Clinical Symptoms (pp. 917-918)

amnesia
anxiety
apathy
autism
compulsion
conversion
delusion
dissociation

dysphoria
euphoria
hallucination
labile
mania
mutism
obsession
paranoia

Personality Disorders (p. 922)

antisocial
borderline
histrionic

narcissistic
paranoid
schizoid

Sexual and Gender Identity Disorders (p. 923)

exhibitionism
fetishism
pedophilia
sexual masochism

sexual sadism
transvestic fetishism
voyeurism

Vocabulary (pp. 930-933)

affect
amnesia
anorexia nervosa
anxiety disorders
apathy
autism

bipolar disorder
bulimia nervosa
cannabis
compulsion
conversion disorder
defense mechanism

Chabner

delirium

delusion

dementia

depression

dissociative disorder

ego

fugue

gender identity disorder

hallucination

id

labile

mania

mood disorders

mutism

obsessive-compulsive disorder

paranoia

paraphilia

personality disorders

phobia

post-traumatic stress disorder

projective (personality) test

psychiatrist

psychologist

psychosis

reality testing

repression

schizophrenia

sexual disorders

somatoform disorder

substance-related disorder

superego

amphetamines

atypical antipsychotics

benzodiazepines

cognitive behavior therapy

electroconvulsive therapy

family therapy

free association

group therapy

hypnosis

insight-oriented therapy

lithium

neuroleptic drug

phenothiazine

play therapy

psychoanalysis

psychodrama

psychopharmacology

sedatives

supportive psychotherapy

transference

tricyclic antidepressants

Terminology (pp. 934-936)

anxi/o

aut/o

hallucin/o

hypn/o

iatr/o

ment/o

neur/o

phil/o

phren/o

psych/o

schiz/o

somat/o

-genic

-leptic

-mania

-phobia

-phoria

-thymia

a-, an-

cata-

hypo-

para-

REFERENCE LIST

PowerPoint slides (CD, Evolve): 1-37

Legend

CD
Companion
CD

iTerms

IRM
Instructor's
Resource Manual
available on CD
and Evolve

Evolve
Evolve
Resources

PPT
PowerPoint
Slides

MTO
Medical
Terminology
Online

Class Activities are indicated in **_bold italic._**

ELSEVIER

Chabner

LESSON 22.1

PRETEST
IRM Exercise Quiz B

BACKGROUND ASSESSMENT
Question: Several types of practitioners help people who have mental health illnesses. What type of practitioner can provide patients drug therapy if needed?
Answer: Psychiatrists are MDs who have the medical training to apply drug therapy in addition to providing psychotherapy. Psychologists are non-medical professionals who do not hold medical degrees and therefore cannot dispense drug therapy. They use methods of psychotherapy and analysis exclusively. It is recommended that patients seeking the services of a psychiatrist look for board-certified physicians.

Question: What are two drugs that are often abused and are readily available at grocery stores? What are their effects, and why are they linked to substance-related disorders?
Answer: Alcohol and nicotine are readily available at grocery stores (in some states) and both are linked to psychological and physical dependence. Psychological dependence is a compulsion to continue taking a drug despite adverse consequences. Physical dependence is characterized by the onset of withdrawal symptoms when the drug is abruptly discontinued. Tolerance is the declining effect of the drug, which leads to an increase in dosage. Unlike alcohol, nicotine addiction does not meet the definition of "abuse," described as "use of a drug for purposes other than those for which it is prescribed."

CRITICAL THINKING QUESTION
Mr. Walden, a high school psychologist, was recently asked to consult with the teachers and parents of Robert, a student who is having academic and social problems. What types of tools would assist Mr. Walden in evaluating this student before the consultation?
Guidelines: School psychologists are generally clinical psychologists who use tests to evaluate various aspects of students' mental health and intelligence. There are several types of intelligence tests, including the Wechsler Adult Intelligence Scale and the Stanford-Binet Intelligence Scale. There are tests to determine personality structure, including one's ability to relate to others, and to help identify psychological disorders in adolescents and adults. There are also tests in which patients view images, drawings, and geometric designs to help reveal their academic abilities, associations, and perceptions. Tests like these will help Mr. Walden formulate and present an objective assessment of Robert.

OBJECTIVES	CONTENT	TEACHING RESOURCES
Differentiate between a psychiatrist, a psychologist, and other mental health specialists.	■ Introduction (p. 916)	PPT 6-8 IRM Multiple Choice Quiz questions 1, 2 MTO Module 22, Section I, Lesson 1 Figure 22-1 Inkblots (p.916) Figure 22-2 Thematic Apperception Test (TAP) (p. 917) Exercise A (p. 940) *Class Activity Have students research the other types of mental health professionals (psychiatric social workers, mental health technicians, etc.) and report their findings to the class.*

Chabner

OBJECTIVES	CONTENT	TEACHING RESOURCES
Learn tests used by clinical psychologists to evaluate a patient's mental health and intelligence.	■ Introduction (p. 916)	▶ MTO Module 22, Section I, Lesson 2 *Class Activity Have students research the variety of psychological testing that may be used to evaluate a patient's mental health and intelligence. Ask each group to report on one new test, describing it and possible results.* *Class Activity Review Figure 22-1 (Rorschach test). Do a demonstration with ink and paper on how to get an image. Have students describe the images that come out on the paper. As an extra credit assignment, have students conduct Internet research on this topic and report how the test is used in clinical practice.*
Define terms that describe psychiatric symptoms.	■ Psychiatric clinical symptoms (p. 917)	PPT 9 IRM Multiple Choice Quiz questions 3-8 IRM Exercise Quiz A IRM Pronunciation Quiz B Exercises B, C (pp. 940-941) *Class Activity Divide the class into three groups and have each choose a "contestant" for a game show. Read the contestants a definition of a psychiatric symptom and ask them to give the correct term. Award a point to the first contestant to answer correctly. When a contestant answers incorrectly, the team chooses a new contestant.* *Class Activity Have a copy of the DSM-IV available. Students should split into four groups. Have each group take four psychiatric terms and compare their definitions in the DSM-IV with the definition in the textbook. Why are there discrepancies between the two sources of the definitions? Which definitions are more precise? Which present overlapping symptoms? How would a doctor deal with overlapping symptoms?*
Identify terms that describe major psychiatric disorders.	■ Psychiatric disorders (p. 918) □ Anxiety disorders (p. 919) □ Delirium and dementia (p. 920) □ Dissociative disorders (p. 920) □ Eating disorders (p. 920)	PPT 10-17 IRM Multiple Choice Quiz questions 9, 11-16 IRM Practical Application A ▶ MTO Module 22, Section I, Lesson 3 ▶ MTO Module 22, Section II, Lessons 1-2

Chabner

OBJECTIVES	CONTENT	TEACHING RESOURCES
	☐ Mood disorders (p. 921) ☐ Personality disorders (p. 922)	➤ MTO Module 22, Section III, Lessons 1 and 4 Exercises F-H (pp. 942-943) ⦿ Companion CD Exercises 22-1, 22-2 *Class Activity Divide the class into two or more competing teams. Give them a class of psychiatric disorder (e.g., anxiety disorders) and ask them to name an example. Award a point to the first contestant to answer correctly. Award an additional point for a definition of the disorder.* *Class Activity Using news articles that refer to a psychiatric disorder, have students group their articles by the disorder mentioned. Then have each group present the disorder to the class and show how it was presented or discussed in the article.*

22.1 Homework/Assignments:

Have students bring in newspaper articles that refer to a psychiatric disorder.

22.1 Teacher's Notes:

ELSEVIER

The Language of Medicine, 9th ed.

Chabner

LESSON 22.2

CRITICAL THINKING QUESTION

Andrea, an extremely thin 19-year-old woman, tells Dr. Versace that she has not been menstruating. Although Andrea appears healthy from her physical exam, Dr. Versace thinks that Andrea may be suffering from anorexia nervosa. However, she notices that Andrea has pitted teeth. Why should that observation cause Dr. Versace to further consider the diagnosis?

Guidelines: Dr. Versace is trying to make a differential diagnosis to determine whether Andrea has anorexia nervosa or bulimia nervosa. Anorexic individuals are intensely afraid of gaining weight and misperceive the shape and size of their bodies. The condition affects mostly female adolescents. Other symptoms may include relentless dieting and compulsive overactivity and exercise. In general, anorexic women do not menstruate. Bulimic individuals usually have low to normal weight. Symptoms include binge eating and purging, which can take the form of induced vomiting or misuse of laxatives or enemas. Andrea's pitted teeth may indicate self-induced and repetitive vomiting because tooth damage results from stomach acids in the mouth.

OBJECTIVES	CONTENT	TEACHING RESOURCES
Define terms that describe major psychiatric disorders.	☐ Schizophrenia (p. 923) ☐ Sexual and gender identity disorders (p. 923) ☐ Somatoform disorders (p. 924) ☐ Substance-related disorders (p. 924)	⊠ PPT 19-24 IRM Multiple Choice Quiz questions 16-25 IRM Practical Application B MTO Module 22, Section II, Lessons 1, 3 MTO Module 22, Section III, Lessons 2-3, 5-6 Figure 22-3 Psychoactive substances (p. 926) Table 22-1 Psychiatric disorders (p. 927) Exercise F (p. 942) Exercise L question 4 (p. 945) *Class Activity Divide the class into two competing teams. Give each team a set of different flash cards with the names of major psychiatric disorders on them. The teams take turns showing a card to the opponent, who must pronounce and then define the disorder. Award a point for each correct answer. However, the first team loses a point for accepting an incorrect answer or rejecting a correct answer.*

Chabner

22.2 Homework/Assignments:

Have students watch the movie *A Beautiful Mind*. Have students write questions about schizophrenia that were prompted by the movie.

Have students go to the National Institute on Drug Abuse Web site. Ask each student to pick a particular abused substance and download relevant information not contained in the text that can be discussed in class.

22.2 Teacher's Notes:

LESSON 22.3

CRITICAL THINKING QUESTION

Julie is receiving selective serotonin reuptake inhibitors (SSRIs) for her depression. Her psychiatrist told her that they would improve her mood and mental alertness and make her more active. Meanwhile, Julie's friend told her that he was prescribed an SSRI for panic attacks. Why are these two ailments being treated with the same class of drugs? Is one of these patients mistaken about the type of drug being taken?

Guidelines: Both individuals are correct about their medication classification. SSRIs prevent the reuptake of the neurotransmitter serotonin into nerve endings, allowing it to produce its effects on nerve cells for a longer period of time. They are used for both anxiety and panic disorder, as well as to treat imbalances of neurotransmitters in the brain that occur during depression. They improve sleep patterns of both patients and produce feelings of well-being.

OBJECTIVES	CONTENT	TEACHING RESOURCES
Compare different types of therapy for psychiatric disorders.	■ Therapeutic Modalities (p. 926) ☐ Psychotherapy (p. 926) ☐ Electroconvulsive therapy (ECT) (p. 928)	PPT 26-27 Exercises I-J (pp. 943-944)
Learn the categories and names of common psychiatric drugs.	☐ Drug therapy (p. 928)	PPT 28 MTO Module 22, Section II, Lesson 4 Figure 22-4 Psychiatric drug therapies and specific drugs (p. 929) *Class Activity Using Figure 22-4, find the common side effects of drugs mentioned in the chart using the* **Physicians' Desk Reference.** *Have students work in groups representative of the major classes of drugs.*
Define combining forms, suffixes, prefixes, and abbreviations related to psychiatry.	■ Terminology (p. 934) ■ Abbreviations (p. 937)	PPT 29-30 IRM Terminology Quiz IRM Abbreviations Quiz IRM Crossword Puzzle Table 22-2 Phobias (p. 935) Exercises K-L (p. 945) Companion CD Exercises 22-3, 22-4 *Class Activity Using Table 22-2, have students make flash cards with phobias on one side and their corresponding medical terms on the other. Alternatively, play bingo using bingo cards with medical terms written on them. Have the leader call out the phobia so that*

OBJECTIVES	CONTENT	TEACHING RESOURCES
		students will need to match phobias to their appropriate medical terms. *Class Activity Have students use the resource* http://www.phobialist.com *to find phobias not listed in the text. Divide the alphabet among the number of groups in the class. Ask each group to select four phobias from their section of the alphabet. Have them report on their findings.*
Apply your new knowledge to understanding medical terms in their proper contexts, such as medical reports and records.	■ Practical applications (p. 938)	IRM Practical Applications MTO Module 22, Section V *Class Activity Ask students to use the American Psychiatric Association Web site* http://www.healthyminds.org *to research their fact sheets. Issues include storm disasters, confidentiality, and the Patients Bill of Rights. Have them report their findings to the class.*
Performance Evaluation		IRM Multiple Choice Quiz IRM Terminology Quiz IRM Abbreviations Quiz IRM Exercise Quiz IRM Dictation and Comprehension Quizzes IRM Spelling Quiz IRM Pronunciation Quiz IRM Vocabulary Quiz IRM Review Sheet Quiz IRM Crossword Puzzle IRM Practical Applications ESLR Student Quiz Chapter 22 MTO Module 22, Sections I-III quizzes MTO Module 22 Exam Companion CD Exercises 22-5, 22-6, 22-7 iTerms Chapter 22

22.3 Homework/Assignments:

Have students do a Medline search on electroconvulsive shock therapy. Have them compare the use of this form of therapy today versus 50 years ago. How has it changed?

22.3 Teacher's Notes:

Slide 1

The Language Of Medicine
9th edition
Davi-Ellen Chabner

Slide 2

Chapter 22
Psychiatry

Slide 3

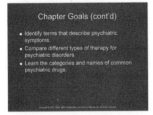

Chapter Goals

- Differentiate among a psychiatrist, a psychologist, and other mental health specialists.
- Learn of tests used by clinical psychologists to evaluate a patient's mental health and intelligence.
- Define terms that describe major psychiatric disorders.

Slide 4

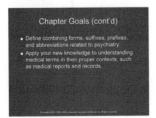

Chapter Goals (cont'd)

- Identify terms that describe psychiatric symptoms.
- Compare different types of therapy for psychiatric disorders.
- Learn the categories and names of common psychiatric drugs.

Slide 5

Chapter Goals (cont'd)

- Define combining forms, suffixes, prefixes, and abbreviations related to psychiatry.
- Apply your new knowledge to understanding medical terms in their proper contexts, such as medical reports and records.

Slide 6

Slide 7

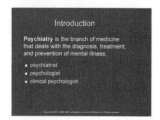

- Which of these health professionals have an MD degree? (*psychiatrists*)

- What's the difference between a psychologist and a clinical psychologist? (*A psychologist is a nonmedical person who is trained in methods of psychotherapy, analysis, and research. He or she completes a masters or PhD degree in a specific field of interest. A clinical psychologist is trained in the use of tests to evaluate various aspects of a patient's mental health and intelligence.*)

Slide 8

- How many years of training do psychoanalysts need to conduct psychoanalysis? (*They need to complete three to five years of training in the special psychotherapeutic technique.*)

- What is psychoanalysis? (*Patients freely relate their thoughts to the analyst, who does not interfere in the flow of thoughts.*)

Slide 9

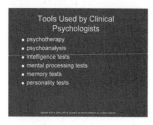

- What are some intelligence tests? (*Examples of I.Q. tests include the Wechsler Adult Intelligence Scale (WAIS) and the Stanford-Binet Intelligence Scale.*)

- What are some examples of personality tests? (*The Rorschach technique, which are inkblots, and the Thematic Apperception Test (TAT), in which pictures are used as stimuli for making up stories. Both tests are especially revealing of personality structure.*)

Slide 10

- This is a good opportunity to not only review, but learn the pronunciations for symptom definitions.

- What is amnesia?

- What is a delusion?

- What is mutism?

- What is paranoia?

Chabner

Slide 11

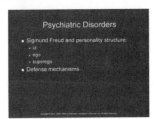

- Which of these three parts of the personality is more like a referee to the other two parts? (*The ego. It is the central coordinating branch of the personality. It is the mediator between the id and the outside world.*)

- In one corner is the id. It represents the unconscious instincts and psychic energy present at birth and thereafter. From the id arises basic drives that seek immediate gratification regardless of the reality of the situation.

- And in the other corner? The superego. It is the internalized conscience and moral part of the personality. Guilt feelings, for instance, arise from behavior and thoughts that do not conform to the standards of the superego.

Slide 12

- Eating disorders predominantly affect adolescent females, and include anorexia and bulimia.

- How many of you have already heard of eating disorders?

- What are some ways to detect whether someone has an eating disorder?

- What are different types of mood disorders? (*Bipolar disorders, depressive disorders, and cyclothymic disorder—a mild form of bipolar disorder characterized by at least two years of hypomania and numerous depressive episodes that do not meet the criteria that define a major depressive episode.*)

Slide 13

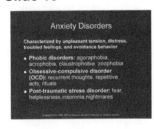

- What are some effective ways to treat OCD? (*Several antidepressant drugs, including clomipramine, have been used to treat OCD with considerable success, particularly when combined with cognitive-behavioral therapy.*)

- Another symptom of PTSD is a diminished response to the external world.

Slide 14

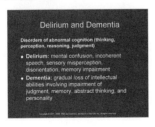

- What delirium is caused by alcohol withdrawal? (*delirium tremens*)

- What are some possible causes of these conditions? (*Dementia is usually due to Alzheimer disease, but it also can be due to cerebrovascular disease, CNS infection, brain trauma, tumors, Parkinson, and Huntington diseases.*)

Slide 15

- What "two" literary figures represent dissociative identity disorder? (*Dr. Jekyll and Mr. Hyde*)

- What does "fugue" mean? (*Flight. The fugue disorder includes the assumption of a new identity and an inability to recall one's previous identity.*)

Slide 16

- Bulimics usually have low to normal body weight. Is that the same with anorexics?

- This condition's principal symptom is a conscious, relentless attempt to diet along with excessive, compulsive overactivity, such as exercise, running, or gymnastics.

Slide 17

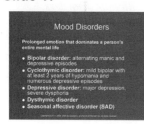

- Major depression involves episodes of dysphoria. What is that? (*Sadness, hopelessness, worry, discouragement.*)

- Depression has other symptoms, including appetite disturbances and changes in weight, sleep, fatigue, sense of worthlessness, hopelessness, inappropriate guilt, difficulty thinking or concentrating, thoughts of death or suicide.

- Dysthymia is a depressive disorder involving a depressed mood that persists over a two-year period, but it is not as severe as major depression.

- What is SAD? (*A regular appearance of depression during low light periods of the year lasting roughly 60 days. In the United States, it tends to occur beginning around October or November every year.*)

Slide 18

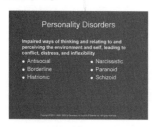

- Review definitions by asking student to define and pronounce these disorders correctly.

Chabner

Slide 19

Slide 20

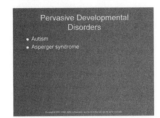

Slide 21

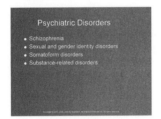

Slide 22

- Go over definitions. Make distinction between positive affect (paranoid psychosis) and negative affect (catatonia) types of symptoms, both constituting the same disease.

- What is flat affect? (*Marked by monotonous voice, immobile face, and no signs of expression.*)

- What are different types of schizophrenia? (*catatonic type, disorganized type, and paranoid type*)

Slide 23

- What are two types of sexual disorders? (*Paraphilias [recurrent intense sexual urges, fantasies or behaviors that involve unusual objects, activities, or situations] and sexual dysfunction [disturbances in sexual desire/psychosexual changes in sexual response, such as premature ejaculation and dyspareunia that are not the result of a general medical condition].*)

- The list includes examples of paraphilias.

Slide 24

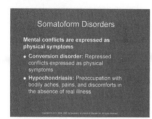

- What is an example of conversion disorder? (*A person with repressed anger and desire to physically harm a family member may suddenly develop a paralysis of the arm.*)

Slide 25

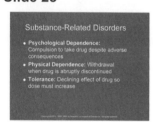

- What are examples of substances associated with drug abuse? (*alcohol; amphetamines; cannabis, such as marijuana; cocaine; hallucinogens, such as LSD and PCP; opioids, such as heroin and morphine; and sedatives, hypnotics, or anxiolytics.*)

Slide 26

- In which of these categories do we place barbiturates?

- What are some examples of barbiturates and benzodiazepines? (*Sleeping pills include barbiturates such as phenobarbital and secobarbital. Other drugs that produce a barbiturate-like effect are benzodiazepines, including temazepam (Restoril), alprazolam (Xanax), and diazepam (Valium).*)

Slide 27

Slide 28

- What is ECT? Does it continue to be a popular form of therapy? (*It is a treatment in which an electric current is applied to the brain while the patient is anesthetized, paralyzed, and being ventilated. This produces convulsions. It is used chiefly for serious depression and the depressive phase of bipolar disorder. With the introduction of antidepressant drug therapy, there are few indications for ECT, although it can be lifesaving when a rapid response is necessary.*)

Chabner

Slide 29

- What is play therapy? (*through play, a child uses toys to express conflicts and feelings that she or he is unable to communicate in a direct manner*)

- What is supportive psychotherapy? (*It offers encouragement, support, and hope to patients facing difficult life transitions and events.*)

- When is hypnosis used? (*Hypnosis is a trance, created to increase the speed of psychotherapy or to help recovery of deeply repressed memories.*)

Slide 30

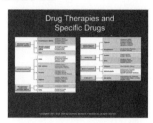

- Go over mechanisms of action of these classes of drugs and then give examples of generic and brand names in each category.

- For example, what are some generic and brand names of SSRIs? (*fluvoxamine [Luvox] and sertraline [Zoloft]*)

- What are some mood stabilizers? (*lithium [Eskalith, Lithane] is an antimanic, while carbamazepine [Tegretol] or valproate [Depakane, Depakote] are anticonvulsants.*)

Slide 31

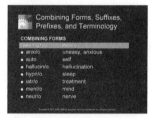

Slide 32

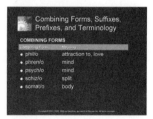

Slide 33

Slide 34

Slide 35

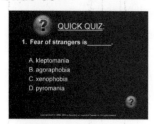

- Correct answer is C: xenophobia

Slide 36

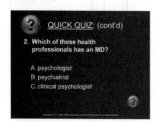

- Correct answer is B: psychiatrist

Slide 37

- Correct answer is B: compulsion

Chabner